Teen Titans spotlight: RAVEN

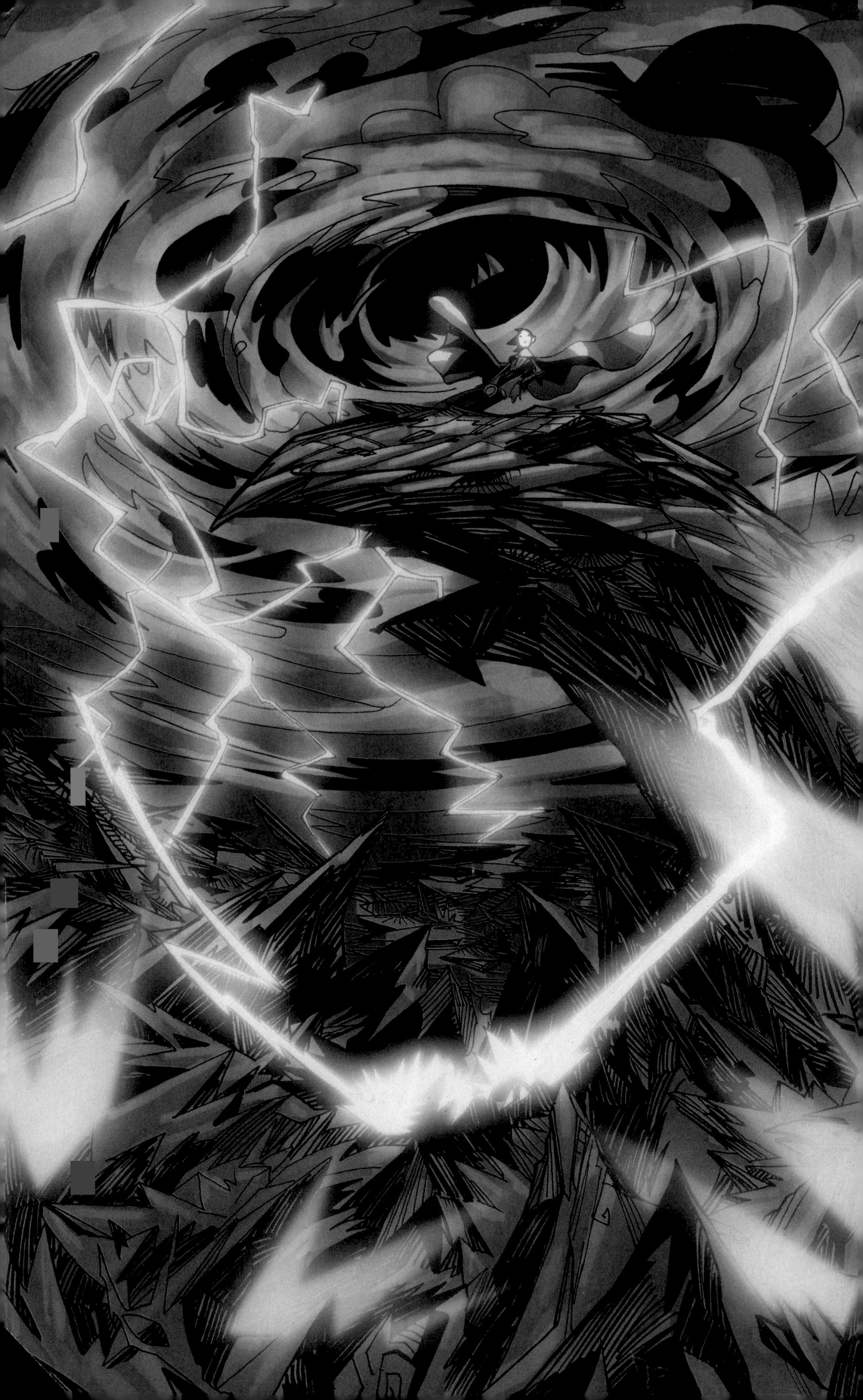

Teen Titans spotlight: Raven

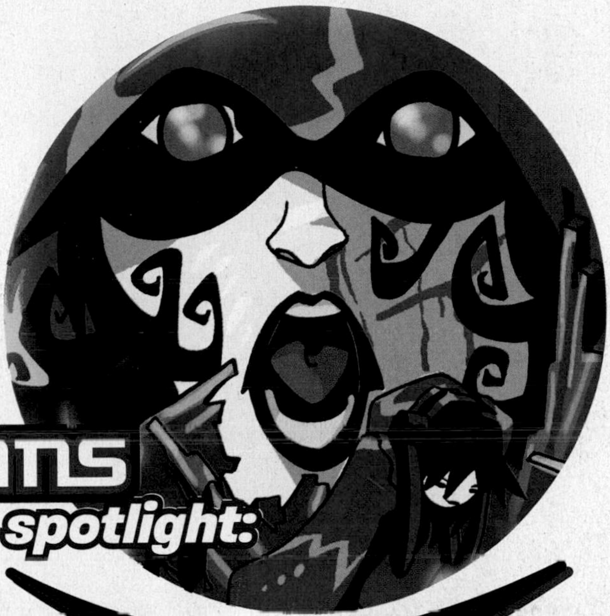

Marv Wolfman Writer

Damion Scott Penciller

Robert Campanella Inker

Sigmund Torre Colorist

John J. Hill Letterer

Scott, Campanella & Torre Original Series Covers

Raven created by **Marv Wolfman & George Pérez**

Dan DiDio Senior VP-Executive Editor
Eddie Berganza Editor-original series
Adam Schlagman Assistant Editor-original series
Sean Mackiewicz Editor-collected edition
Robbin Brosterman Senior Art Director
Nadina Simon Art Director
Paul Levitz President & Publisher
Georg Brewer VP-Design & DC Direct Creative
Richard Bruning Senior VP-Creative Director
Patrick Caldon Executive VP-Finance & Operations
Chris Caramalis VP-Finance
John Cunningham VP-Marketing
Terri Cunningham VP-Managing Editor
Amy Genkins Senior VP-Business & Legal Affairs
Alison Gill VP-Manufacturing
David Hyde VP-Publicity
Hank Kanalz VP-General Manager, WildStorm
Jim Lee Editorial Director-WildStorm
Gregory Noveck Senior VP-Creative Affairs
Sue Pohja VP-Book Trade Sales
Steve Rotterdam Senior VP-Sales & Marketing
Cheryl Rubin Senior VP-Brand Management
Alysse Soll VP-Advertising & Custom Publishing
Jeff Trojan VP-Business Development, DC Direct
Bob Wayne VP-Sales

Cover by Damion Scott, Robert Campanella and Sigmund Torre.

TEEN TITANS SPOTLIGHT: RAVEN

DC Comics, 1700 Broadway, New York, NY 10019
A Warner Bros. Entertainment Company
Printed in Canada. First Printing.
ISBN: 978-1-4012-1953-6

Part 1: Inside Out

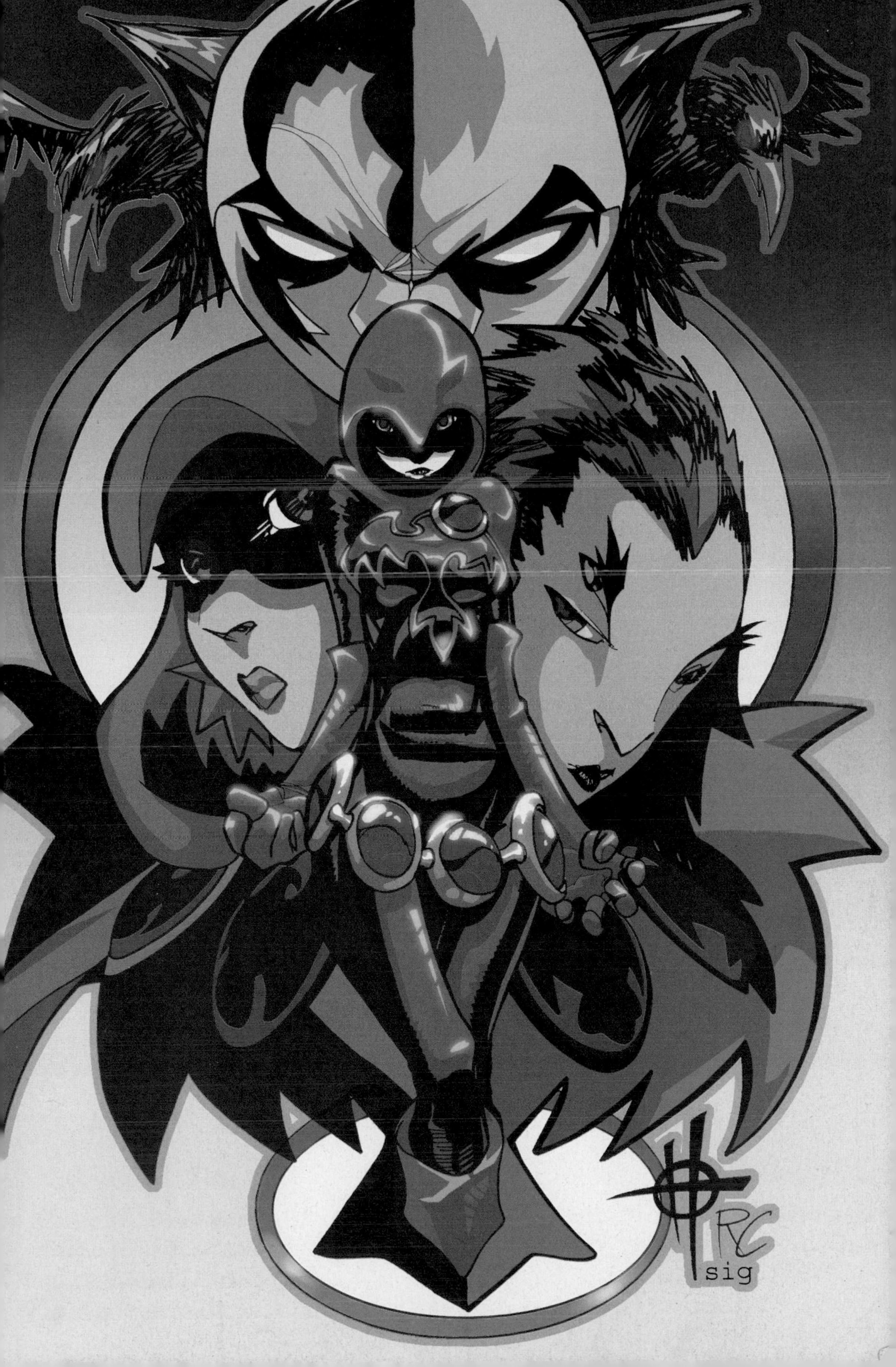

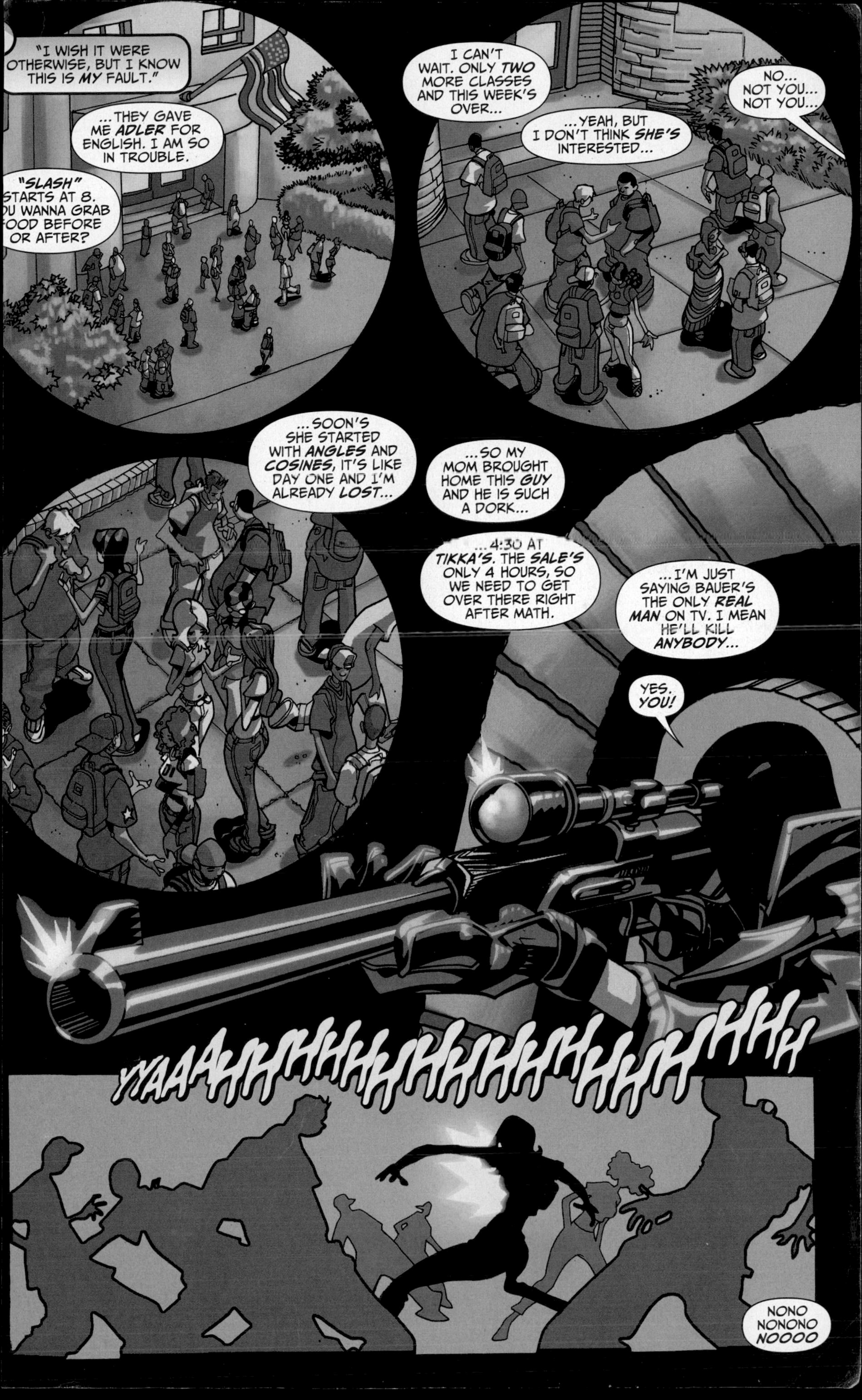
"I WISH IT WERE OTHERWISE, BUT I KNOW THIS IS MY FAULT."
...THEY GAVE ME ADLER FOR ENGLISH. I AM SO IN TROUBLE.
"SLASH" STARTS AT 8. OU WANNA GRAB OOD BEFORE OR AFTER?
I CAN'T WAIT. ONLY TWO MORE CLASSES AND THIS WEEK'S OVER...
...YEAH, BUT I DON'T THINK SHE'S INTERESTED...
NO... NOT YOU... NOT YOU...
...SOON'S SHE STARTED WITH ANGLES AND COSINES, IT'S LIKE DAY ONE AND I'M ALREADY LOST...
...SO MY MOM BROUGHT HOME THIS GUY AND HE IS SUCH A DORK...
...4:30 AT TIKKA'S. THE SALE'S ONLY 4 HOURS, SO WE NEED TO GET OVER THERE RIGHT AFTER MATH.
...I'M JUST SAYING BAUER'S THE ONLY REAL MAN ON TV. I MEAN HE'LL KILL ANYBODY...
YES. YOU!
YYAAAHHHHHHHHHHHHHHHHHHHHH
NONO NONONO NOOOO

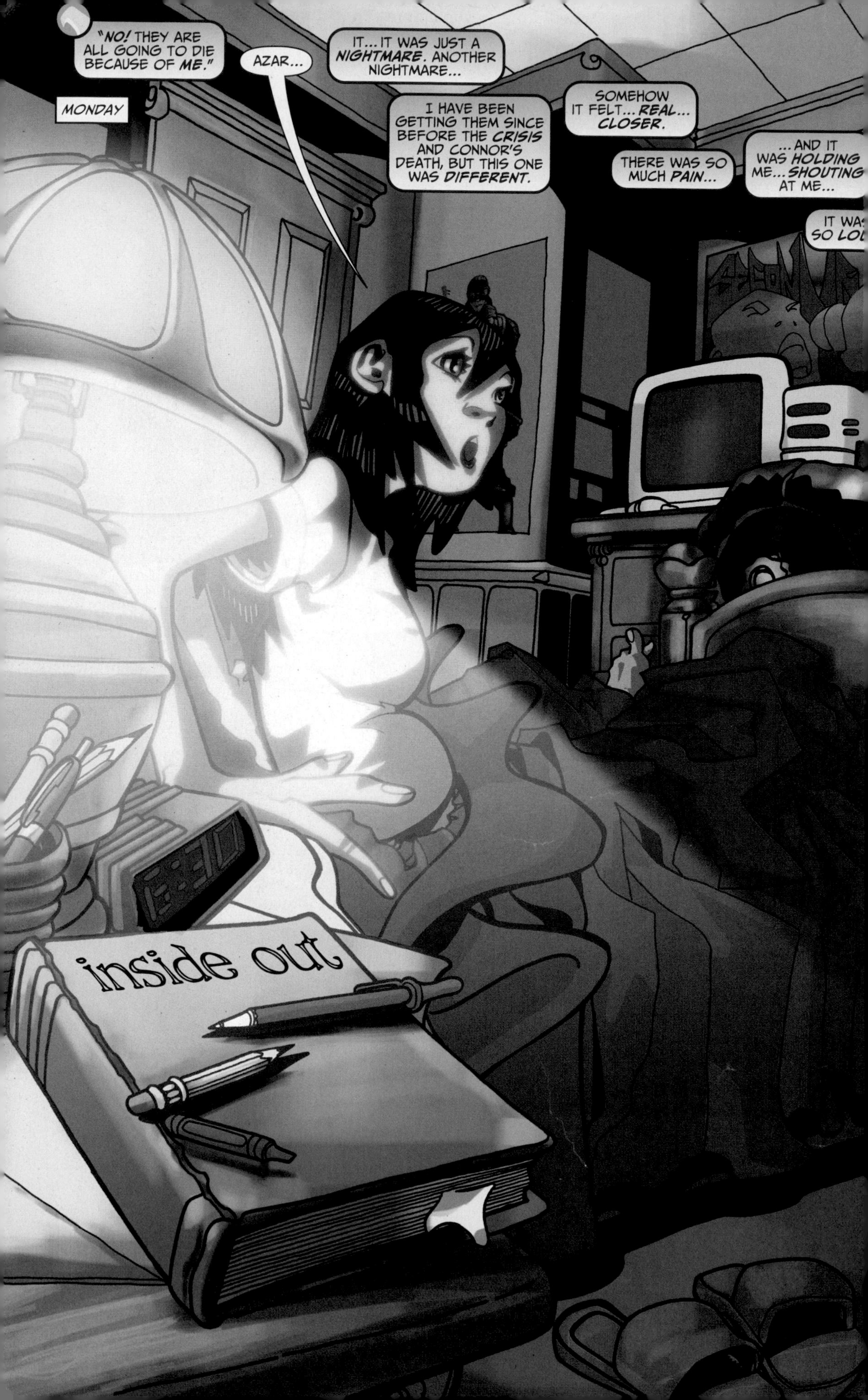
"NO! THEY ARE ALL GOING TO DIE BECAUSE OF ME."
MONDAY
AZAR...
IT... IT WAS JUST A NIGHTMARE. ANOTHER NIGHTMARE...
I HAVE BEEN GETTING THEM SINCE BEFORE THE CRISIS AND CONNOR'S DEATH, BUT THIS ONE WAS DIFFERENT.
SOMEHOW IT FELT... REAL... CLOSER.
THERE WAS SO MUCH PAIN...
...AND IT WAS HOLDING ME... SHOUTING AT ME...
inside out

"SO MANY EMOTIONS, ALL CONFLICTING, ALL SO POWERFUL. I CAN'T STOP THEM, AND I CAN'T *ABSORB* THEM... BUT WORST OF ALL, I CAN'T *CONTROL* THEM..."

HYPER-VENTILATING... BREATHE IN. *MEDITATE.* KEEP REPEATING, "IT WAS ONLY A *DREAM*..."

I--

HUHH HUNHHHH HUHH HUNHHHH

ALTHOUGH I KNOW IT WAS NOT.

FRIDAY. *THIS* FRIDAY...

BREATHE...

"IT FELT REAL."

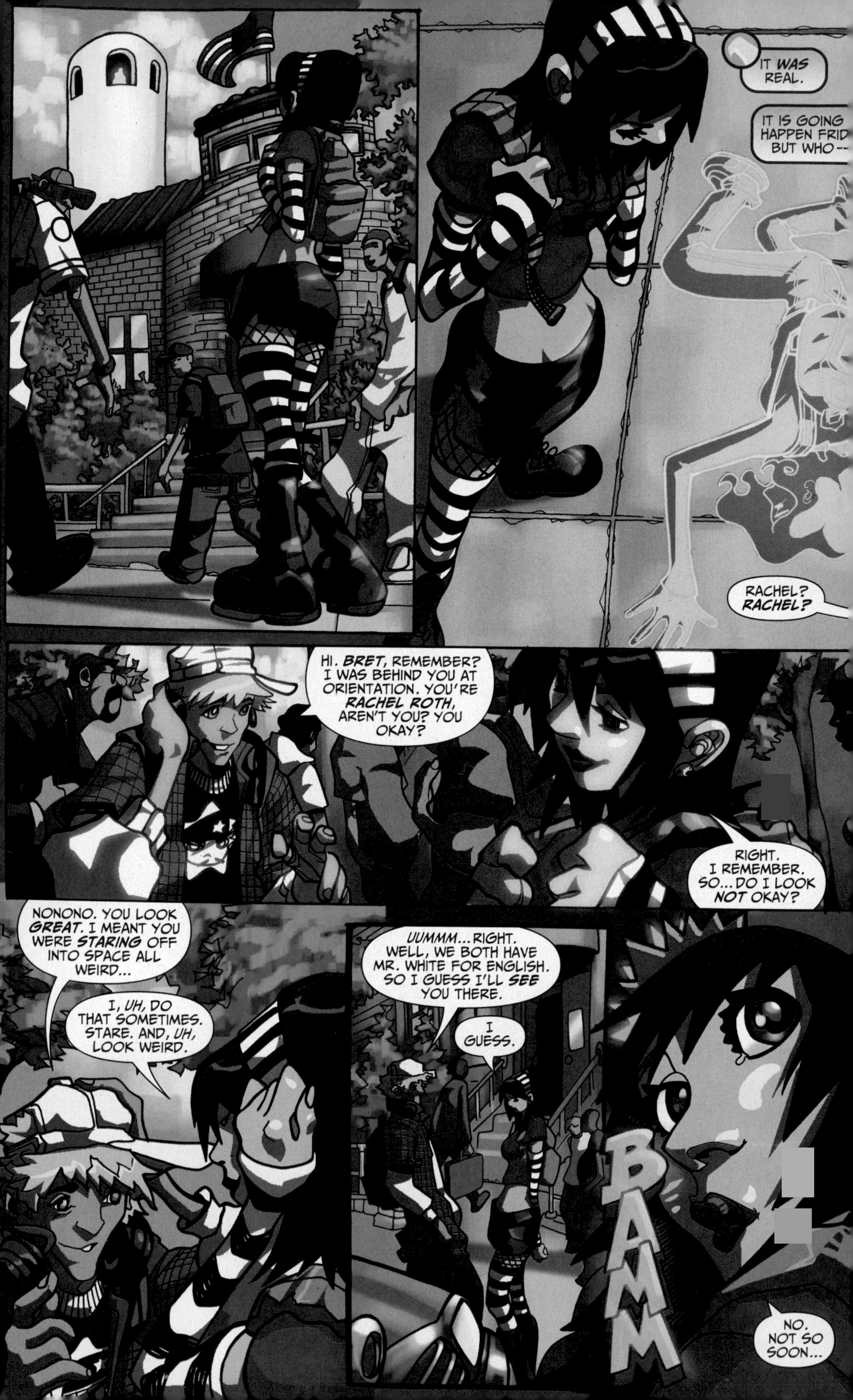
IT WAS REAL.
IT IS GOING HAPPEN FRID BUT WHO--
RACHEL? RACHEL?
HI. BRET, REMEMBER? I WAS BEHIND YOU AT ORIENTATION. YOU'RE RACHEL ROTH, AREN'T YOU? YOU OKAY?
RIGHT. I REMEMBER. SO...DO I LOOK NOT OKAY?
NONONO. YOU LOOK GREAT. I MEANT YOU WERE STARING OFF INTO SPACE ALL WEIRD...
I, UH, DO THAT SOMETIMES. STARE. AND, UH, LOOK WEIRD.
UUMMM...RIGHT. WELL, WE BOTH HAVE MR. WHITE FOR ENGLISH. SO I GUESS I'LL SEE YOU THERE.
I GUESS.
BAMM
NO. NOT SO SOON...

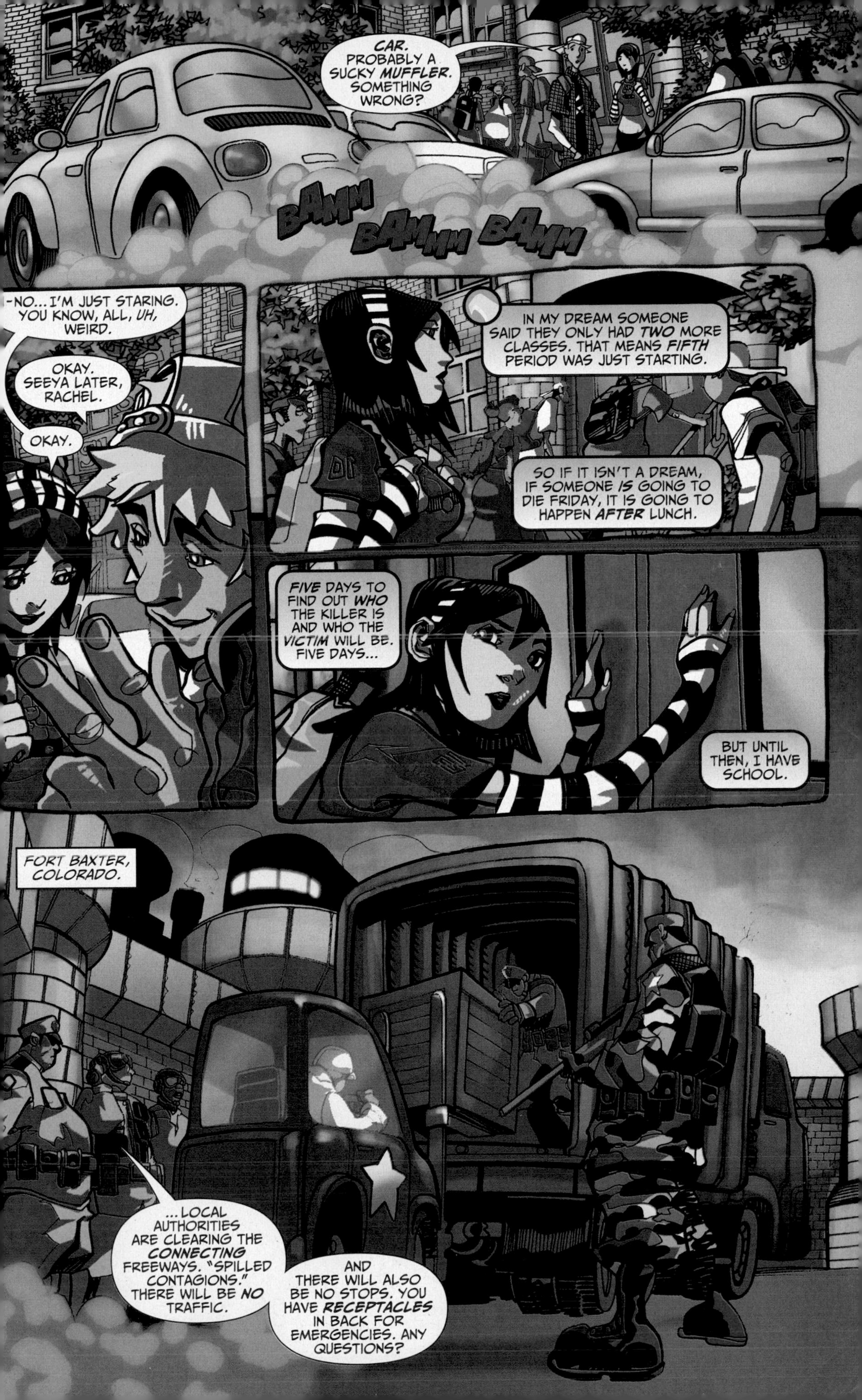
CAR. PROBABLY A SUCKY MUFFLER. SOMETHING WRONG?
BAMM BAMMM BAMM
-NO... I'M JUST STARING. YOU KNOW, ALL, UH, WEIRD.
OKAY. SEEYA LATER, RACHEL.
OKAY.
IN MY DREAM SOMEONE SAID THEY ONLY HAD TWO MORE CLASSES. THAT MEANS FIFTH PERIOD WAS JUST STARTING.
SO IF IT ISN'T A DREAM, IF SOMEONE IS GOING TO DIE FRIDAY, IT IS GOING TO HAPPEN AFTER LUNCH.
FIVE DAYS TO FIND OUT WHO THE KILLER IS AND WHO THE VICTIM WILL BE. FIVE DAYS...
BUT UNTIL THEN, I HAVE SCHOOL.
FORT BAXTER, COLORADO.
...LOCAL AUTHORITIES ARE CLEARING THE CONNECTING FREEWAYS. "SPILLED CONTAGIONS." THERE WILL BE NO TRAFFIC.
AND THERE WILL ALSO BE NO STOPS. YOU HAVE RECEPTACLES IN BACK FOR EMERGENCIES. ANY QUESTIONS?

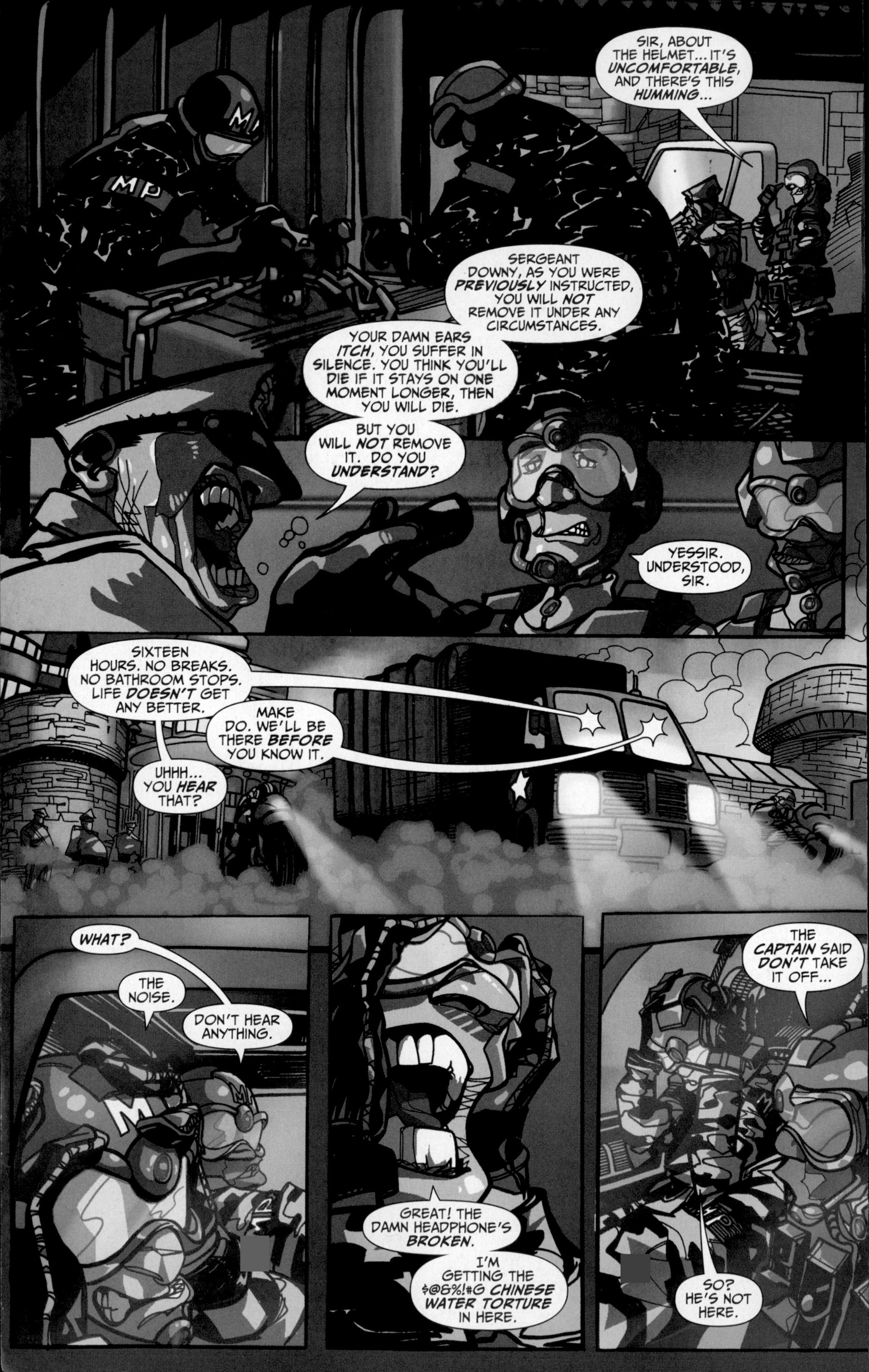
SIR, ABOUT THE HELMET... IT'S UNCOMFORTABLE, AND THERE'S THIS HUMMING...
SERGEANT DOWNY, AS YOU WERE PREVIOUSLY INSTRUCTED, YOU WILL NOT REMOVE IT UNDER ANY CIRCUMSTANCES.
YOUR DAMN EARS ITCH, YOU SUFFER IN SILENCE. YOU THINK YOU'LL DIE IF IT STAYS ON ONE MOMENT LONGER, THEN YOU WILL DIE.
BUT YOU WILL NOT REMOVE IT. DO YOU UNDERSTAND?
YESSIR. UNDERSTOOD, SIR.
SIXTEEN HOURS. NO BREAKS. NO BATHROOM STOPS. LIFE DOESN'T GET ANY BETTER.
MAKE DO. WE'LL BE THERE BEFORE YOU KNOW IT.
UHHH... YOU HEAR THAT?
WHAT?
THE NOISE.
DON'T HEAR ANYTHING.
GREAT! THE DAMN HEADPHONE'S BROKEN.
I'M GETTING THE $@&%!#G CHINESE WATER TORTURE IN HERE.
THE CAPTAIN SAID DON'T TAKE IT OFF...
SO? HE'S NOT HERE.

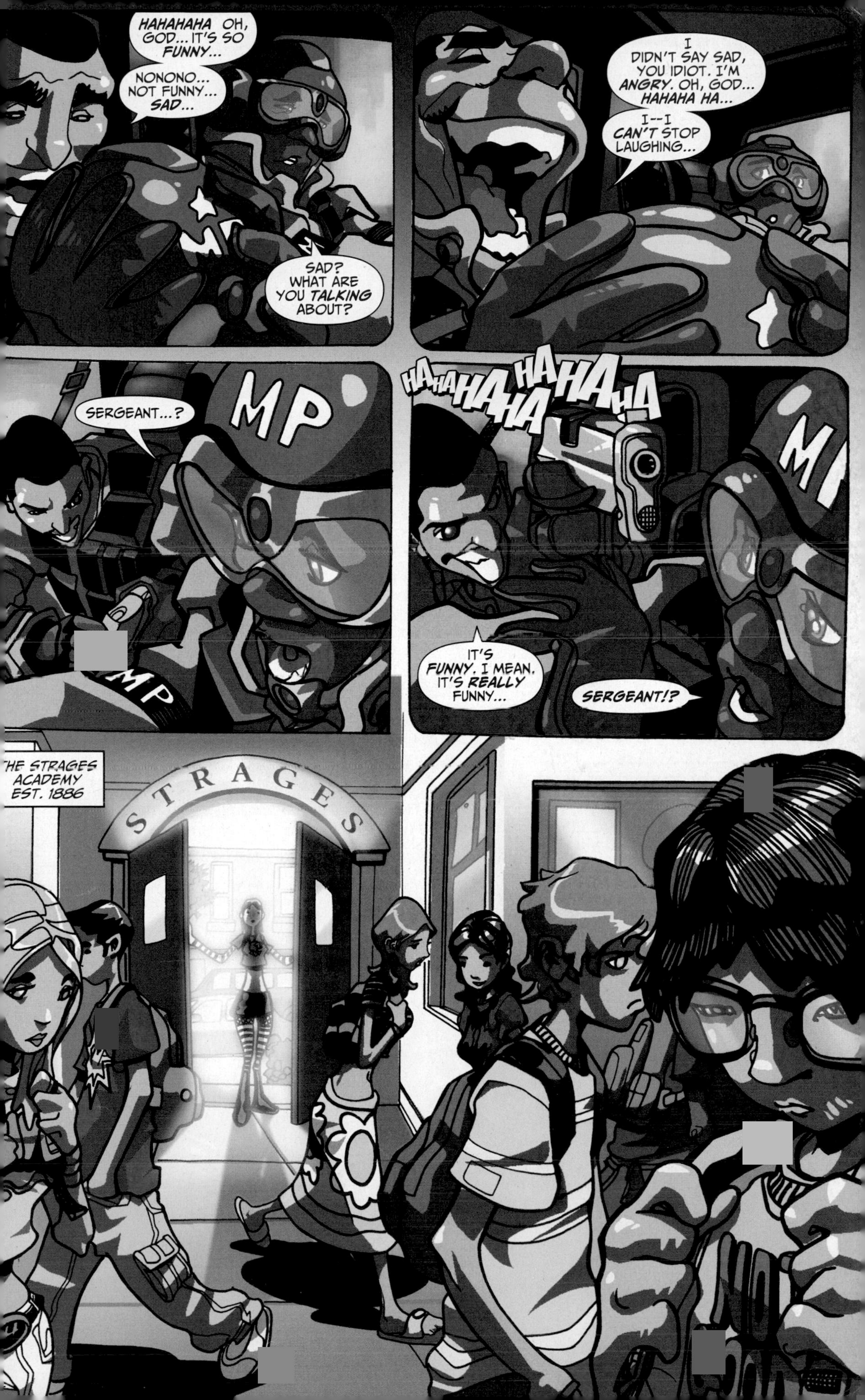
HAHAHAHA OH, GOD... IT'S SO FUNNY...
NONONO... NOT FUNNY... SAD...
SAD? WHAT ARE YOU TALKING ABOUT?
I DIDN'T SAY SAD, YOU IDIOT. I'M ANGRY. OH, GOD... HAHAHA HA...
I--I CAN'T STOP LAUGHING...
SERGEANT...?
MP
HAHAHAHAHAHAHAHAHA
IT'S FUNNY. I MEAN, IT'S REALLY FUNNY...
SERGEANT!?
THE STRAGES ACADEMY EST. 1886
STRAGES

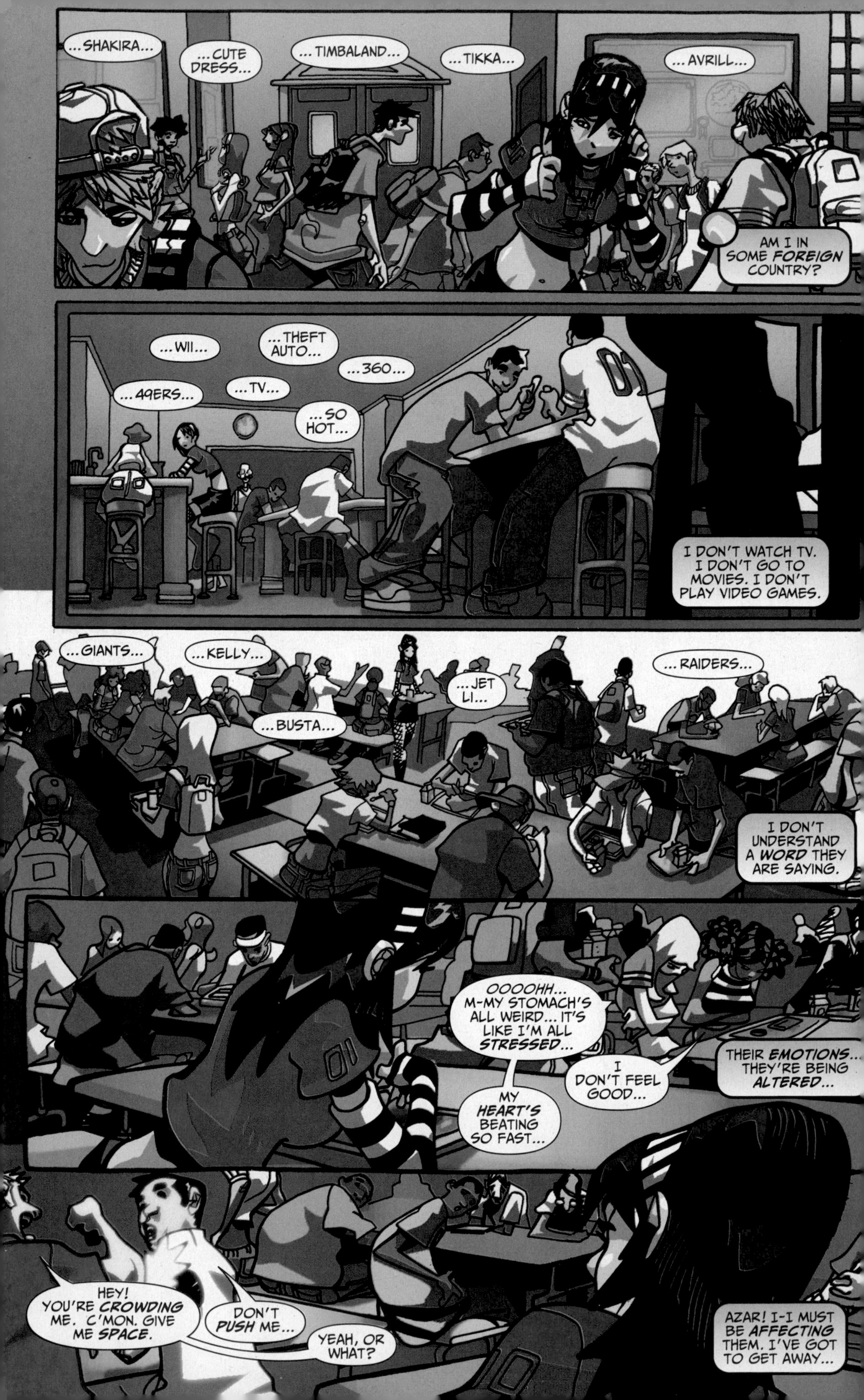
...SHAKIRA...
...CUTE DRESS...
...TIMBALAND...
...TIKKA...
...AVRILL...
AM I IN SOME FOREIGN COUNTRY?
...WII...
...THEFT AUTO...
...360...
...49ERS...
...TV...
...SO HOT...
I DON'T WATCH TV. I DON'T GO TO MOVIES. I DON'T PLAY VIDEO GAMES.
...GIANTS...
...KELLY...
...JET LI...
...BUSTA...
...RAIDERS...
I DON'T UNDERSTAND A WORD THEY ARE SAYING.
OOOOHH... M-MY STOMACH'S ALL WEIRD... IT'S LIKE I'M ALL STRESSED...
MY HEART'S BEATING SO FAST...
I DON'T FEEL GOOD...
THEIR EMOTIONS... THEY'RE BEING ALTERED...
HEY! YOU'RE CROWDING ME. C'MON. GIVE ME SPACE.
DON'T PUSH ME...
YEAH, OR WHAT?
AZAR! I-I MUST BE AFFECTING THEM. I'VE GOT TO GET AWAY...

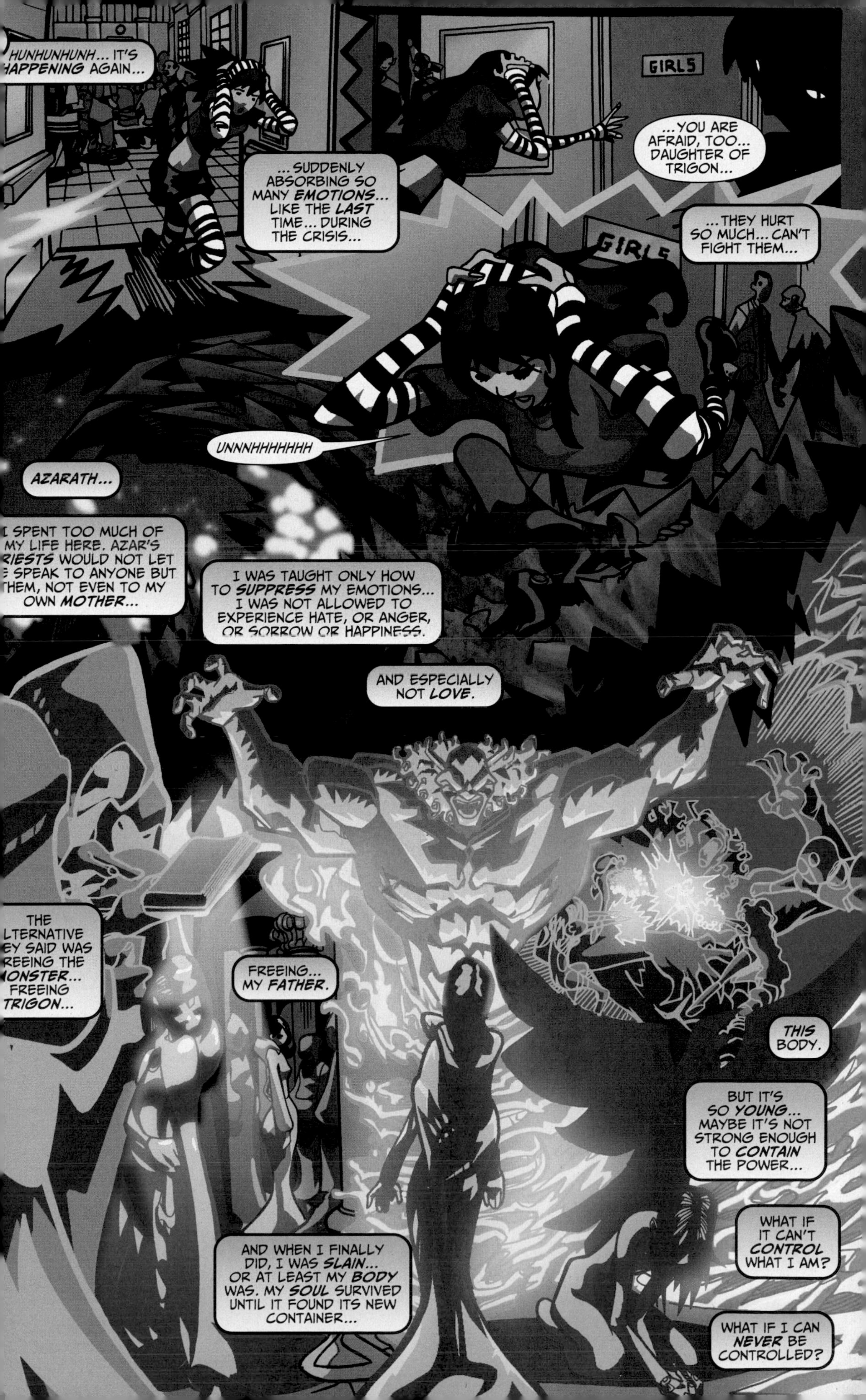
HUNHUNHUNH... IT'S
HAPPENING AGAIN...
GIRLS
...SUDDENLY ABSORBING SO MANY EMOTIONS... LIKE THE LAST TIME... DURING THE CRISIS...
...YOU ARE AFRAID, TOO... DAUGHTER OF TRIGON...
GIRLS
...THEY HURT SO MUCH... CAN'T FIGHT THEM...
UNNNHHHHHHH
AZARATH...
I SPENT TOO MUCH OF MY LIFE HERE. AZAR'S PRIESTS WOULD NOT LET ME SPEAK TO ANYONE BUT THEM, NOT EVEN TO MY OWN MOTHER...
I WAS TAUGHT ONLY HOW TO SUPPRESS MY EMOTIONS... I WAS NOT ALLOWED TO EXPERIENCE HATE, OR ANGER, OR SORROW OR HAPPINESS.
AND ESPECIALLY NOT LOVE.
THE ALTERNATIVE THEY SAID WAS FREEING THE MONSTER... FREEING TRIGON...
FREEING... MY FATHER.
AND WHEN I FINALLY DID, I WAS SLAIN... OR AT LEAST MY BODY WAS. MY SOUL SURVIVED UNTIL IT FOUND ITS NEW CONTAINER...
THIS BODY.
BUT IT'S SO YOUNG... MAYBE IT'S NOT STRONG ENOUGH TO CONTAIN THE POWER...
WHAT IF IT CAN'T CONTROL WHAT I AM?
WHAT IF I CAN NEVER BE CONTROLLED?

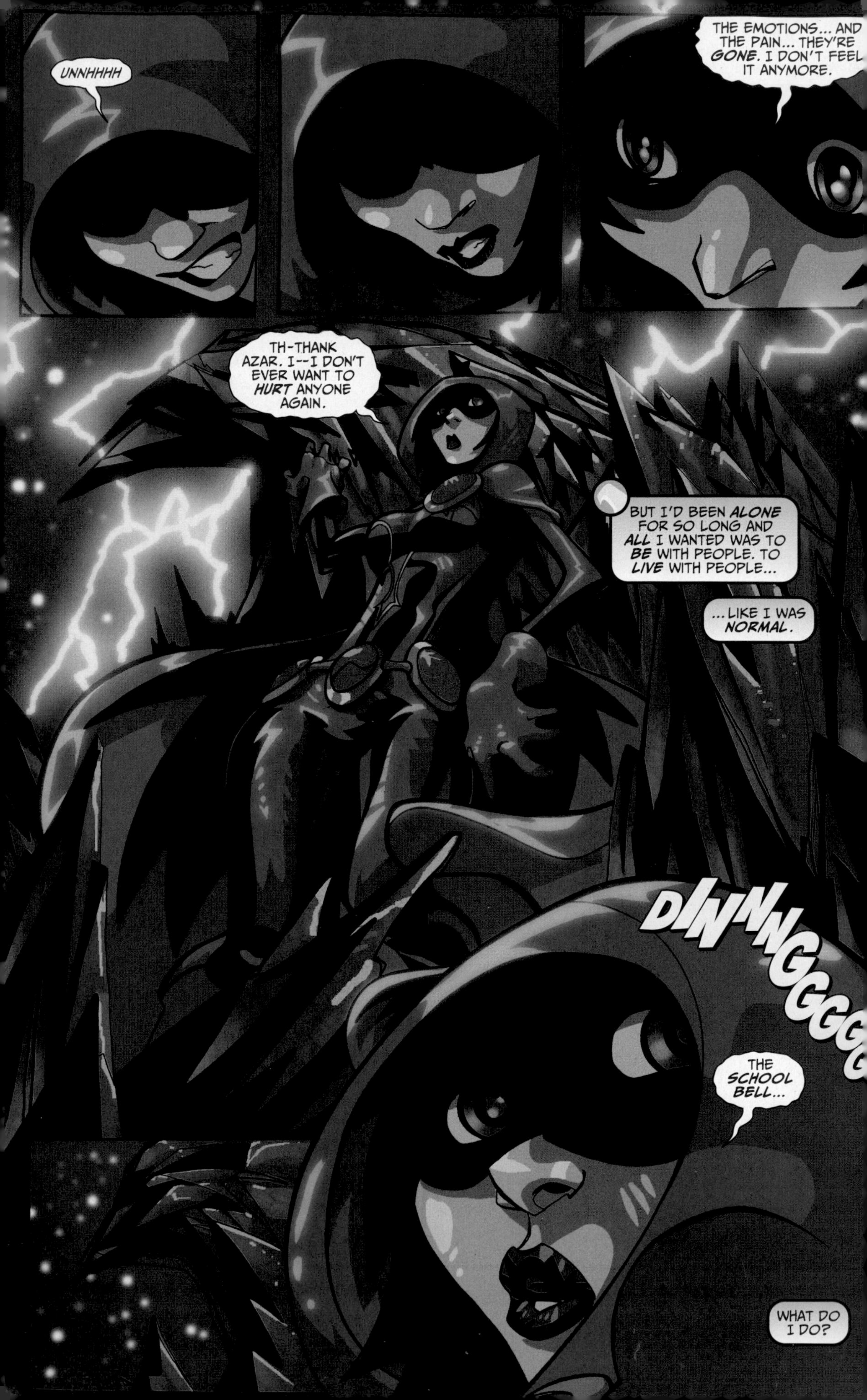
UNNHHHH
THE EMOTIONS... AND THE PAIN... THEY'RE GONE. I DON'T FEEL IT ANYMORE.
TH-THANK AZAR. I--I DON'T EVER WANT TO HURT ANYONE AGAIN.
BUT I'D BEEN ALONE FOR SO LONG AND ALL I WANTED WAS TO BE WITH PEOPLE. TO LIVE WITH PEOPLE...
...LIKE I WAS NORMAL.
DINNNGGGGG
THE SCHOOL BELL...
WHAT DO I DO?

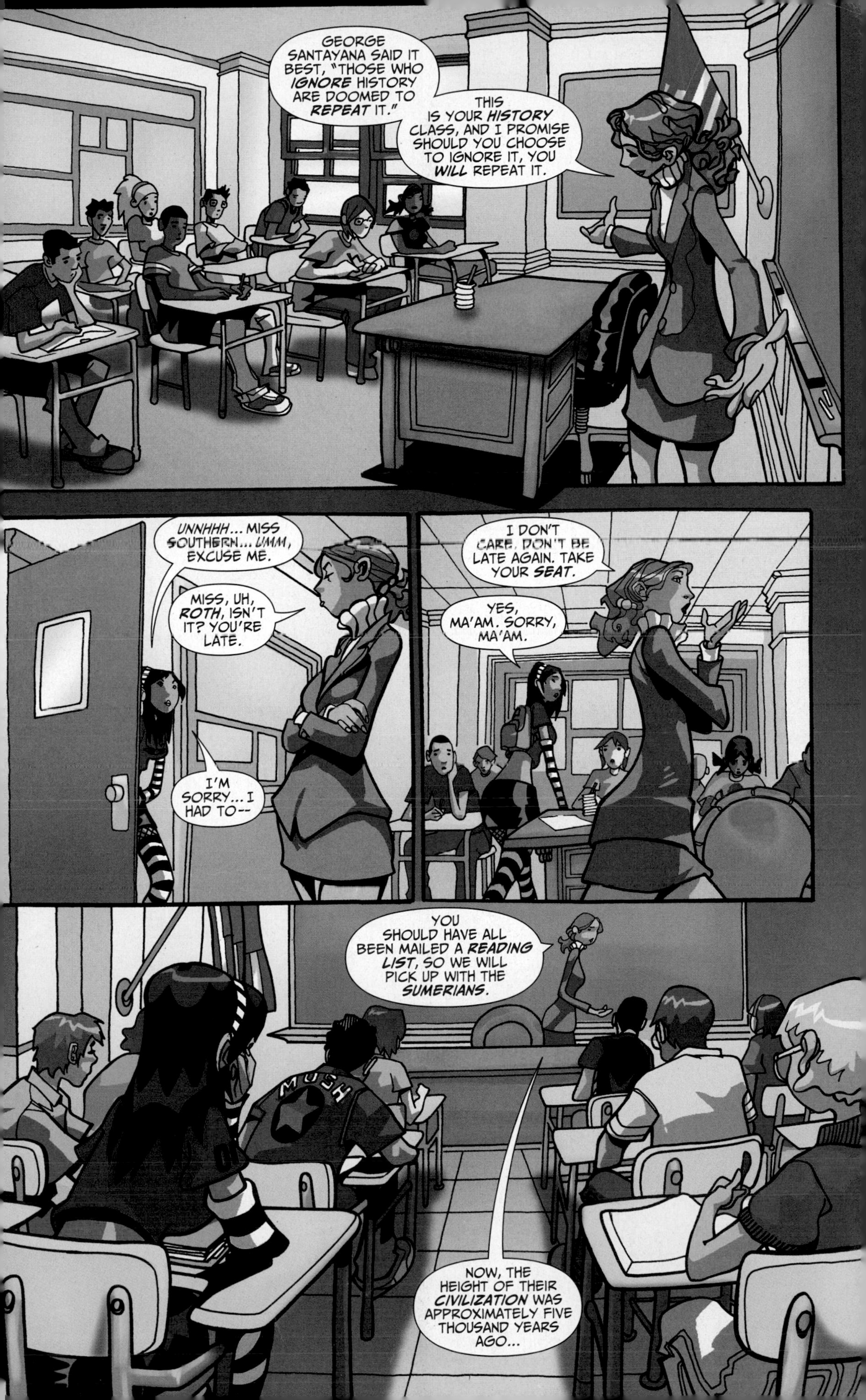
GEORGE SANTAYANA SAID IT BEST, "THOSE WHO IGNORE HISTORY ARE DOOMED TO REPEAT IT."
THIS IS YOUR HISTORY CLASS, AND I PROMISE SHOULD YOU CHOOSE TO IGNORE IT, YOU WILL REPEAT IT.
UNNHHH... MISS SOUTHERN... UMM, EXCUSE ME.
MISS, UH, ROTH, ISN'T IT? YOU'RE LATE.
I'M SORRY... I HAD TO--
I DON'T CARE. DON'T BE LATE AGAIN. TAKE YOUR SEAT.
YES, MA'AM. SORRY, MA'AM.
YOU SHOULD HAVE ALL BEEN MAILED A READING LIST, SO WE WILL PICK UP WITH THE SUMERIANS.
MUSH
NOW, THE HEIGHT OF THEIR CIVILIZATION WAS APPROXIMATELY FIVE THOUSAND YEARS AGO...

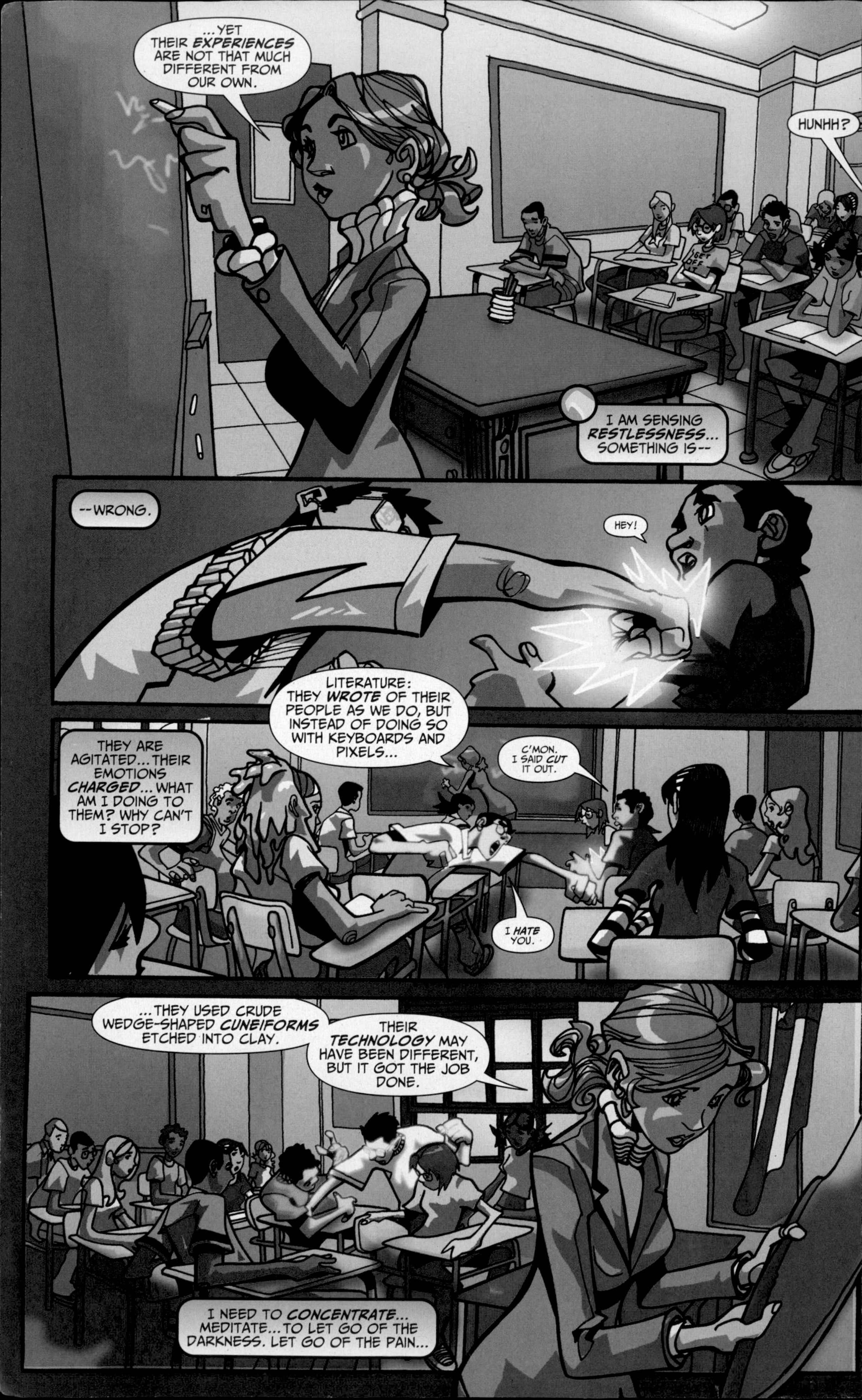
...YET THEIR EXPERIENCES ARE NOT THAT MUCH DIFFERENT FROM OUR OWN.
HUNHH?
I AM SENSING RESTLESSNESS... SOMETHING IS--
--WRONG.
HEY!
LITERATURE: THEY WROTE OF THEIR PEOPLE AS WE DO, BUT INSTEAD OF DOING SO WITH KEYBOARDS AND PIXELS...
THEY ARE AGITATED... THEIR EMOTIONS CHARGED... WHAT AM I DOING TO THEM? WHY CAN'T I STOP?
C'MON. I SAID CUT IT OUT.
I HATE YOU.
...THEY USED CRUDE WEDGE-SHAPED CUNEIFORMS ETCHED INTO CLAY.
THEIR TECHNOLOGY MAY HAVE BEEN DIFFERENT, BUT IT GOT THE JOB DONE.
I NEED TO CONCENTRATE... MEDITATE... TO LET GO OF THE DARKNESS. LET GO OF THE PAIN...

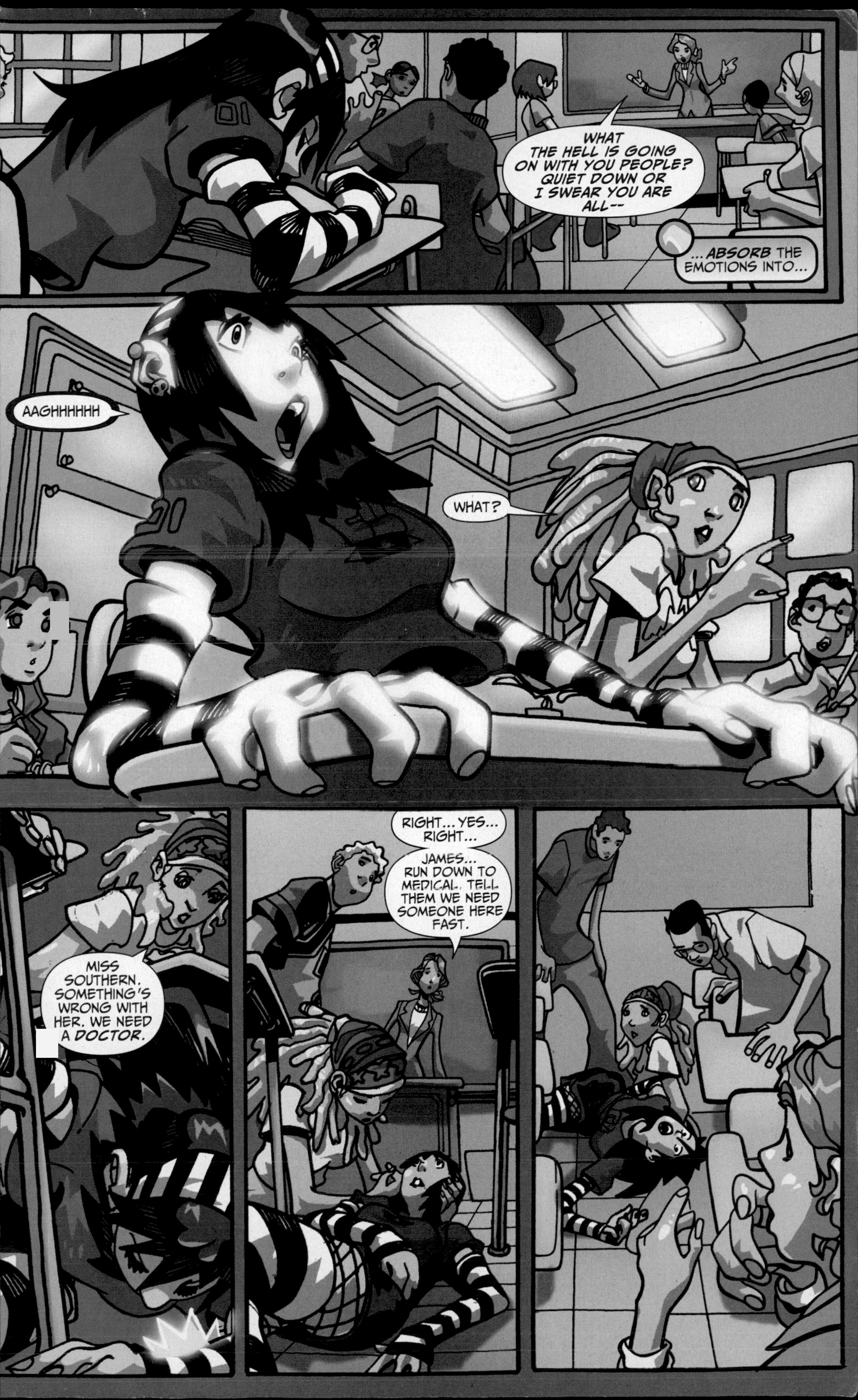
WHAT THE HELL IS GOING ON WITH YOU PEOPLE? QUIET DOWN OR I SWEAR YOU ARE ALL--
...ABSORB THE EMOTIONS INTO...
AAGHHHHHH
WHAT?
MISS SOUTHERN. SOMETHING'S WRONG WITH HER. WE NEED A DOCTOR.
RIGHT... YES... RIGHT...
JAMES... RUN DOWN TO MEDICAL. TELL THEM WE NEED SOMEONE HERE FAST.

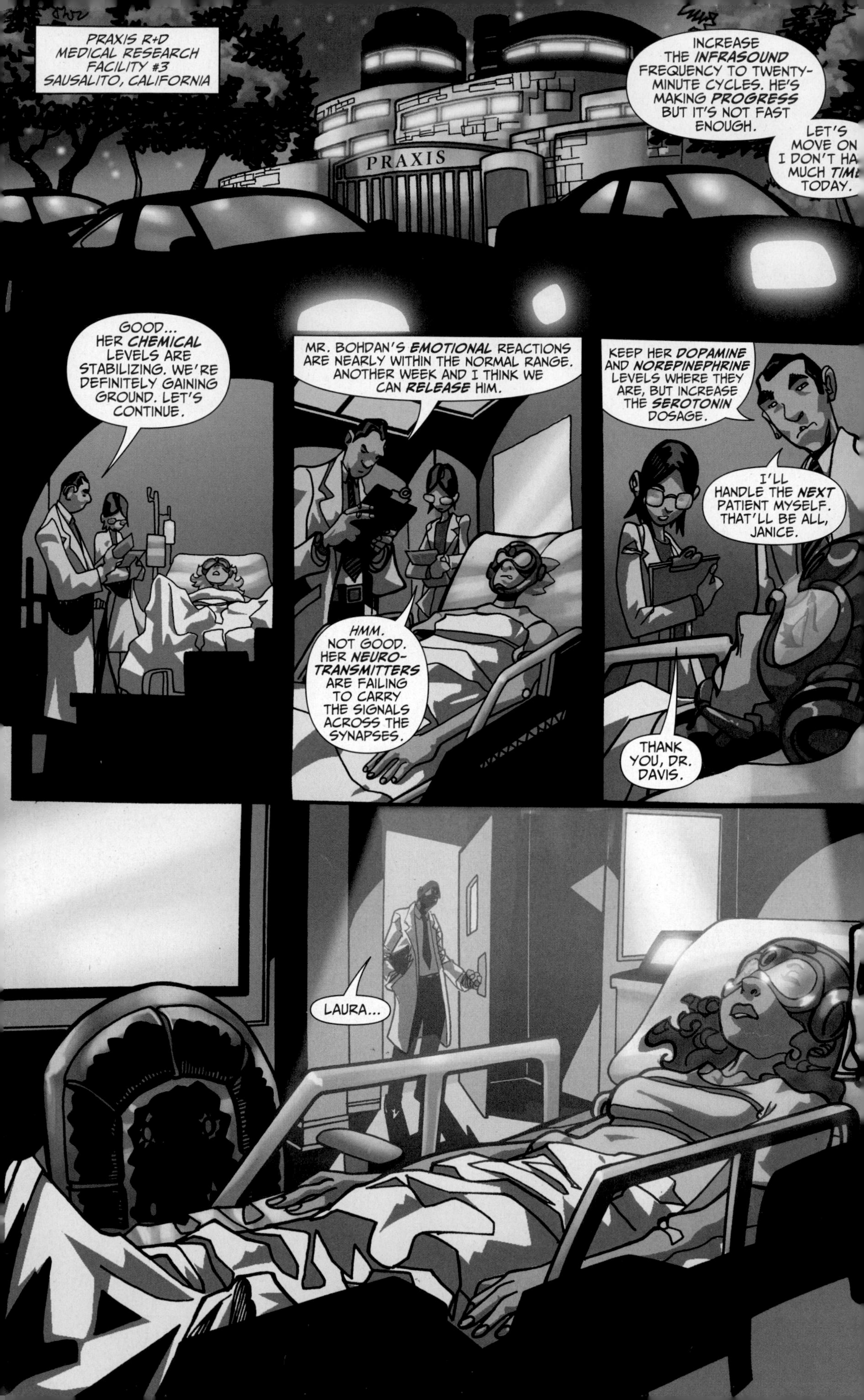
PRAXIS R+D MEDICAL RESEARCH FACILITY #3 SAUSALITO, CALIFORNIA
PRAXIS
INCREASE THE INFRASOUND FREQUENCY TO TWENTY-MINUTE CYCLES. HE'S MAKING PROGRESS BUT IT'S NOT FAST ENOUGH.
LET'S MOVE ON I DON'T HA MUCH TIME TODAY.
GOOD... HER CHEMICAL LEVELS ARE STABILIZING. WE'RE DEFINITELY GAINING GROUND. LET'S CONTINUE.
MR. BOHDAN'S EMOTIONAL REACTIONS ARE NEARLY WITHIN THE NORMAL RANGE. ANOTHER WEEK AND I THINK WE CAN RELEASE HIM.
HMM. NOT GOOD. HER NEURO-TRANSMITTERS ARE FAILING TO CARRY THE SIGNALS ACROSS THE SYNAPSES.
KEEP HER DOPAMINE AND NOREPINEPHRINE LEVELS WHERE THEY ARE, BUT INCREASE THE SEROTONIN DOSAGE.
I'LL HANDLE THE NEXT PATIENT MYSELF. THAT'LL BE ALL, JANICE.
THANK YOU, DR. DAVIS.
LAURA...

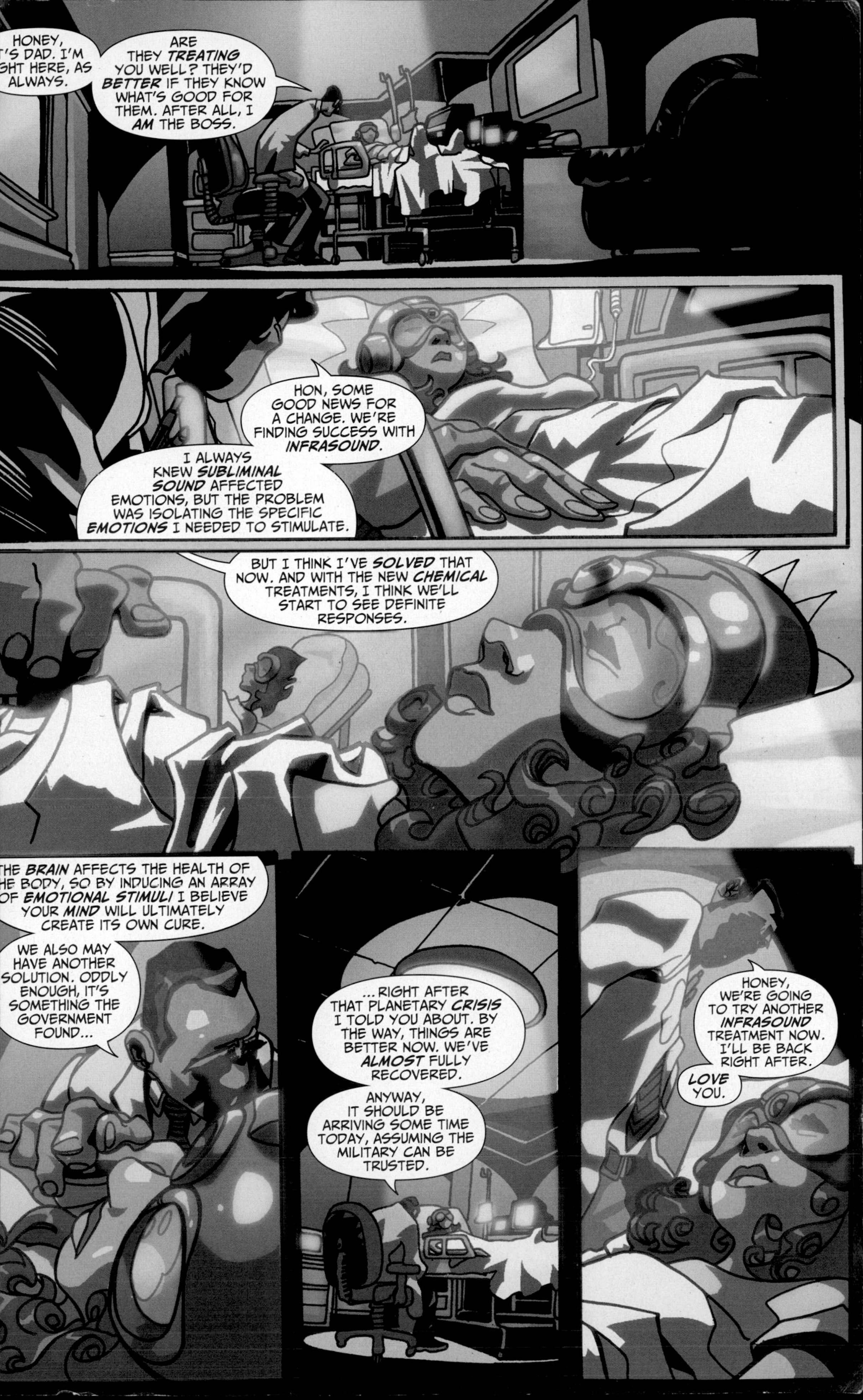
HONEY, IT'S DAD. I'M RIGHT HERE, AS ALWAYS.
ARE THEY TREATING YOU WELL? THEY'D BETTER IF THEY KNOW WHAT'S GOOD FOR THEM. AFTER ALL, I AM THE BOSS.
HON, SOME GOOD NEWS FOR A CHANGE. WE'RE FINDING SUCCESS WITH INFRASOUND.
I ALWAYS KNEW SUBLIMINAL SOUND AFFECTED EMOTIONS, BUT THE PROBLEM WAS ISOLATING THE SPECIFIC EMOTIONS I NEEDED TO STIMULATE.
BUT I THINK I'VE SOLVED THAT NOW. AND WITH THE NEW CHEMICAL TREATMENTS, I THINK WE'LL START TO SEE DEFINITE RESPONSES.
THE BRAIN AFFECTS THE HEALTH OF THE BODY, SO BY INDUCING AN ARRAY OF EMOTIONAL STIMULI I BELIEVE YOUR MIND WILL ULTIMATELY CREATE ITS OWN CURE.
WE ALSO MAY HAVE ANOTHER SOLUTION. ODDLY ENOUGH, IT'S SOMETHING THE GOVERNMENT FOUND...
...RIGHT AFTER THAT PLANETARY CRISIS I TOLD YOU ABOUT. BY THE WAY, THINGS ARE BETTER NOW. WE'VE ALMOST FULLY RECOVERED.
ANYWAY, IT SHOULD BE ARRIVING SOME TIME TODAY, ASSUMING THE MILITARY CAN BE TRUSTED.
HONEY, WE'RE GOING TO TRY ANOTHER INFRASOUND TREATMENT NOW. I'LL BE BACK RIGHT AFTER.
LOVE YOU.

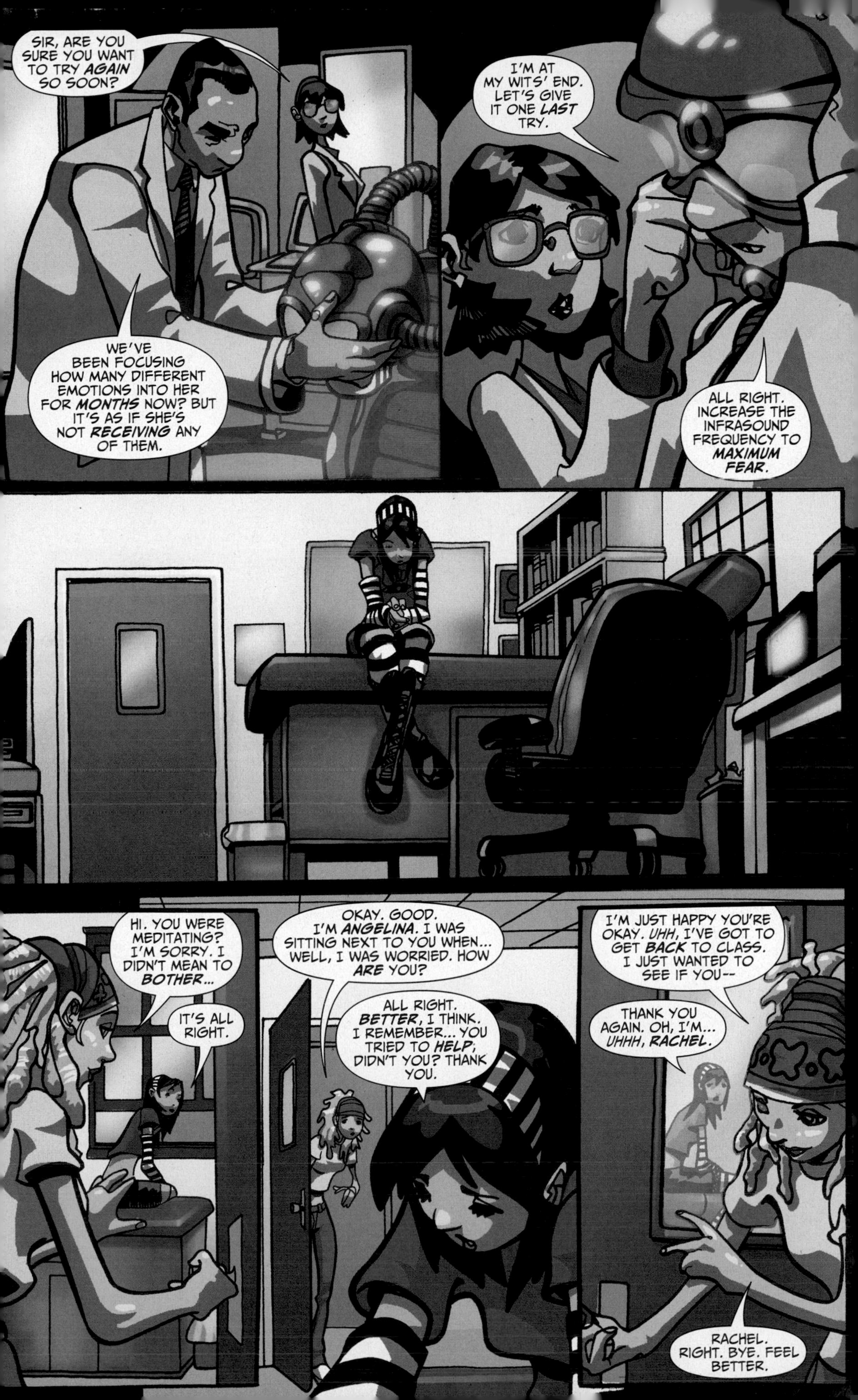
SIR, ARE YOU SURE YOU WANT TO TRY AGAIN SO SOON?
WE'VE BEEN FOCUSING HOW MANY DIFFERENT EMOTIONS INTO HER FOR MONTHS NOW? BUT IT'S AS IF SHE'S NOT RECEIVING ANY OF THEM.
I'M AT MY WITS' END. LET'S GIVE IT ONE LAST TRY.
ALL RIGHT. INCREASE THE INFRASOUND FREQUENCY TO MAXIMUM FEAR.
HI. YOU WERE MEDITATING? I'M SORRY. I DIDN'T MEAN TO BOTHER...
IT'S ALL RIGHT.
OKAY. GOOD. I'M ANGELINA. I WAS SITTING NEXT TO YOU WHEN... WELL, I WAS WORRIED. HOW ARE YOU?
ALL RIGHT. BETTER, I THINK. I REMEMBER... YOU TRIED TO HELP, DIDN'T YOU? THANK YOU.
I'M JUST HAPPY YOU'RE OKAY. UHH, I'VE GOT TO GET BACK TO CLASS. I JUST WANTED TO SEE IF YOU--
THANK YOU AGAIN. OH, I'M... UHHH, RACHEL.
RACHEL. RIGHT. BYE. FEEL BETTER.

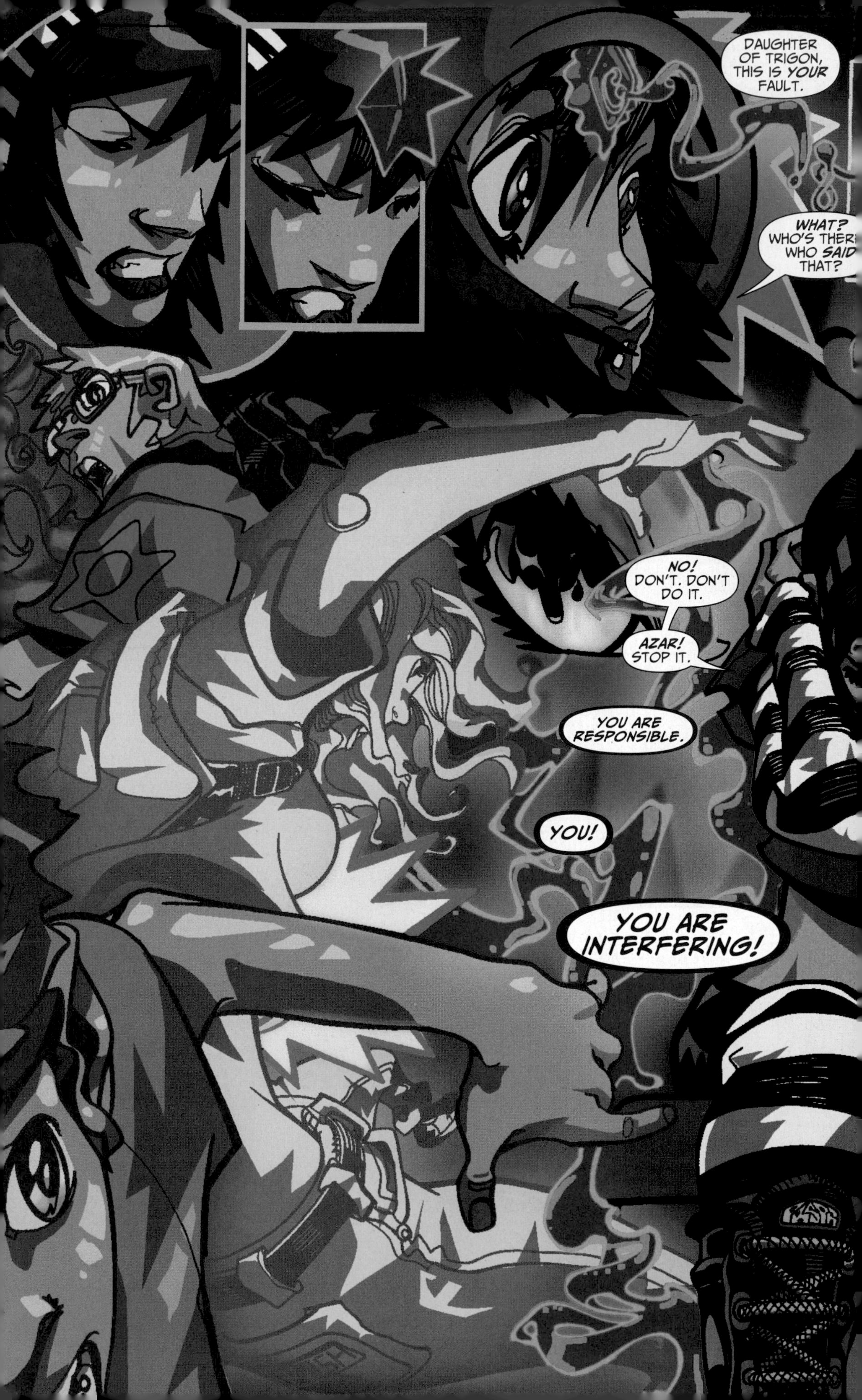
DAUGHTER OF TRIGON, THIS IS *YOUR* FAULT.
WHAT? WHO'S THERE WHO *SAID* THAT?
NO! DON'T. DON'T DO IT.
AZAR! STOP IT.
YOU ARE RESPONSIBLE.
YOU!
YOU ARE INTERFERING!

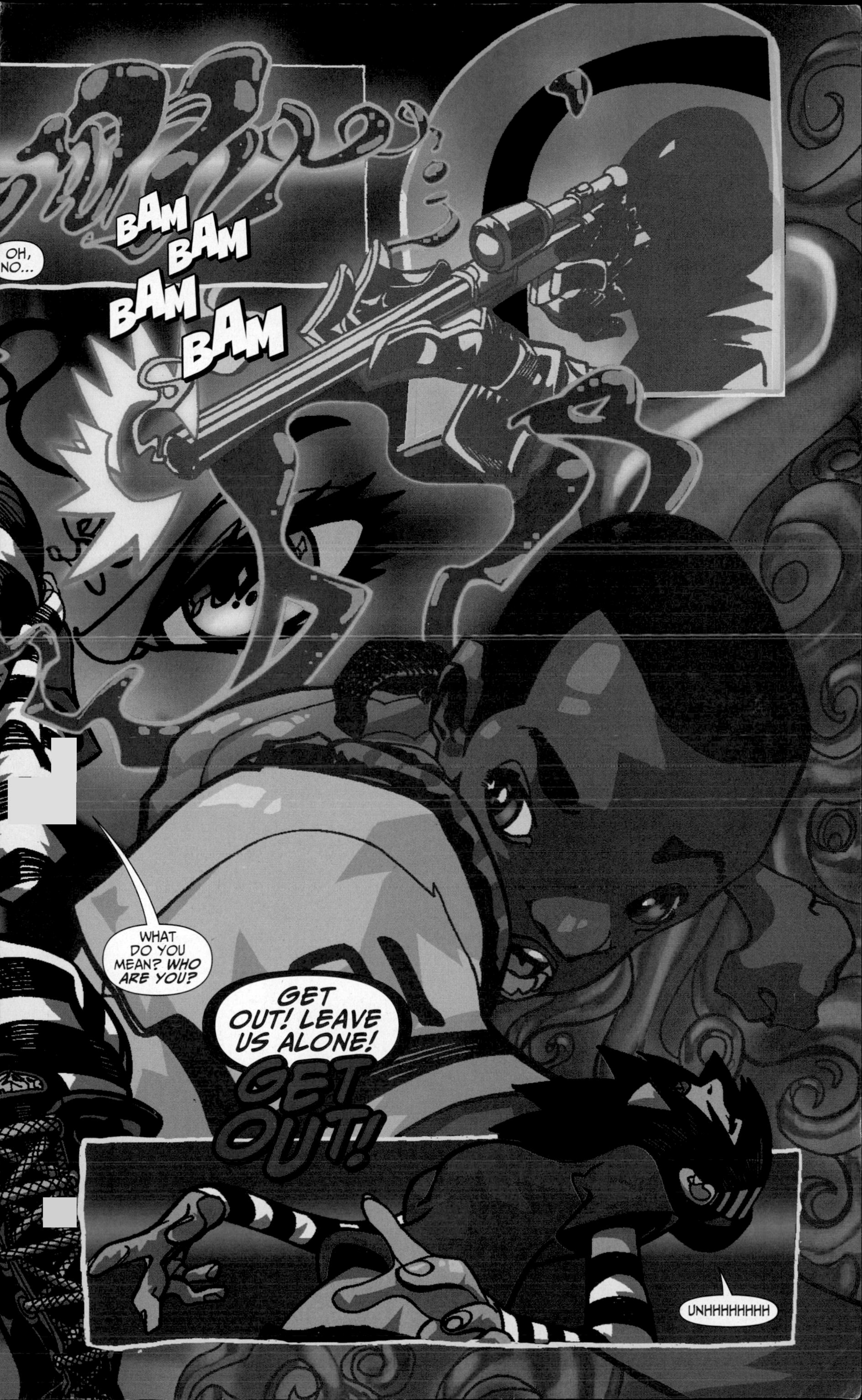
OH, NO...
BAM BAM BAM BAM
WHAT DO YOU MEAN? WHO ARE YOU?
GET OUT! LEAVE US ALONE!
GET OUT!
UNHHHHHHHH

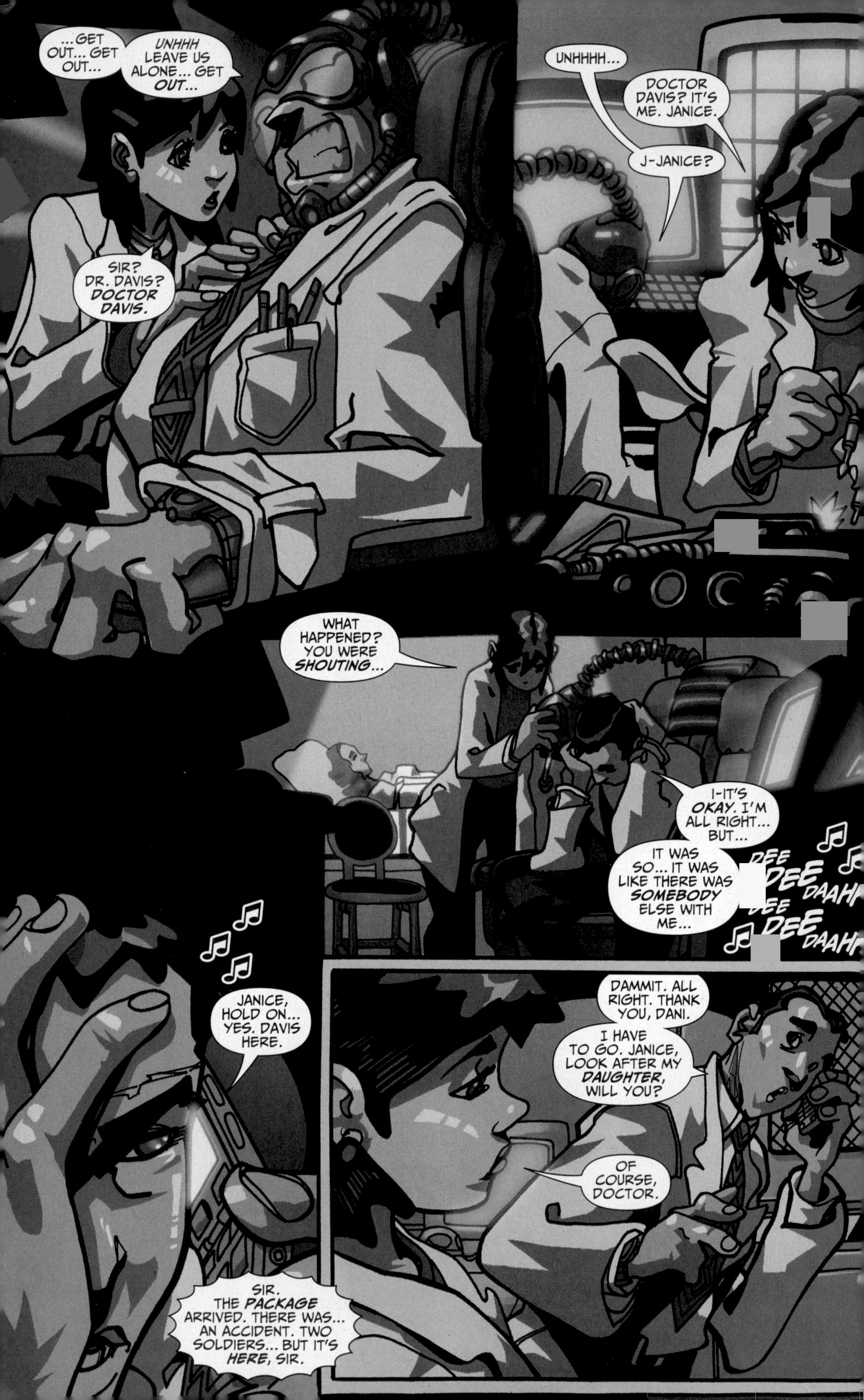
...GET OUT... GET OUT...
UNHHH LEAVE US ALONE... GET OUT...
SIR? DR. DAVIS? DOCTOR DAVIS.
UNHHHH...
DOCTOR DAVIS? IT'S ME. JANICE.
J-JANICE?
WHAT HAPPENED? YOU WERE SHOUTING...
I-IT'S OKAY. I'M ALL RIGHT... BUT...
IT WAS SO... IT WAS LIKE THERE WAS SOMEBODY ELSE WITH ME...
DEE DEE DAAH
DEE DEE DAAH
JANICE, HOLD ON... YES. DAVIS HERE.
SIR. THE PACKAGE ARRIVED. THERE WAS... AN ACCIDENT. TWO SOLDIERS... BUT IT'S HERE, SIR.
DAMMIT. ALL RIGHT. THANK YOU, DANI.
I HAVE TO GO. JANICE, LOOK AFTER MY DAUGHTER, WILL YOU?
OF COURSE, DOCTOR.

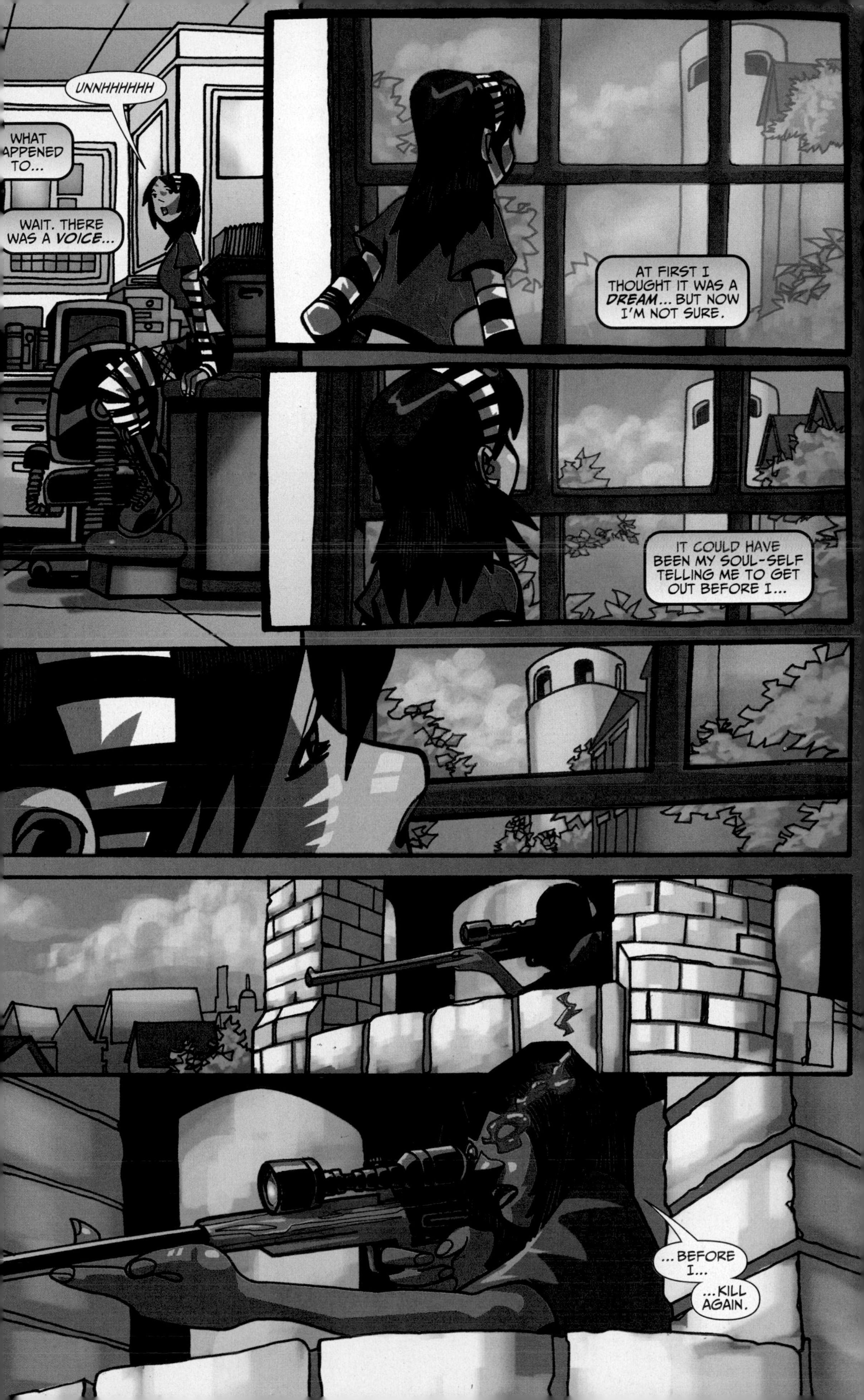
UNNHHHHHH
WHAT APPENED TO...
WAIT. THERE WAS A VOICE...
AT FIRST I THOUGHT IT WAS A DREAM... BUT NOW I'M NOT SURE.
IT COULD HAVE BEEN MY SOUL-SELF TELLING ME TO GET OUT BEFORE I...
...BEFORE I...
...KILL AGAIN.

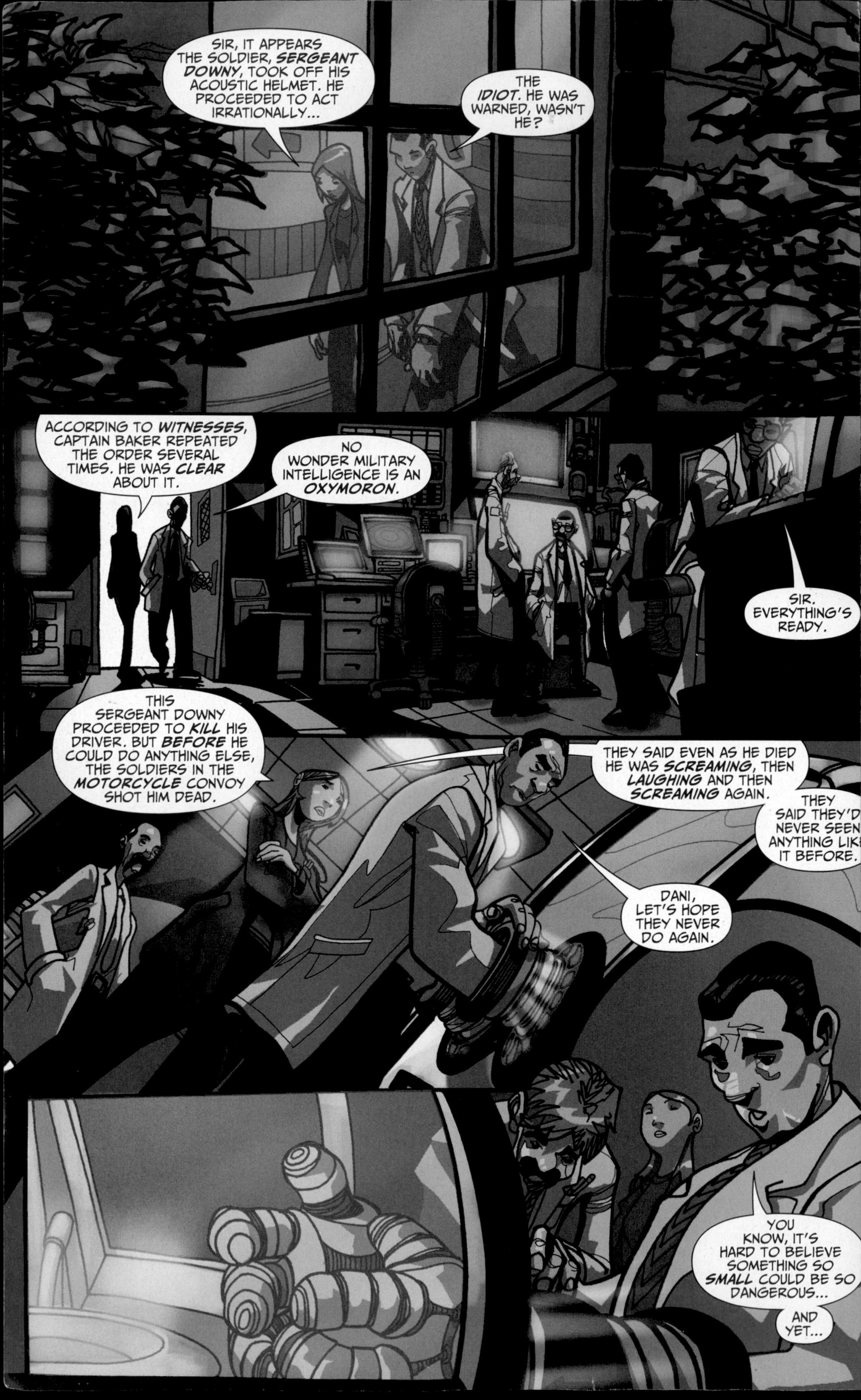
SIR, IT APPEARS THE SOLDIER, SERGEANT DOWNY, TOOK OFF HIS ACOUSTIC HELMET. HE PROCEEDED TO ACT IRRATIONALLY...
THE IDIOT. HE WAS WARNED, WASN'T HE?
ACCORDING TO WITNESSES, CAPTAIN BAKER REPEATED THE ORDER SEVERAL TIMES. HE WAS CLEAR ABOUT IT.
NO WONDER MILITARY INTELLIGENCE IS AN OXYMORON.
SIR. EVERYTHING'S READY.
THIS SERGEANT DOWNY PROCEEDED TO KILL HIS DRIVER. BUT BEFORE HE COULD DO ANYTHING ELSE, THE SOLDIERS IN THE MOTORCYCLE CONVOY SHOT HIM DEAD.
THEY SAID EVEN AS HE DIED HE WAS SCREAMING, THEN LAUGHING AND THEN SCREAMING AGAIN.
THEY SAID THEY'D NEVER SEEN ANYTHING LIKE IT BEFORE.
DANI, LET'S HOPE THEY NEVER DO AGAIN.
YOU KNOW, IT'S HARD TO BELIEVE SOMETHING SO SMALL COULD BE SO DANGEROUS...
AND YET...

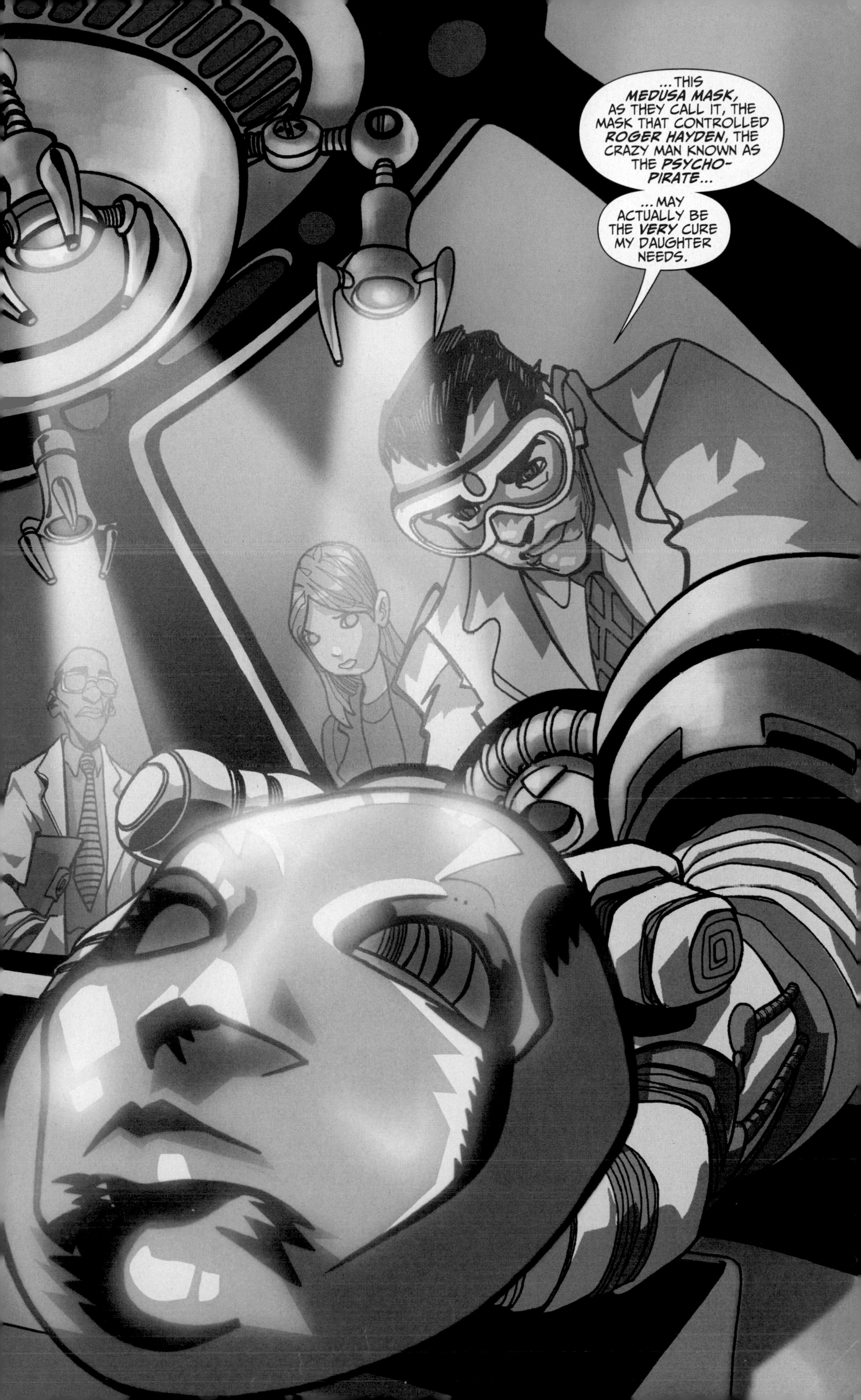
...THIS **MEDUSA MASK,** AS THEY CALL IT, THE MASK THAT CONTROLLED **ROGER HAYDEN,** THE CRAZY MAN KNOWN AS THE **PSYCHO-PIRATE...**
...MAY ACTUALLY BE THE **VERY** CURE MY DAUGHTER NEEDS.

Part 2: Shadows

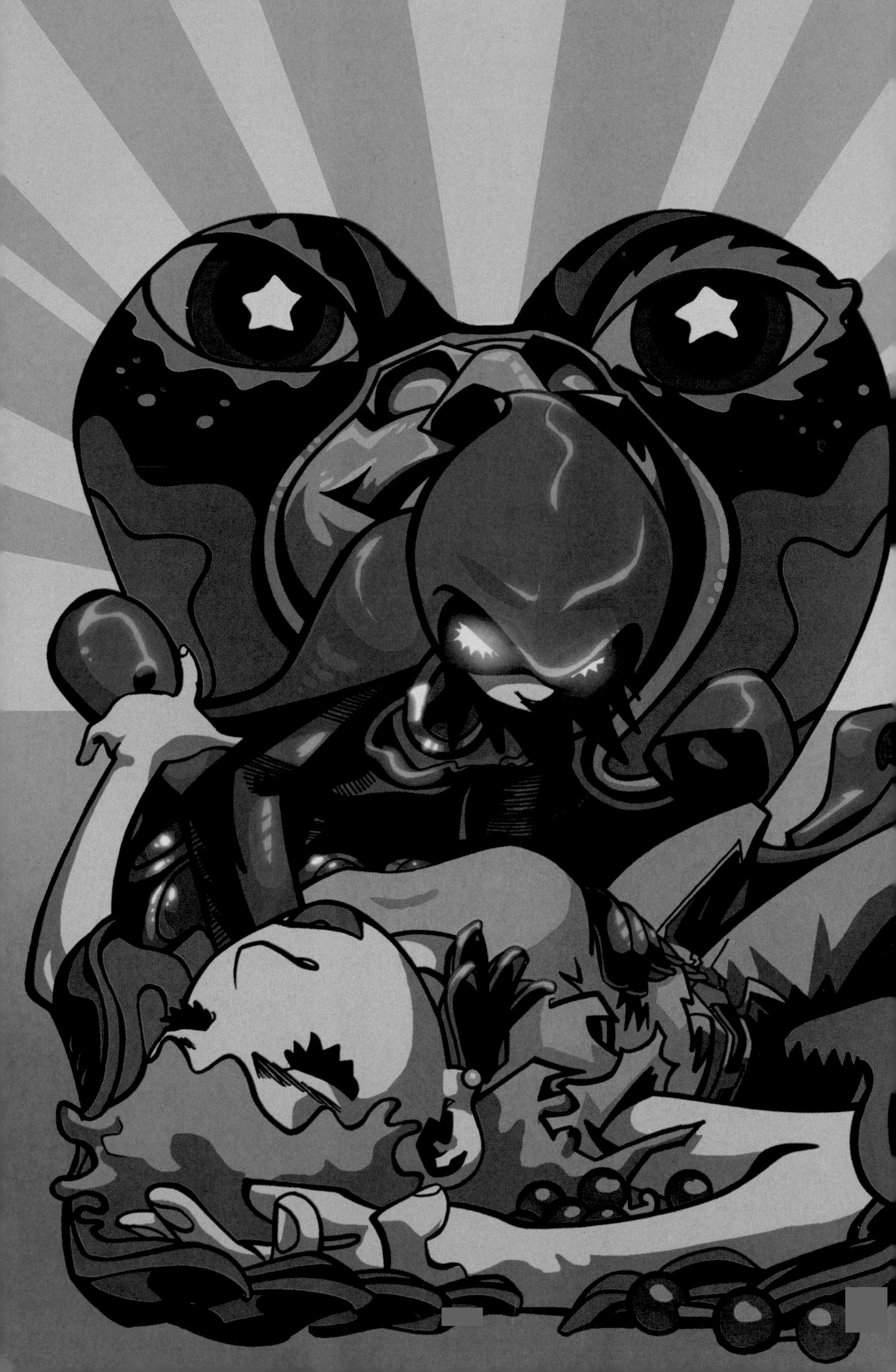

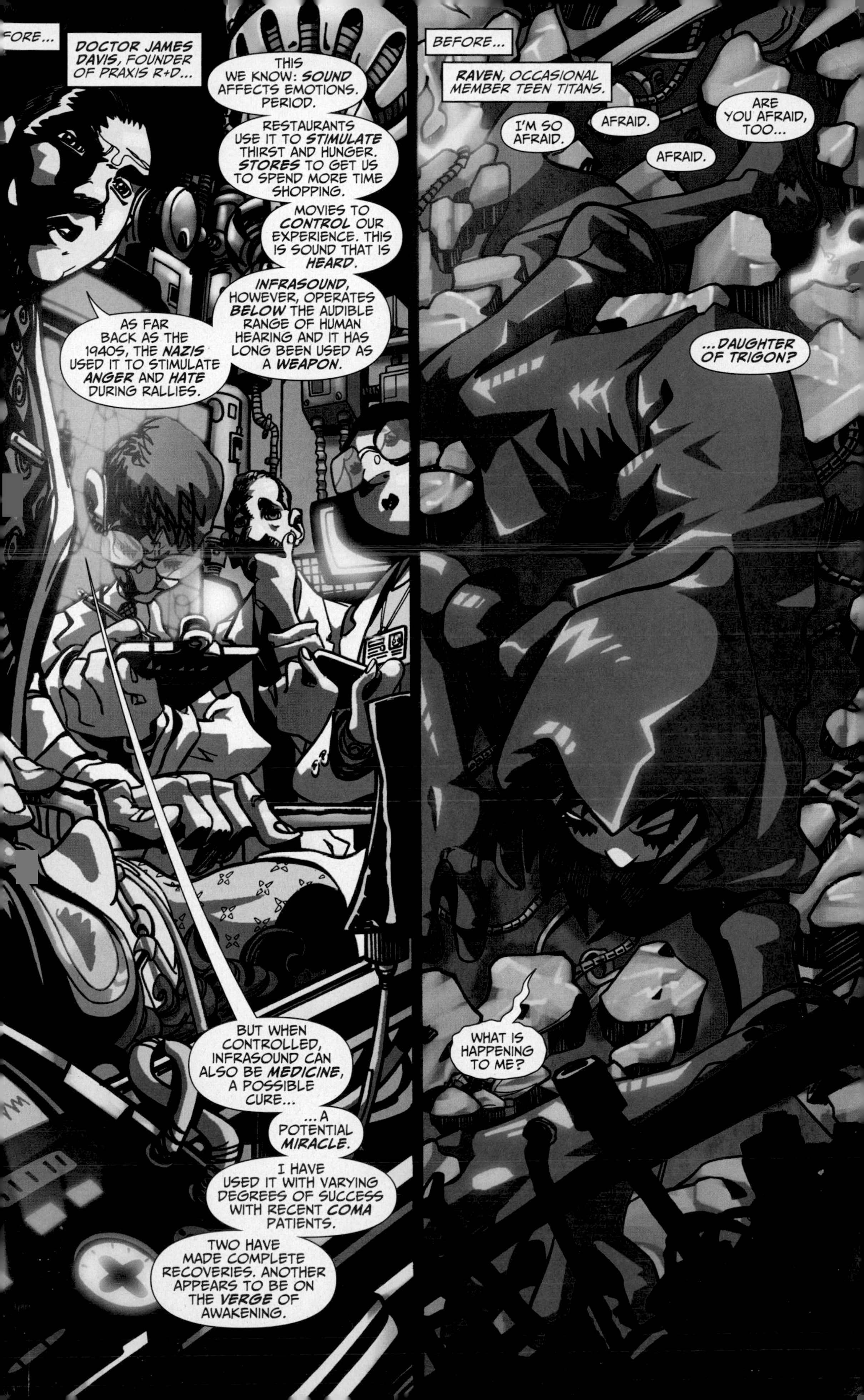

FORE...
DOCTOR JAMES DAVIS, FOUNDER OF PRAXIS R+D...
THIS WE KNOW: SOUND AFFECTS EMOTIONS. PERIOD.
RESTAURANTS USE IT TO STIMULATE THIRST AND HUNGER. STORES TO GET US TO SPEND MORE TIME SHOPPING.
MOVIES TO CONTROL OUR EXPERIENCE. THIS IS SOUND THAT IS HEARD.
INFRASOUND, HOWEVER, OPERATES BELOW THE AUDIBLE RANGE OF HUMAN HEARING AND IT HAS LONG BEEN USED AS A WEAPON.
AS FAR BACK AS THE 1940S, THE NAZIS USED IT TO STIMULATE ANGER AND HATE DURING RALLIES.
BUT WHEN CONTROLLED, INFRASOUND CAN ALSO BE MEDICINE, A POSSIBLE CURE...
...A POTENTIAL MIRACLE.
I HAVE USED IT WITH VARYING DEGREES OF SUCCESS WITH RECENT COMA PATIENTS.
TWO HAVE MADE COMPLETE RECOVERIES. ANOTHER APPEARS TO BE ON THE VERGE OF AWAKENING.
BEFORE...
RAVEN, OCCASIONAL MEMBER TEEN TITANS.
I'M SO AFRAID.
AFRAID.
AFRAID.
ARE YOU AFRAID, TOO...
...DAUGHTER OF TRIGON?
WHAT IS HAPPENING TO ME?

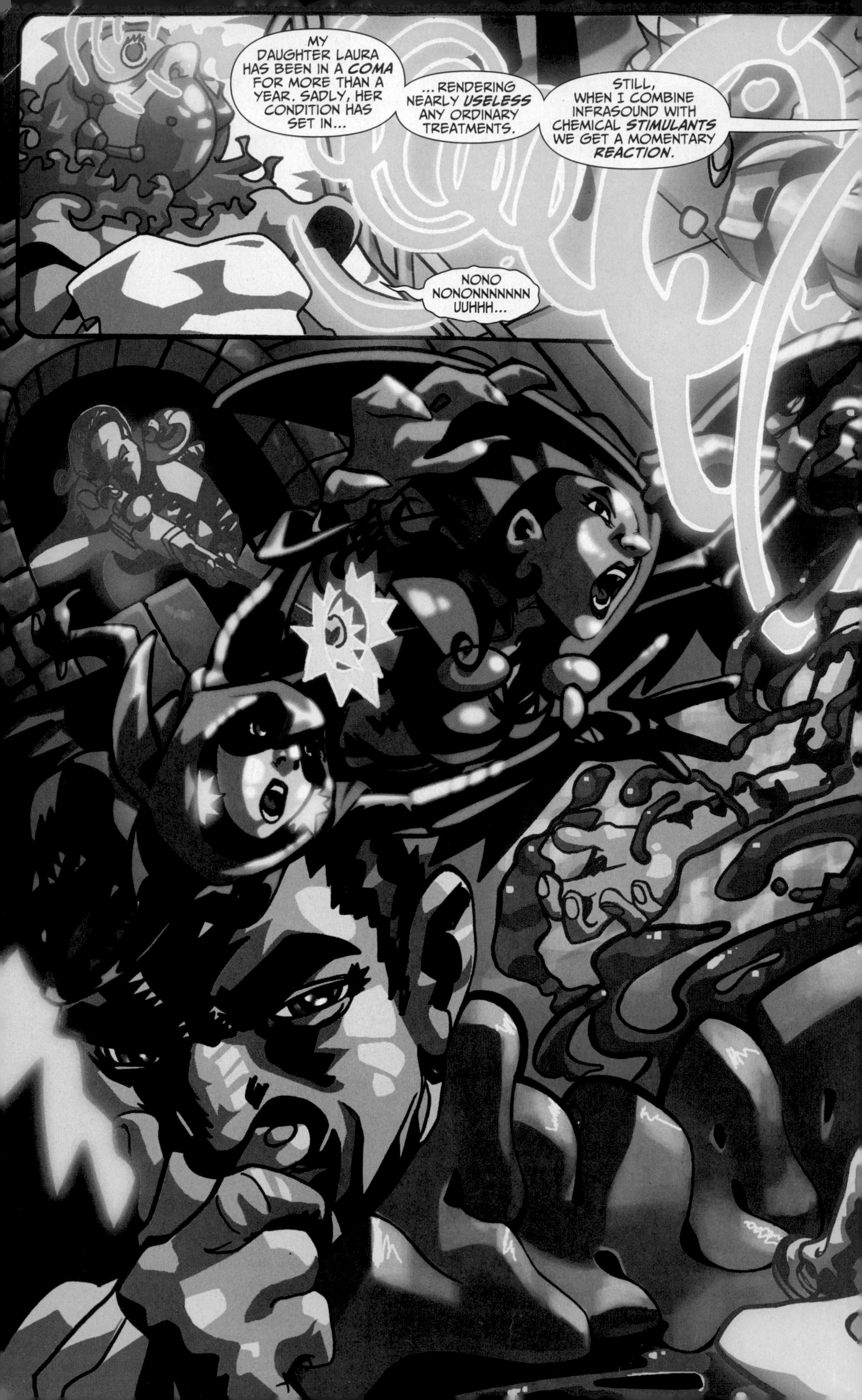
MY DAUGHTER LAURA HAS BEEN IN A COMA FOR MORE THAN A YEAR. SADLY, HER CONDITION HAS SET IN...
...RENDERING NEARLY USELESS ANY ORDINARY TREATMENTS.
STILL, WHEN I COMBINE INFRASOUND WITH CHEMICAL STIMULANTS WE GET A MOMENTARY REACTION.
NONO NONONNNNNNN UUHHH...

I BELIEVE HIDDEN BEHIND A BLOCK WHICH PREVENTS HER FROM ACCESSING HER OWN MIND, MY DAUGHTER IS ALIVE AND AWARE.
I FURTHER BELIEVE THAT BLOCK CAN BE SHATTERED BY SPECIFIC FORCED EMOTIONS THAT ARE CONTROLLED AND FOCUSED.
UNTIL NOW EVEN INFRASOUND WAS INCAPABLE OF SUCH PRECISION TARGETING. BUT DUE TO A RECENT FIND BY THE GOVERNMENT...
...WE ARE AT THE THRESHOLD OF A MAJOR BREAKTHROUGH IN THE TREATMENT OF ALL MENTAL AND EMOTIONAL DISORDERS.
MY NIGHTMARE...
AZARRRRRRR!
DAUGHTER OF TRIGON, IT IS ALL YOUR FAULT.

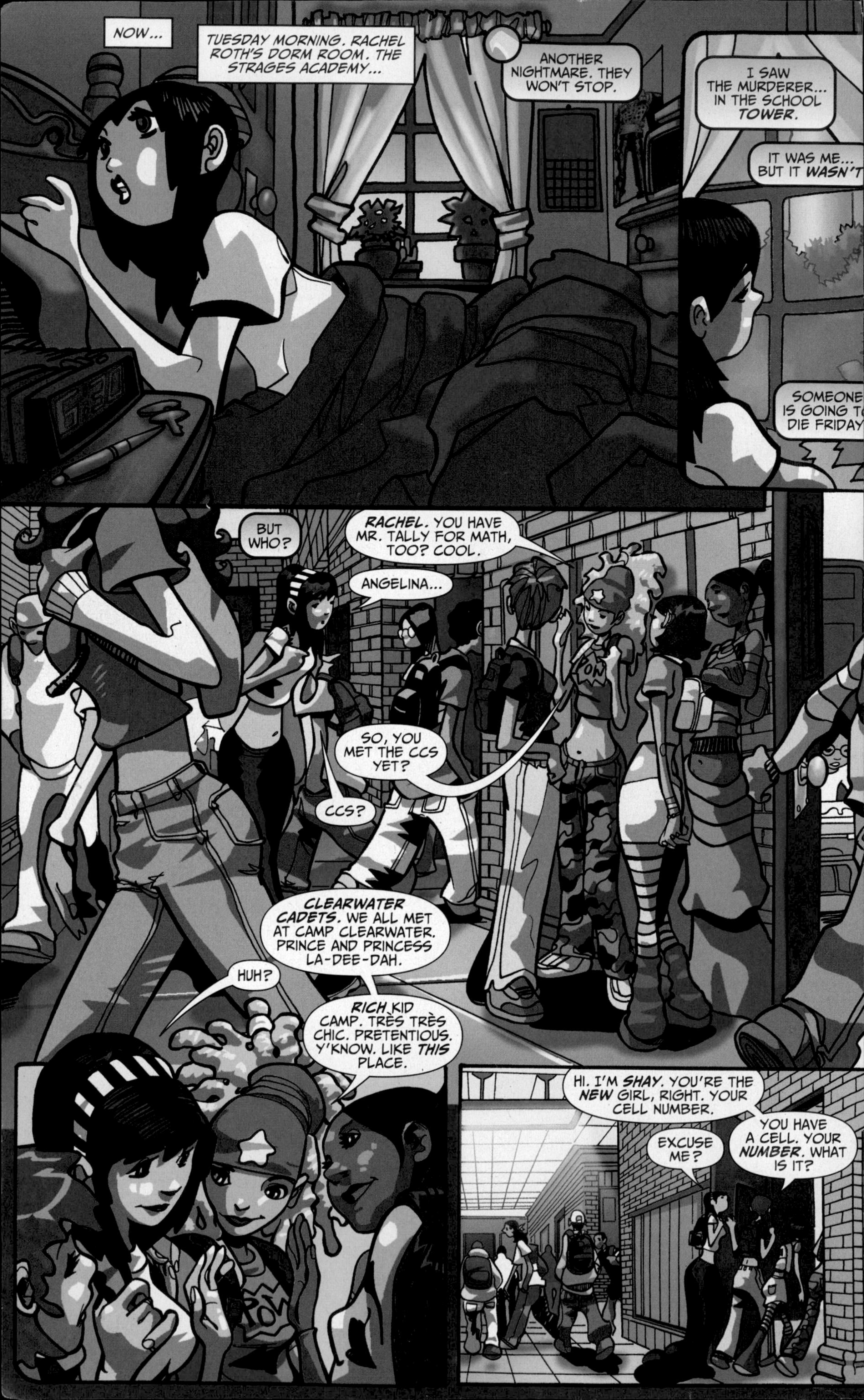
NOW...
TUESDAY MORNING. RACHEL ROTH'S DORM ROOM. THE STRAGES ACADEMY...
ANOTHER NIGHTMARE. THEY WON'T STOP.
I SAW THE MURDERER... IN THE SCHOOL TOWER.
IT WAS ME... BUT IT WASN'T
SOMEONE IS GOING TO DIE FRIDAY
BUT WHO?
RACHEL. YOU HAVE MR. TALLY FOR MATH, TOO? COOL.
ANGELINA...
SO, YOU MET THE CCS YET?
CCS?
CLEARWATER CADETS. WE ALL MET AT CAMP CLEARWATER. PRINCE AND PRINCESS LA-DEE-DAH.
HUH?
RICH KID CAMP. TRÈS TRÈS CHIC. PRETENTIOUS. Y'KNOW. LIKE THIS PLACE.
HI. I'M SHAY. YOU'RE THE NEW GIRL, RIGHT. YOUR CELL NUMBER.
EXCUSE ME?
YOU HAVE A CELL. YOUR NUMBER. WHAT IS IT?

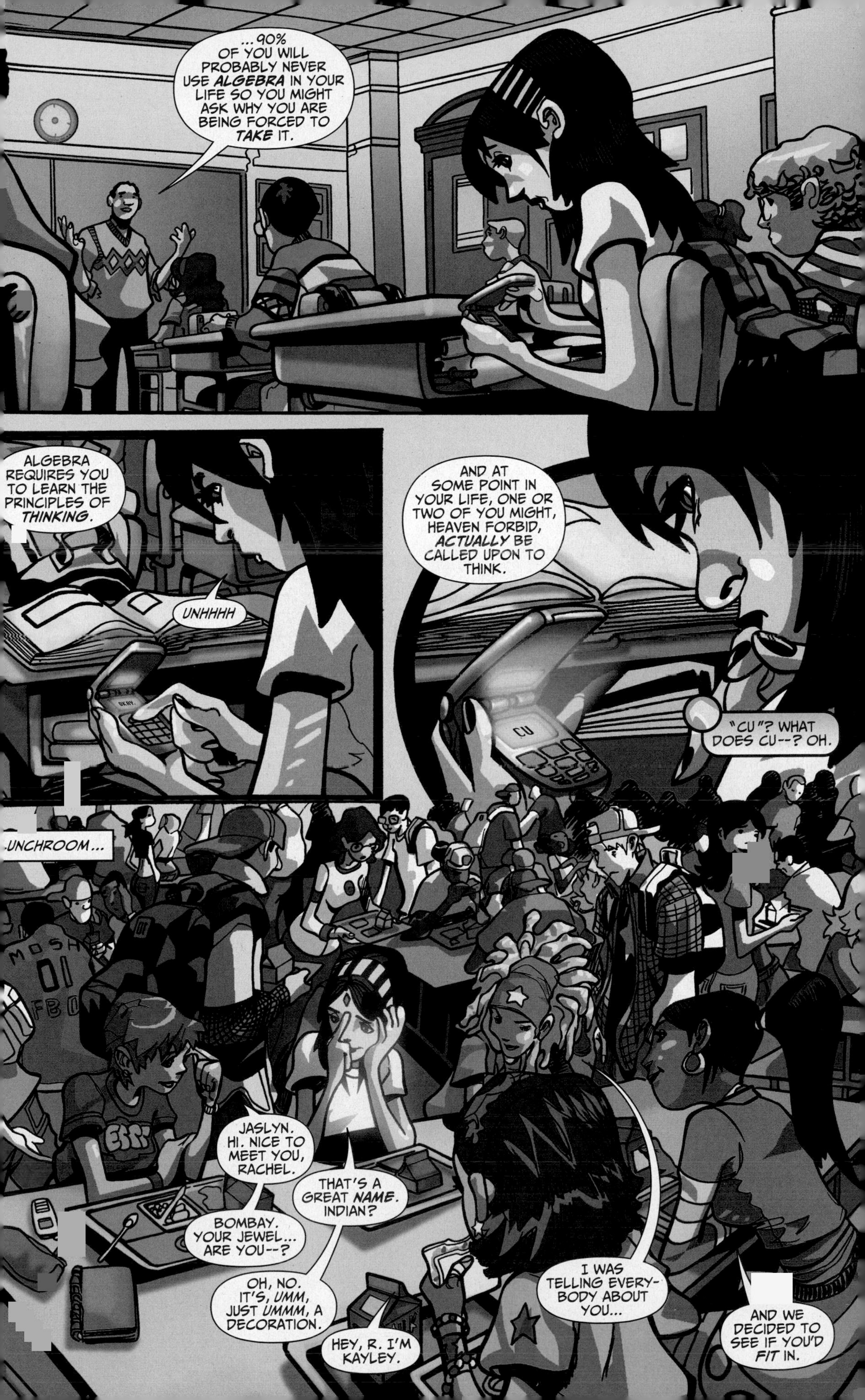

...90% OF YOU WILL PROBABLY NEVER USE ALGEBRA IN YOUR LIFE SO YOU MIGHT ASK WHY YOU ARE BEING FORCED TO TAKE IT.
ALGEBRA REQUIRES YOU TO LEARN THE PRINCIPLES OF THINKING.
UNHHHH
AND AT SOME POINT IN YOUR LIFE, ONE OR TWO OF YOU MIGHT, HEAVEN FORBID, ACTUALLY BE CALLED UPON TO THINK.
CU
"CU"? WHAT DOES CU--? OH.
UNCHROOM...
JASLYN. HI. NICE TO MEET YOU, RACHEL.
THAT'S A GREAT NAME. INDIAN?
BOMBAY. YOUR JEWEL... ARE YOU--?
OH, NO. IT'S, UMM, JUST UMMM, A DECORATION.
HEY, R. I'M KAYLEY.
I WAS TELLING EVERY-BODY ABOUT YOU...
AND WE DECIDED TO SEE IF YOU'D FIT IN.

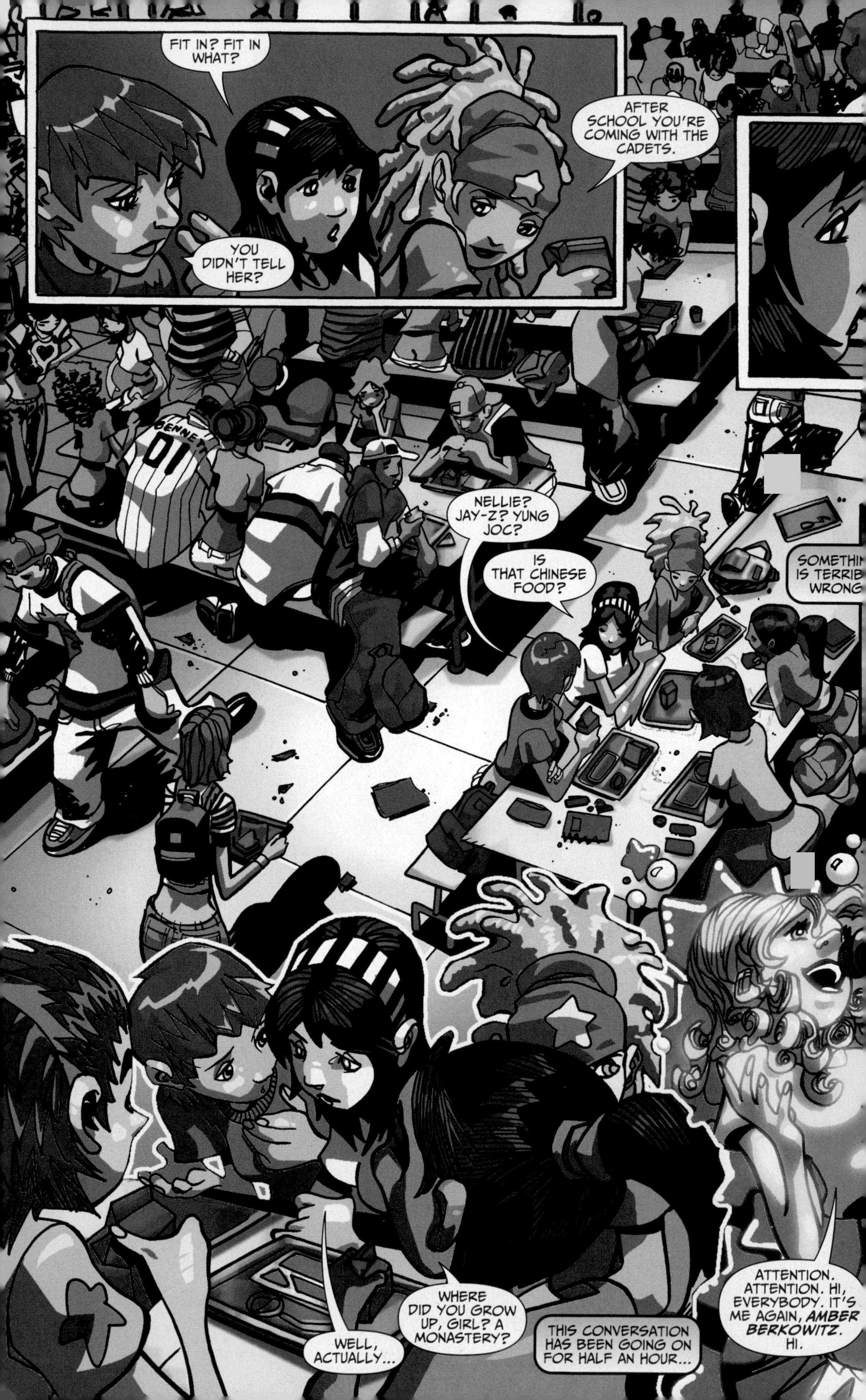
FIT IN? FIT IN WHAT?
YOU DIDN'T TELL HER?
AFTER SCHOOL YOU'RE COMING WITH THE CADETS.
NELLIE? JAY-Z? YUNG JOC?
IS THAT CHINESE FOOD?
SOMETHIN IS TERRIB WRONG
WHERE DID YOU GROW UP, GIRL? A MONASTERY?
WELL, ACTUALLY...
THIS CONVERSATION HAS BEEN GOING ON FOR HALF AN HOUR...
ATTENTION. ATTENTION. HI, EVERYBODY. IT'S ME AGAIN, *AMBER BERKOWITZ*. HI.

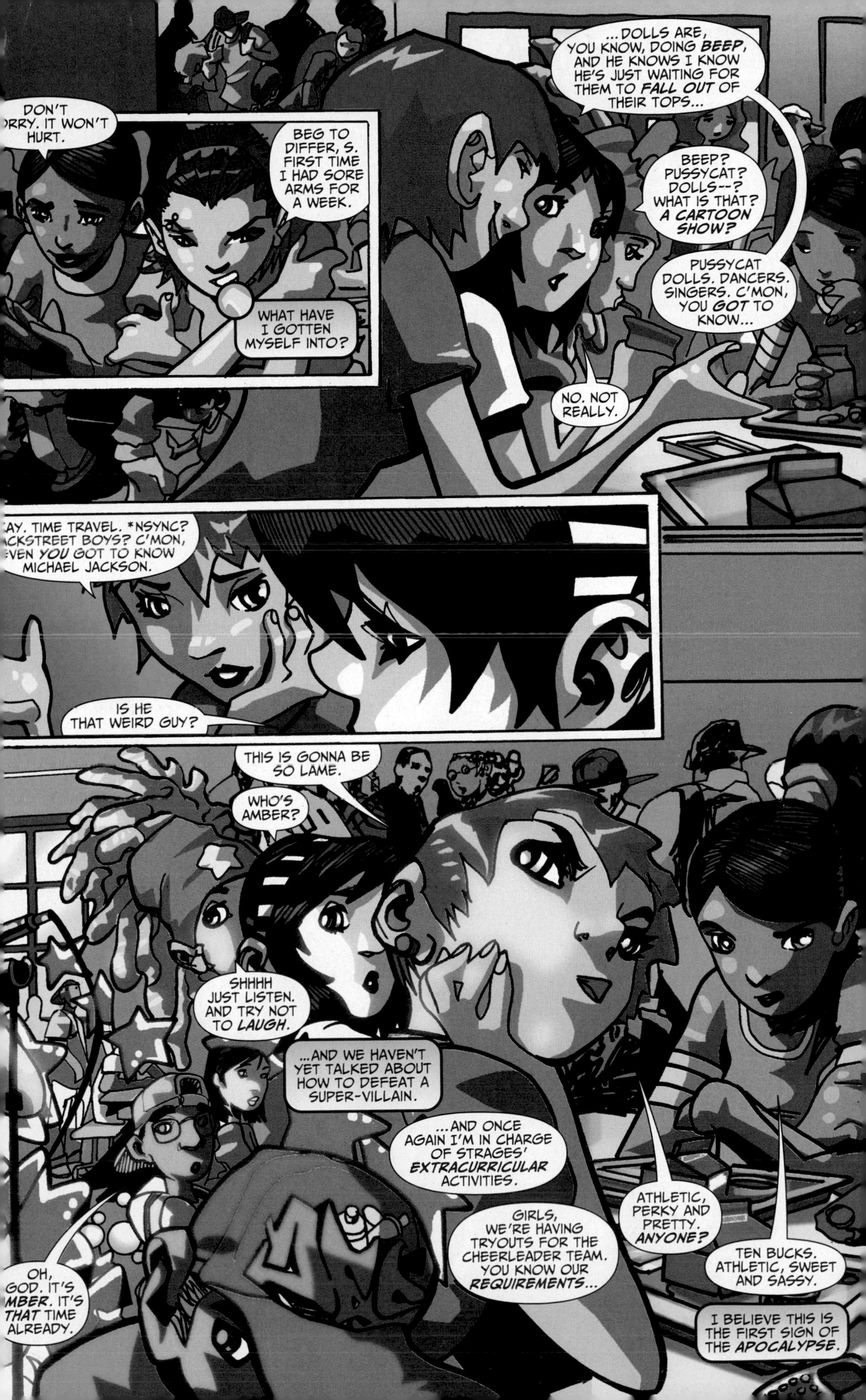

...DOLLS ARE, YOU KNOW, DOING BEEP, AND HE KNOWS I KNOW HE'S JUST WAITING FOR THEM TO FALL OUT OF THEIR TOPS...
DON'T RRY. IT WON'T HURT.
BEG TO DIFFER, S. FIRST TIME I HAD SORE ARMS FOR A WEEK.
WHAT HAVE I GOTTEN MYSELF INTO?
BEEP? PUSSYCAT? DOLLS--? WHAT IS THAT? A CARTOON SHOW?
PUSSYCAT DOLLS. DANCERS. SINGERS. C'MON, YOU GOT TO KNOW...
NO. NOT REALLY.
AY. TIME TRAVEL. *NSYNC? ACKSTREET BOYS? C'MON, EVEN YOU GOT TO KNOW MICHAEL JACKSON.
IS HE THAT WEIRD GUY?
THIS IS GONNA BE SO LAME.
WHO'S AMBER?
SHHHH JUST LISTEN. AND TRY NOT TO LAUGH.
...AND WE HAVEN'T YET TALKED ABOUT HOW TO DEFEAT A SUPER-VILLAIN.
...AND ONCE AGAIN I'M IN CHARGE OF STRAGES' EXTRACURRICULAR ACTIVITIES.
OH, GOD. IT'S MBER. IT'S THAT TIME ALREADY.
GIRLS, WE'RE HAVING TRYOUTS FOR THE CHEERLEADER TEAM. YOU KNOW OUR REQUIREMENTS...
ATHLETIC, PERKY AND PRETTY. ANYONE?
TEN BUCKS. ATHLETIC, SWEET AND SASSY.
I BELIEVE THIS IS THE FIRST SIGN OF THE APOCALYPSE.

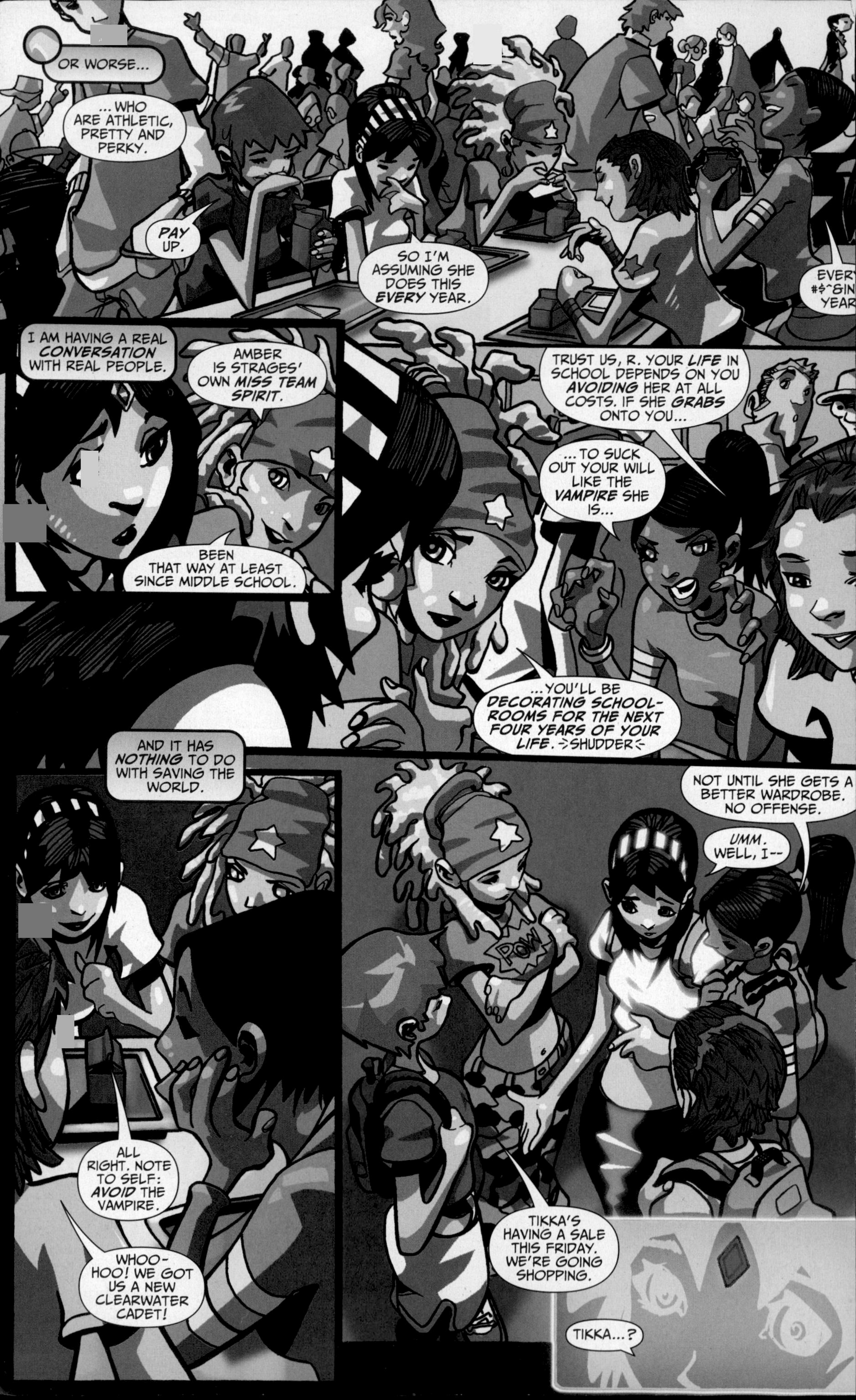
OR WORSE...
...WHO ARE ATHLETIC, PRETTY AND PERKY.
PAY UP.
SO I'M ASSUMING SHE DOES THIS EVERY YEAR.
EVERY #$^&IN YEAR
I AM HAVING A REAL CONVERSATION WITH REAL PEOPLE.
AMBER IS STRAGES' OWN MISS TEAM SPIRIT.
BEEN THAT WAY AT LEAST SINCE MIDDLE SCHOOL.
TRUST US, R. YOUR LIFE IN SCHOOL DEPENDS ON YOU AVOIDING HER AT ALL COSTS. IF SHE GRABS ONTO YOU...
...TO SUCK OUT YOUR WILL LIKE THE VAMPIRE SHE IS...
...YOU'LL BE DECORATING SCHOOL-ROOMS FOR THE NEXT FOUR YEARS OF YOUR LIFE. >SHUDDER<
AND IT HAS NOTHING TO DO WITH SAVING THE WORLD.
ALL RIGHT. NOTE TO SELF: AVOID THE VAMPIRE.
WHOO-HOO! WE GOT US A NEW CLEARWATER CADET!
NOT UNTIL SHE GETS A BETTER WARDROBE. NO OFFENSE.
UMM. WELL, I--
TIKKA'S HAVING A SALE THIS FRIDAY. WE'RE GOING SHOPPING.
TIKKA...?

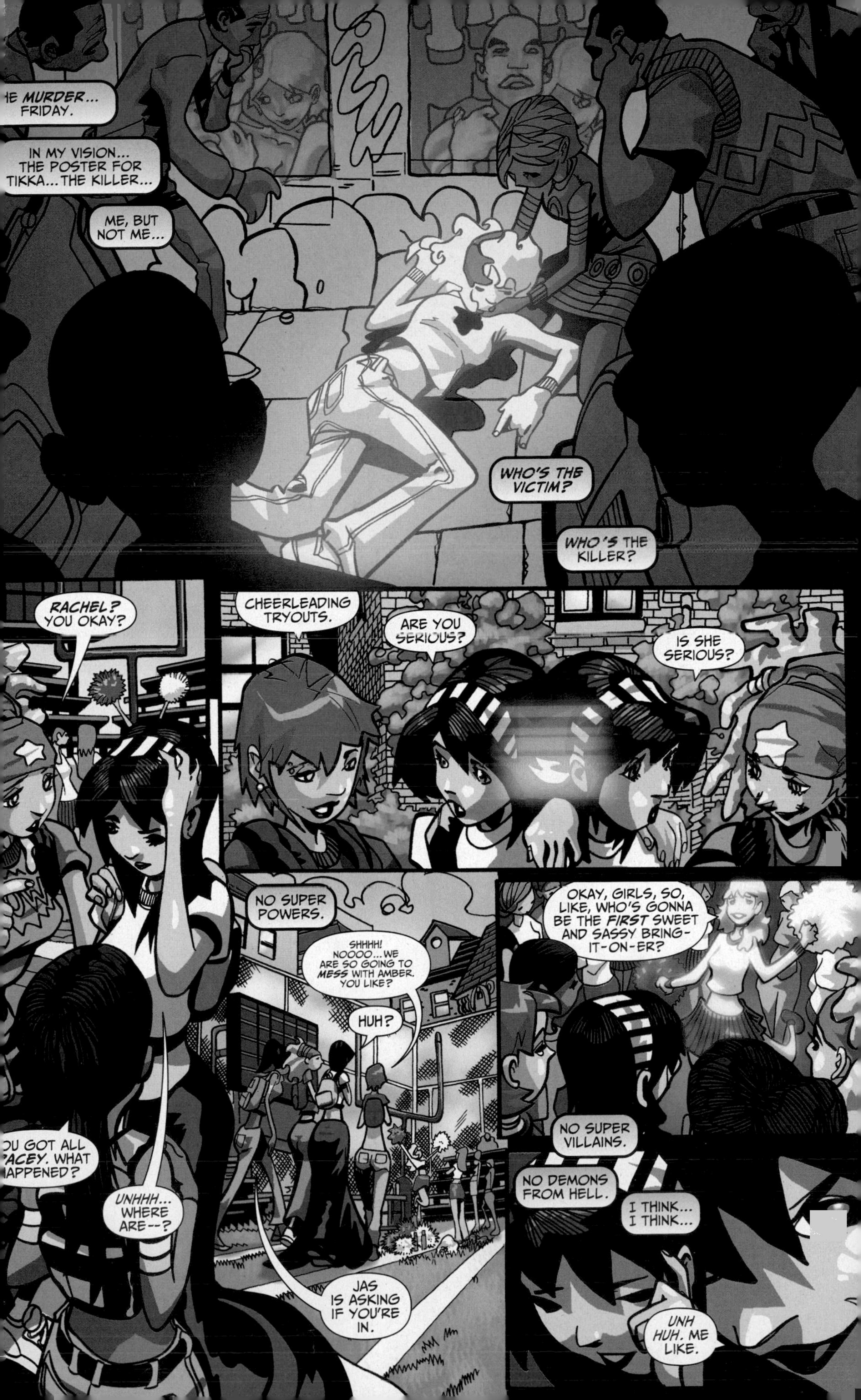

HE MURDER... FRIDAY.
IN MY VISION... THE POSTER FOR TIKKA... THE KILLER...
ME, BUT NOT ME...
WHO'S THE VICTIM?
WHO'S THE KILLER?
RACHEL? YOU OKAY?
CHEERLEADING TRYOUTS.
ARE YOU SERIOUS?
IS SHE SERIOUS?
OU GOT ALL ACEY. WHAT APPENED?
UNHHH... WHERE ARE--?
NO SUPER POWERS.
SHHHH! NOOOO...WE ARE SO GOING TO MESS WITH AMBER. YOU LIKE?
HUH?
JAS IS ASKING IF YOU'RE IN.
OKAY, GIRLS, SO, LIKE, WHO'S GONNA BE THE FIRST SWEET AND SASSY BRING-IT-ON-ER?
NO SUPER VILLAINS.
NO DEMONS FROM HELL.
I THINK... I THINK...
UNH HUH. ME LIKE.

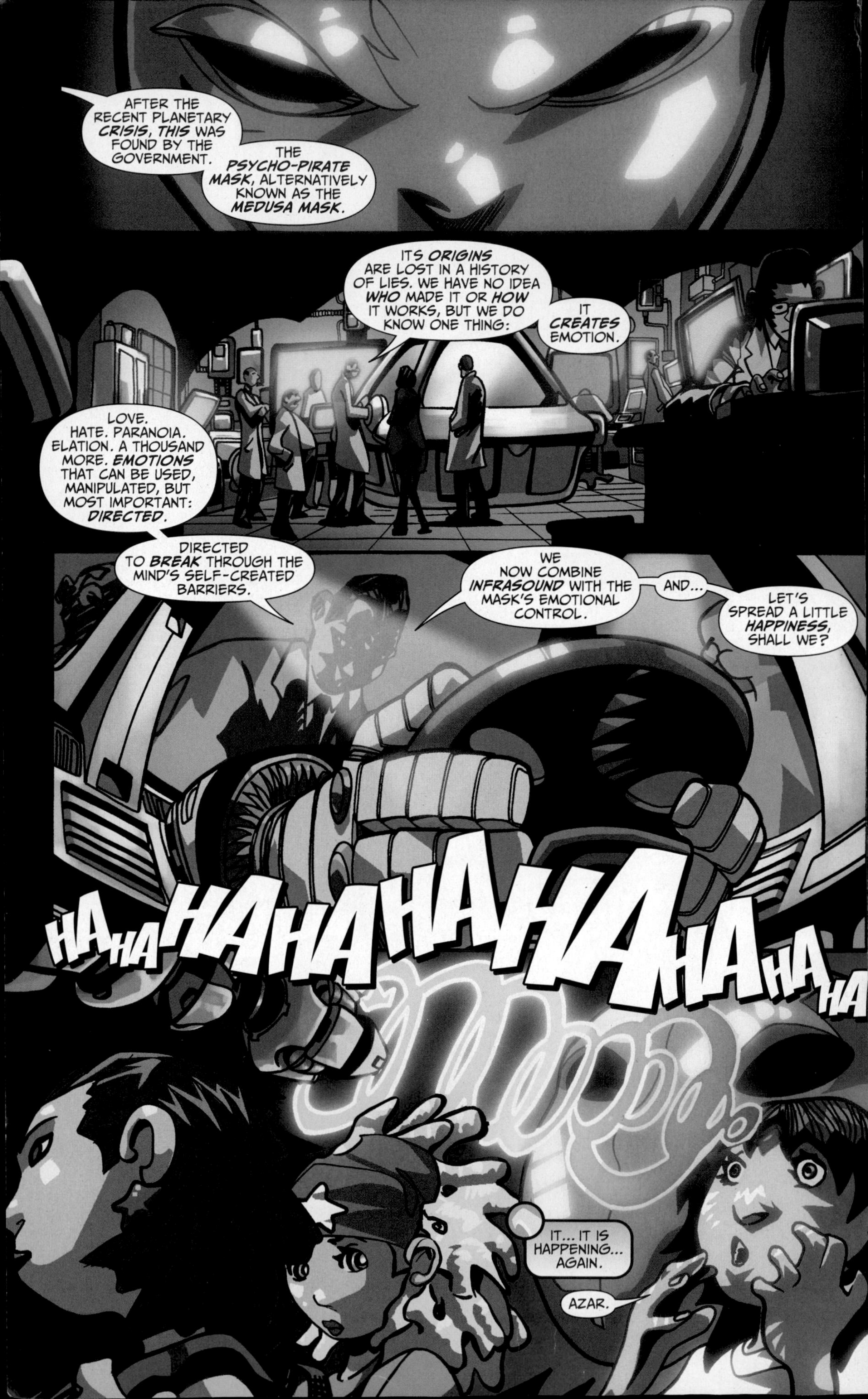
AFTER THE RECENT PLANETARY CRISIS, THIS WAS FOUND BY THE GOVERNMENT.
THE PSYCHO-PIRATE MASK, ALTERNATIVELY KNOWN AS THE MEDUSA MASK.
ITS ORIGINS ARE LOST IN A HISTORY OF LIES. WE HAVE NO IDEA WHO MADE IT OR HOW IT WORKS, BUT WE DO KNOW ONE THING:
IT CREATES EMOTION.
LOVE. HATE. PARANOIA. ELATION. A THOUSAND MORE. EMOTIONS THAT CAN BE USED, MANIPULATED, BUT MOST IMPORTANT: DIRECTED.
DIRECTED TO BREAK THROUGH THE MIND'S SELF-CREATED BARRIERS.
WE NOW COMBINE INFRASOUND WITH THE MASK'S EMOTIONAL CONTROL.
AND...
LET'S SPREAD A LITTLE HAPPINESS, SHALL WE?
HAHAHAHAHAHAHAHAHAHAHAHA
IT... IT IS HAPPENING... AGAIN.
AZAR.

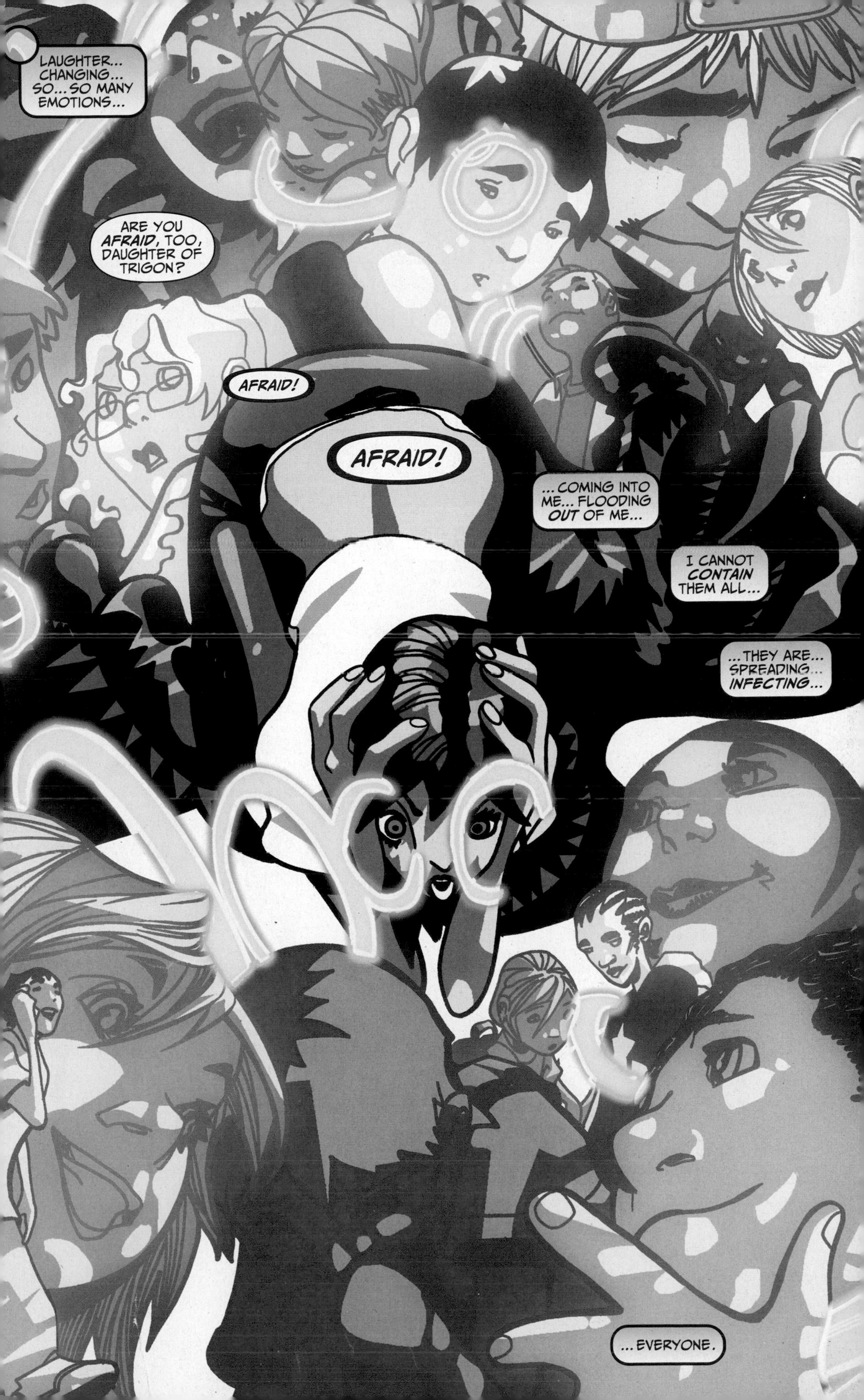

LAUGHTER... CHANGING... SO... SO MANY EMOTIONS...
ARE YOU *AFRAID*, TOO, DAUGHTER OF TRIGON?
AFRAID!
AFRAID!
...COMING INTO ME... FLOODING *OUT* OF ME...
I CANNOT *CONTAIN* THEM ALL...
...THEY ARE... SPREADING... *INFECTING*...
...EVERYONE.

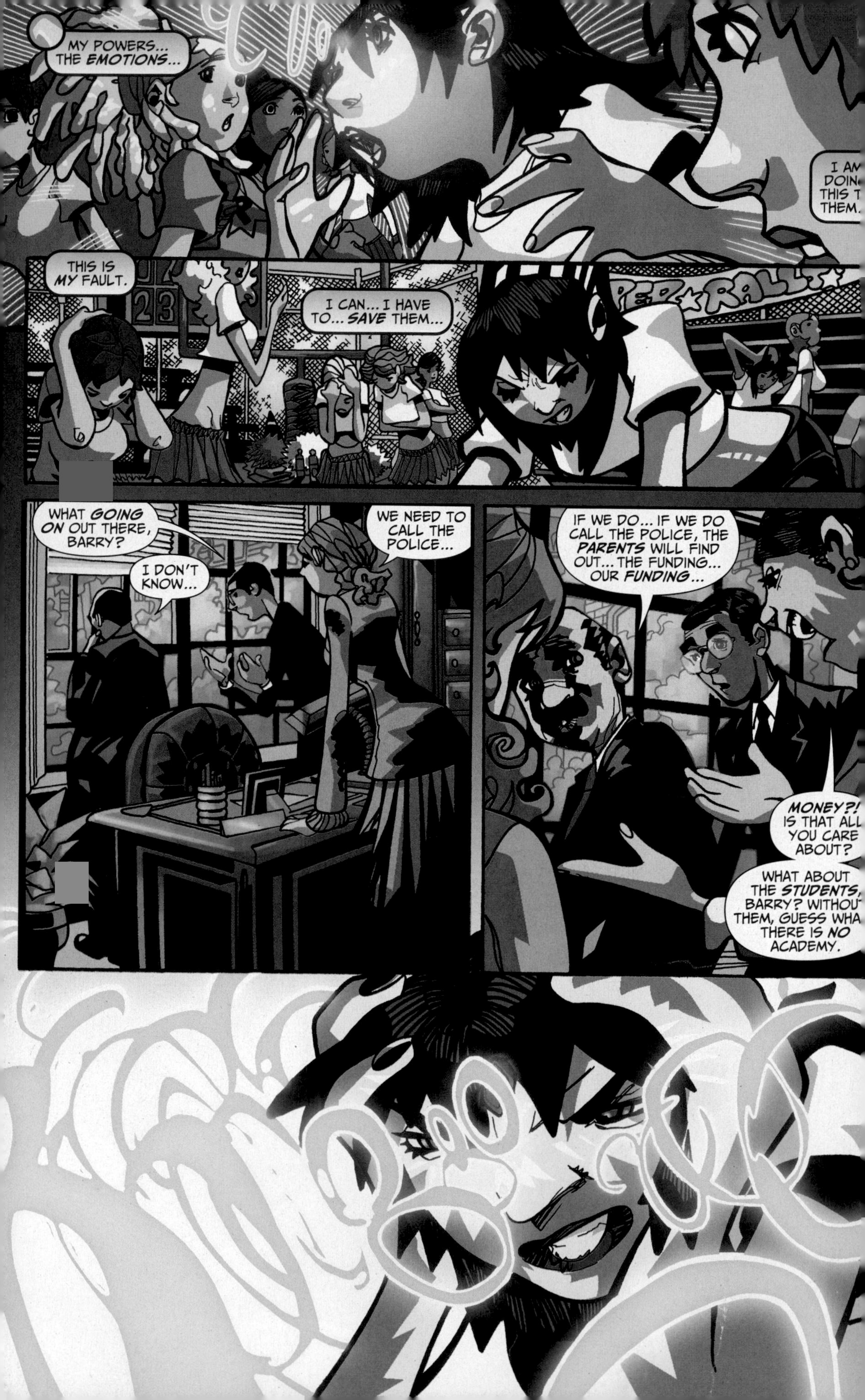
MY POWERS... THE EMOTIONS...
I AM DOIN THIS T THEM.
THIS IS MY FAULT.
I CAN... I HAVE TO... SAVE THEM...
WHAT GOING ON OUT THERE, BARRY?
I DON'T KNOW...
WE NEED TO CALL THE POLICE...
IF WE DO... IF WE DO CALL THE POLICE, THE PARENTS WILL FIND OUT... THE FUNDING... OUR FUNDING...
MONEY?! IS THAT ALL YOU CARE ABOUT?
WHAT ABOUT THE STUDENTS, BARRY? WITHOU THEM, GUESS WHA THERE IS NO ACADEMY.

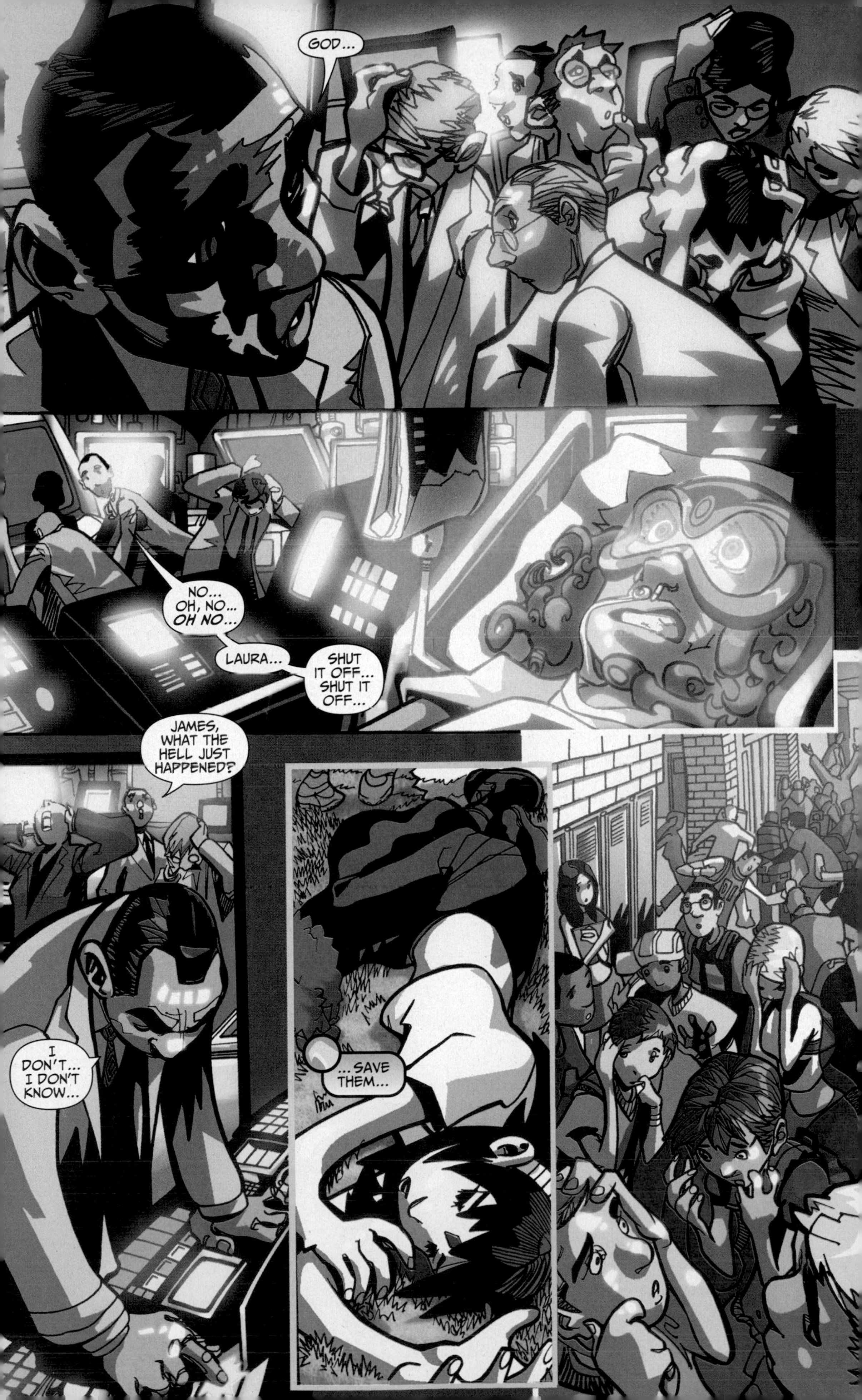
GOD...
NO... OH, NO... OH NO...
LAURA...
SHUT IT OFF... SHUT IT OFF...
JAMES, WHAT THE HELL JUST HAPPENED?
I DON'T... I DON'T KNOW...
...SAVE THEM...

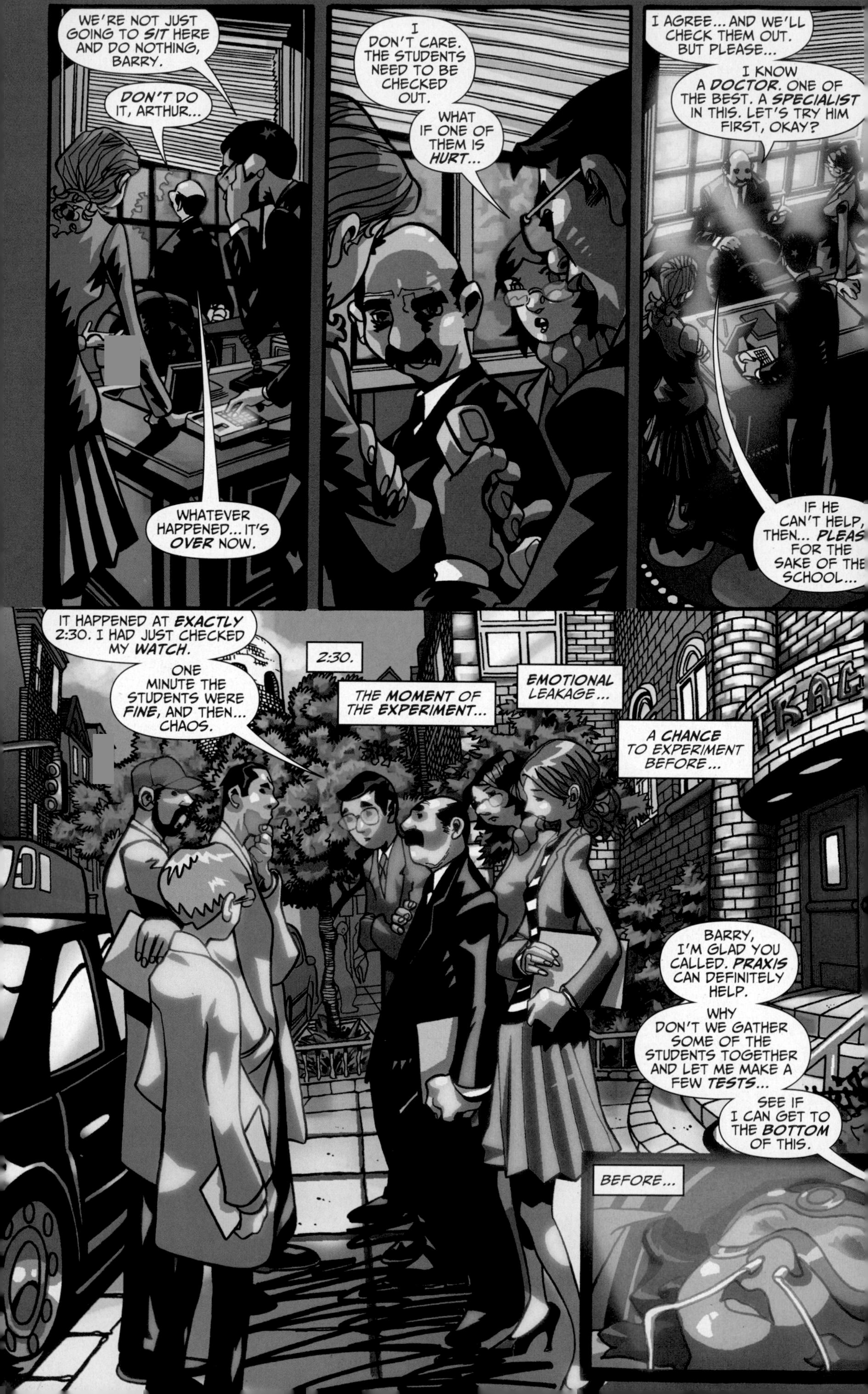

WE'RE NOT JUST GOING TO *SIT* HERE AND DO NOTHING, BARRY.
DON'T DO IT, ARTHUR...
WHATEVER HAPPENED... IT'S ***OVER*** NOW.
I DON'T CARE. THE STUDENTS NEED TO BE CHECKED OUT.
WHAT IF ONE OF THEM IS ***HURT***...
I AGREE... AND WE'LL CHECK THEM OUT. BUT PLEASE...
I KNOW A ***DOCTOR***. ONE OF THE BEST. A ***SPECIALIST*** IN THIS. LET'S TRY HIM FIRST, OKAY?
IF HE CAN'T HELP, THEN... ***PLEAS***
FOR THE SAKE OF THE SCHOOL...
IT HAPPENED AT ***EXACTLY*** 2:30. I HAD JUST CHECKED MY ***WATCH***.
ONE MINUTE THE STUDENTS WERE ***FINE***, AND THEN... CHAOS.
2:30.
*THE **MOMENT** OF THE **EXPERIMENT**...*
***EMOTIONAL** LEAKAGE...*
*A **CHANCE** TO EXPERIMENT BEFORE...*
BARRY, I'M GLAD YOU CALLED. ***PRAXIS*** CAN DEFINITELY HELP.
WHY DON'T WE GATHER SOME OF THE STUDENTS TOGETHER AND LET ME MAKE A FEW ***TESTS***...
SEE IF I CAN GET TO THE ***BOTTOM*** OF THIS.
BEFORE...

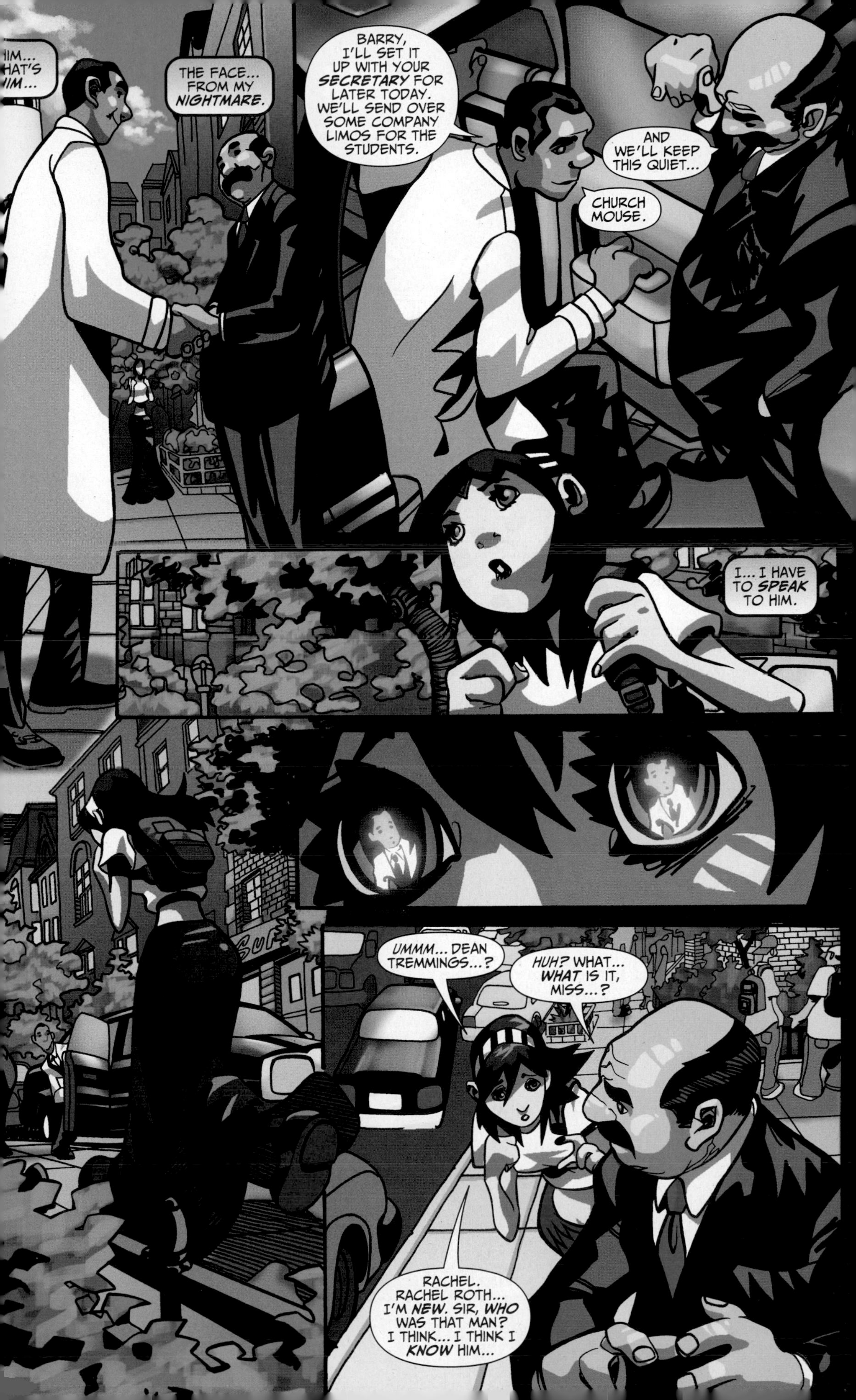
HIM... THAT'S HIM...
THE FACE... FROM MY NIGHTMARE.
BARRY, I'LL SET IT UP WITH YOUR SECRETARY FOR LATER TODAY. WE'LL SEND OVER SOME COMPANY LIMOS FOR THE STUDENTS.
AND WE'LL KEEP THIS QUIET...
CHURCH MOUSE.
I... I HAVE TO SPEAK TO HIM.
UMMM... DEAN TREMMINGS...?
HUH? WHAT... WHAT IS IT, MISS...?
RACHEL. RACHEL ROTH... I'M NEW. SIR, WHO WAS THAT MAN? I THINK... I THINK I KNOW HIM...

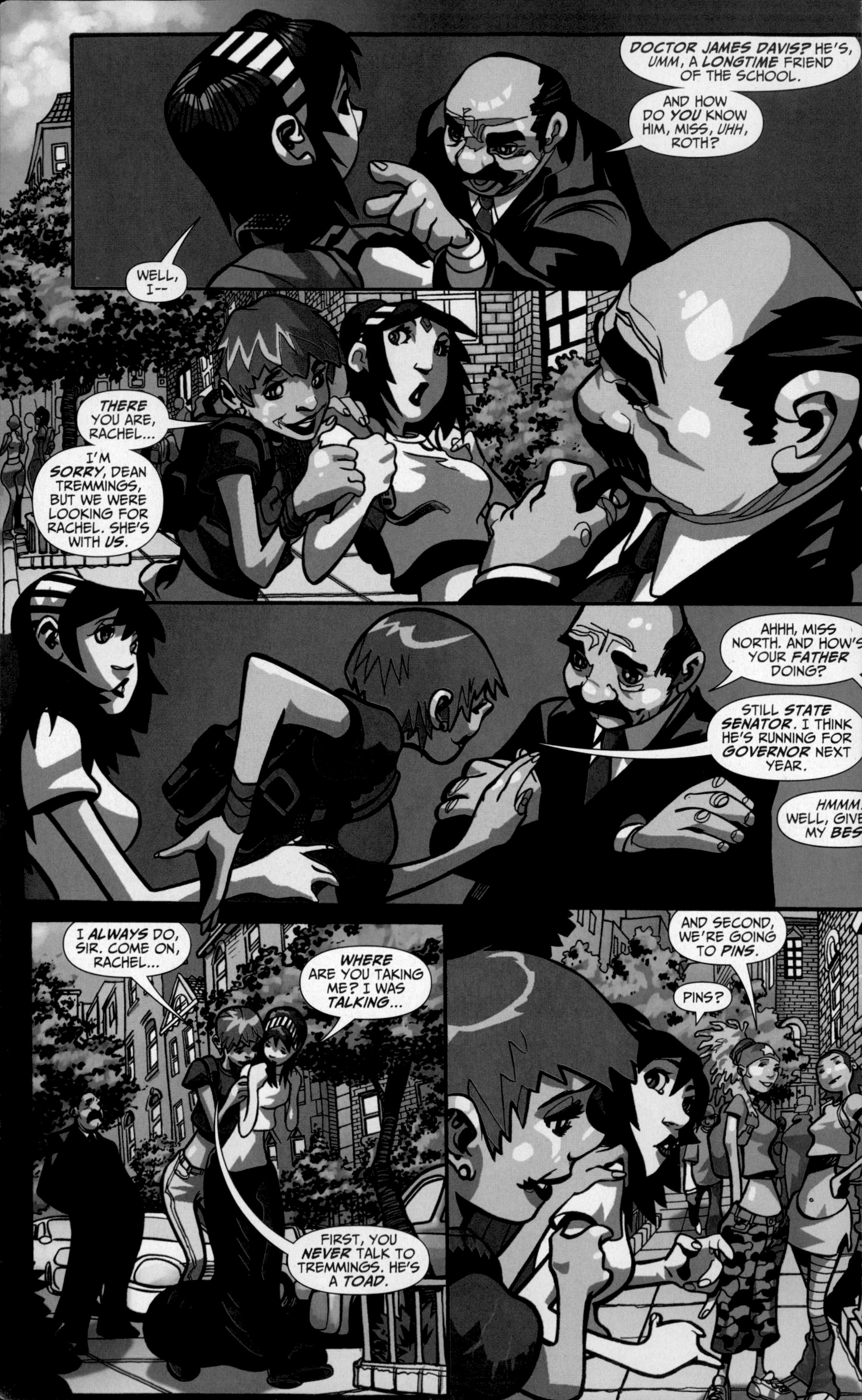
DOCTOR JAMES DAVIS? HE'S, UMM, A LONGTIME FRIEND OF THE SCHOOL.
AND HOW DO YOU KNOW HIM, MISS, UHH, ROTH?
WELL, I--
THERE YOU ARE, RACHEL...
I'M SORRY, DEAN TREMMINGS, BUT WE WERE LOOKING FOR RACHEL. SHE'S WITH US.
AHHH, MISS NORTH. AND HOW'S YOUR FATHER DOING?
STILL STATE SENATOR. I THINK HE'S RUNNING FOR GOVERNOR NEXT YEAR.
I ALWAYS DO, SIR. COME ON, RACHEL...
WHERE ARE YOU TAKING ME? I WAS TALKING...
FIRST, YOU NEVER TALK TO TREMMINGS. HE'S A TOAD.
AND SECOND, WE'RE GOING TO PINS.
PINS?

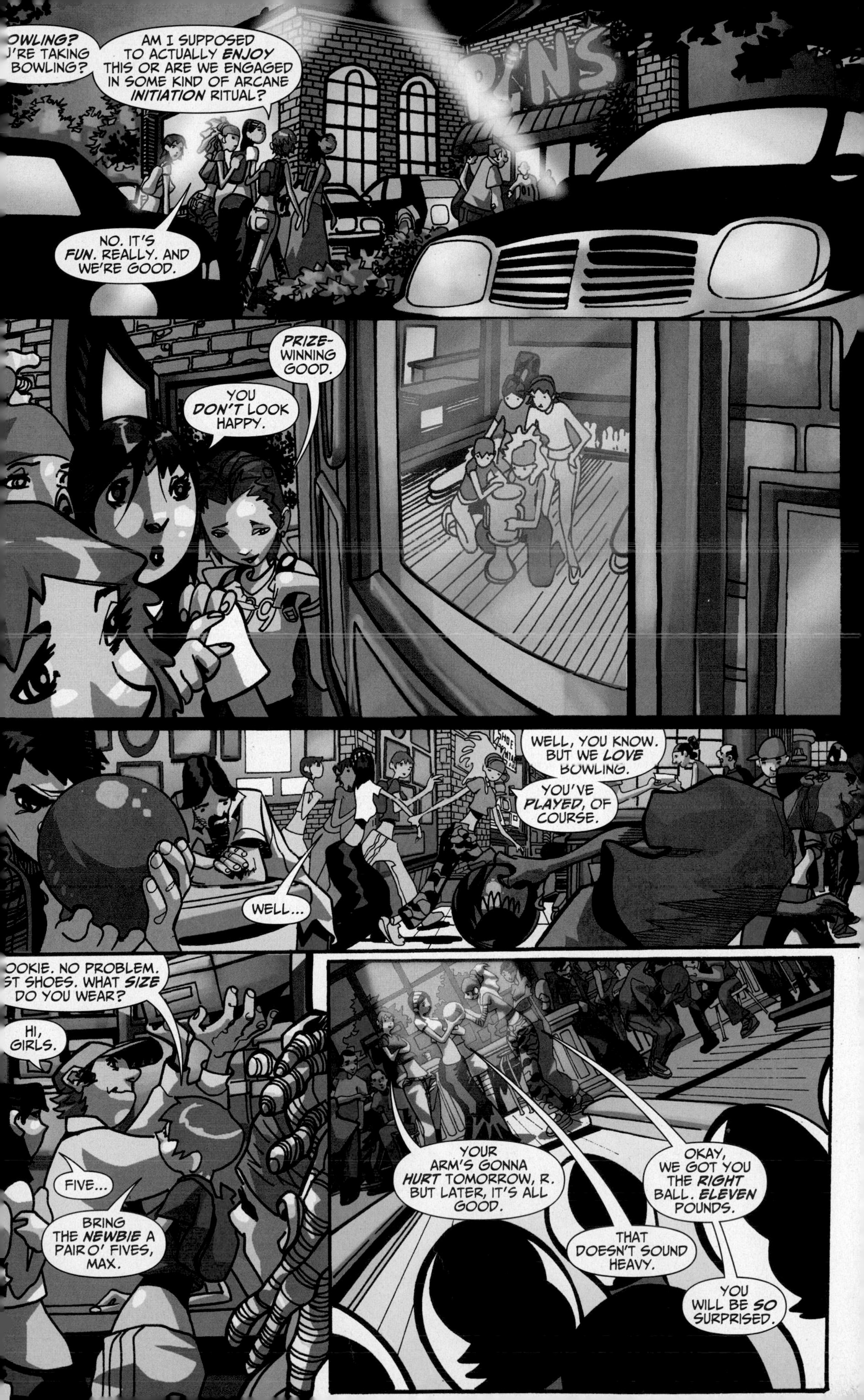
OWLING?
'RE TAKING BOWLING?
AM I SUPPOSED TO ACTUALLY *ENJOY* THIS OR ARE WE ENGAGED IN SOME KIND OF ARCANE *INITIATION* RITUAL?
NO. IT'S *FUN*. REALLY. AND WE'RE GOOD.
*PRIZE-*WINNING GOOD.
YOU *DON'T* LOOK HAPPY.
WELL, YOU KNOW. BUT WE *LOVE* BOWLING.
YOU'VE *PLAYED*, OF COURSE.
WELL...
OOKIE. NO PROBLEM.
ST SHOES. WHAT *SIZE* DO YOU WEAR?
HI, GIRLS.
FIVE...
BRING THE *NEWBIE* A PAIR O' FIVES, MAX.
OKAY, WE GOT YOU THE *RIGHT* BALL. *ELEVEN* POUNDS.
THAT DOESN'T SOUND HEAVY.
YOU WILL BE *SO* SURPRISED.
YOUR ARM'S GONNA *HURT* TOMORROW, R. BUT LATER, IT'S ALL GOOD.

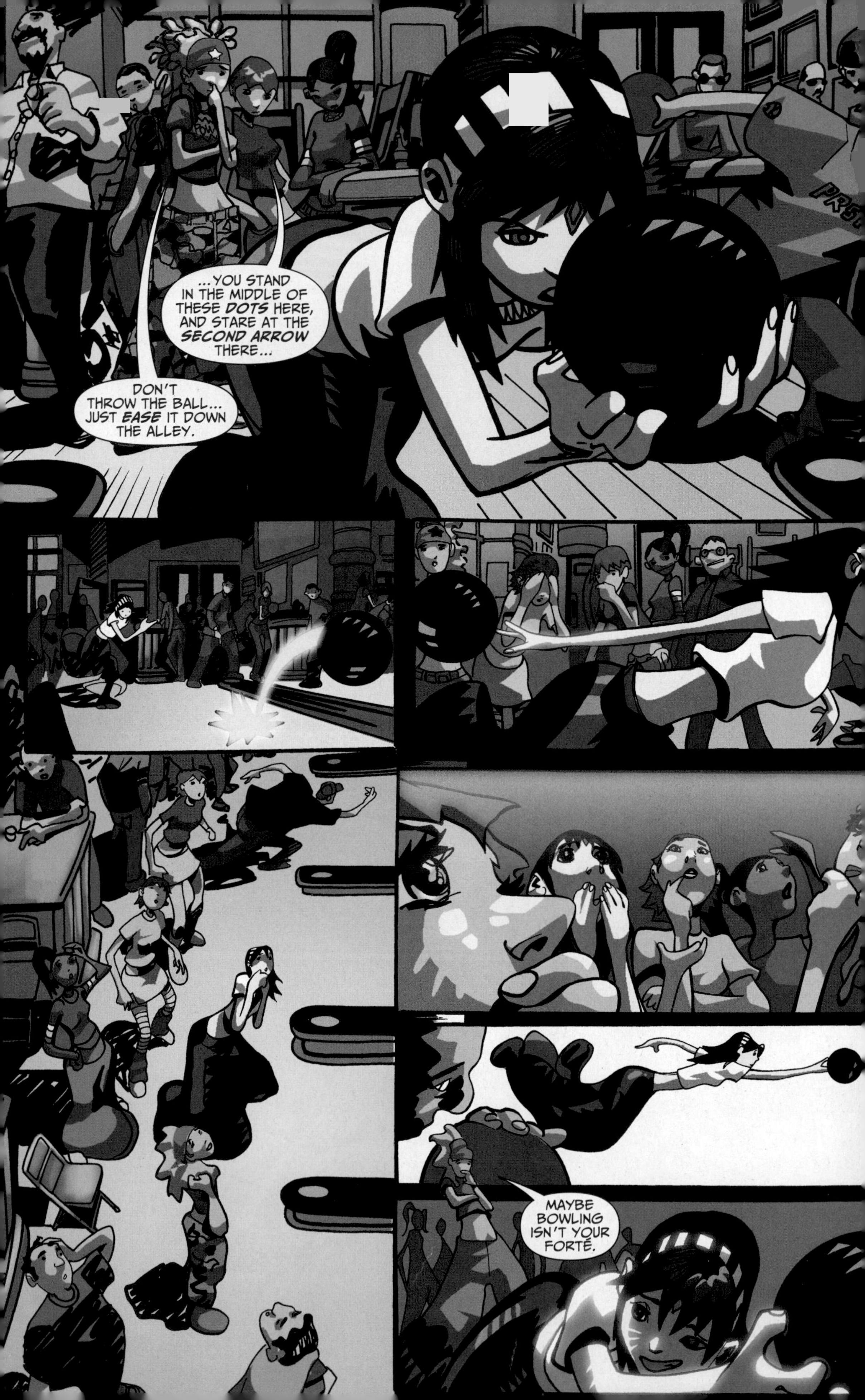
...YOU STAND IN THE MIDDLE OF THESE *DOTS* HERE, AND STARE AT THE *SECOND ARROW* THERE...
DON'T THROW THE BALL... JUST *EASE* IT DOWN THE ALLEY.
MAYBE BOWLING ISN'T YOUR FORTÉ.

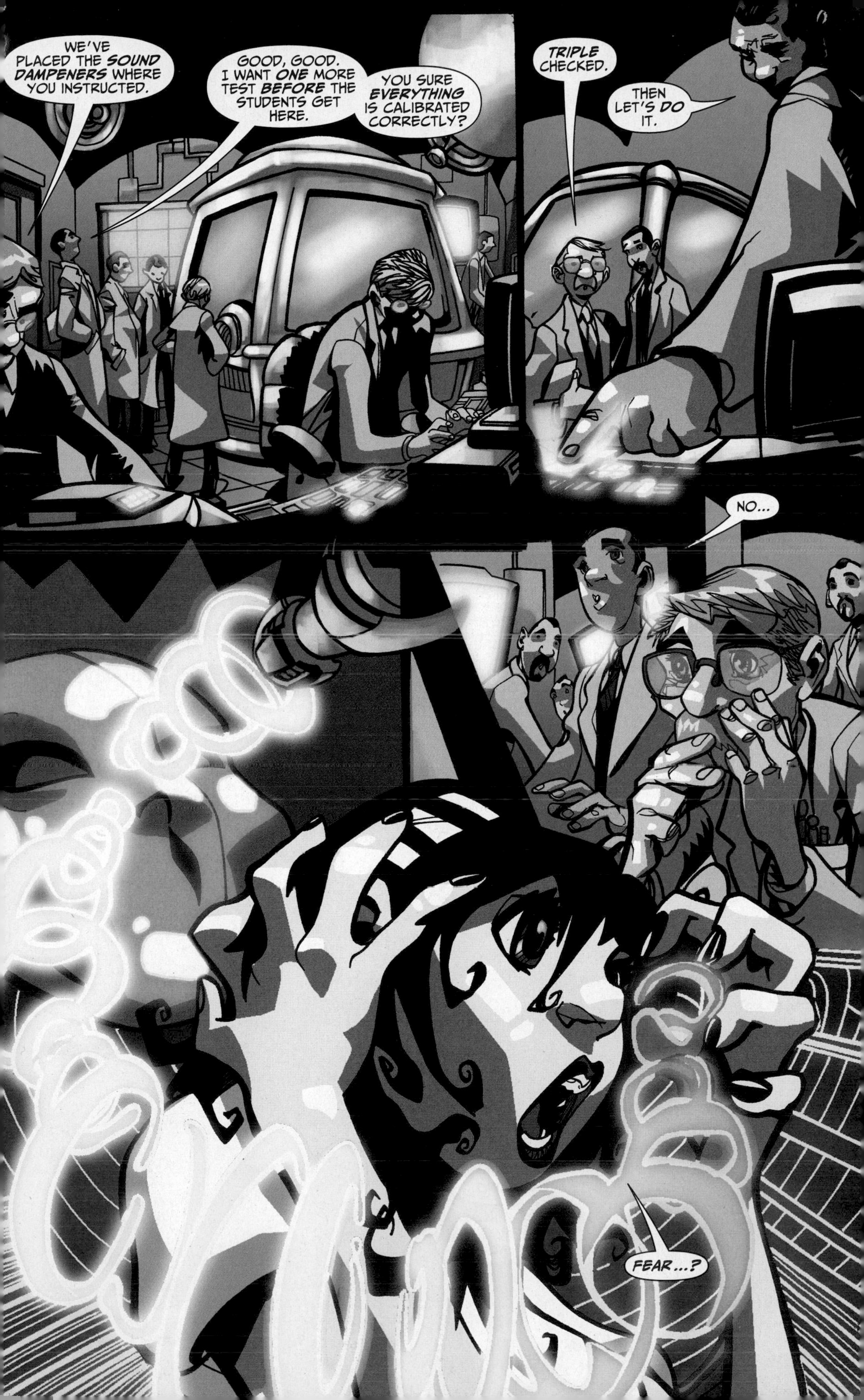
WE'VE PLACED THE SOUND DAMPENERS WHERE YOU INSTRUCTED.
GOOD, GOOD. I WANT ONE MORE TEST BEFORE THE STUDENTS GET HERE.
YOU SURE EVERYTHING IS CALIBRATED CORRECTLY?
TRIPLE CHECKED.
THEN LET'S DO IT.
NO...
FEAR...?

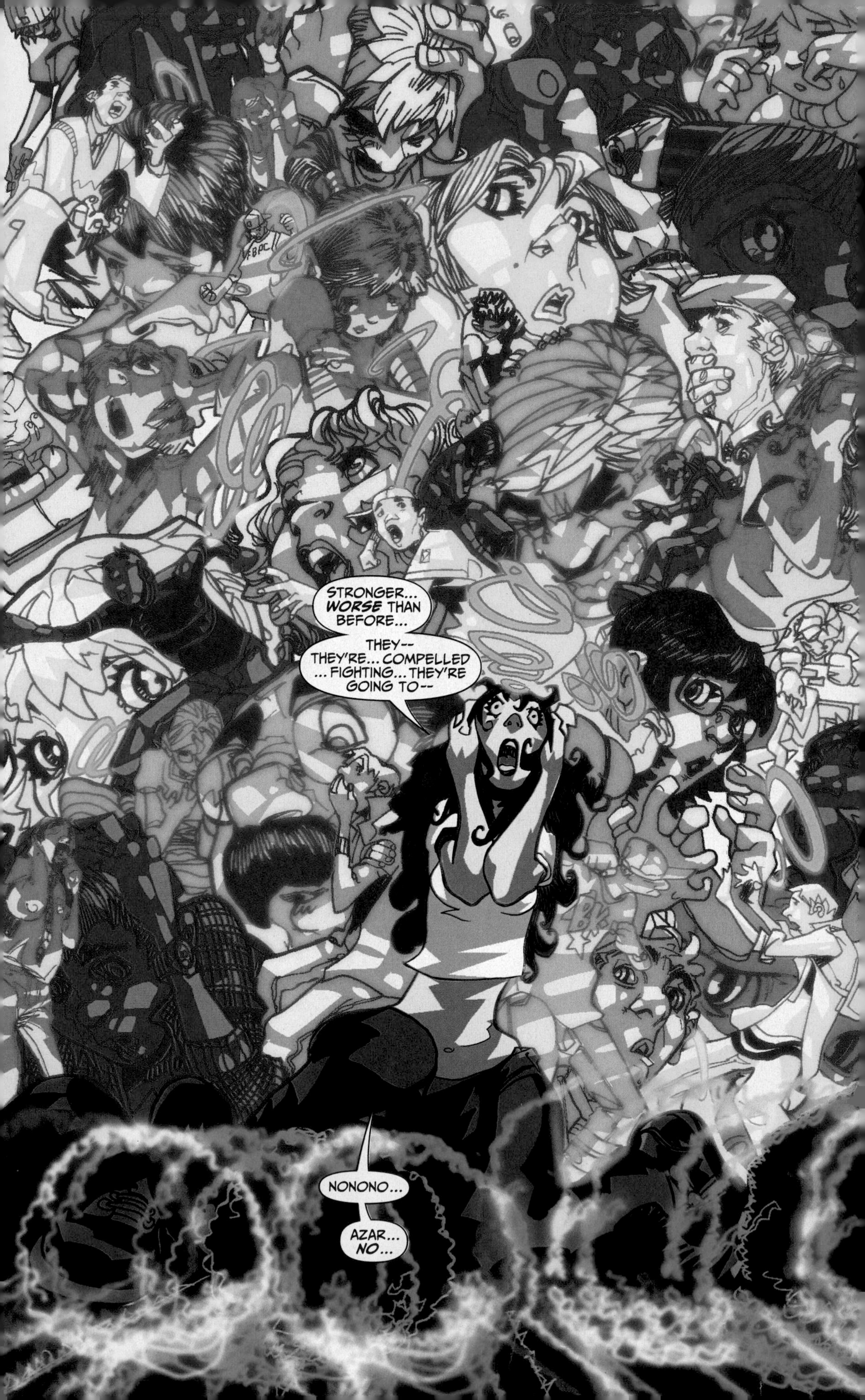
STRONGER... WORSE THAN BEFORE...
THEY-- THEY'RE... COMPELLED ... FIGHTING... THEY'RE GOING TO--
NONONO...
AZAR... NO...

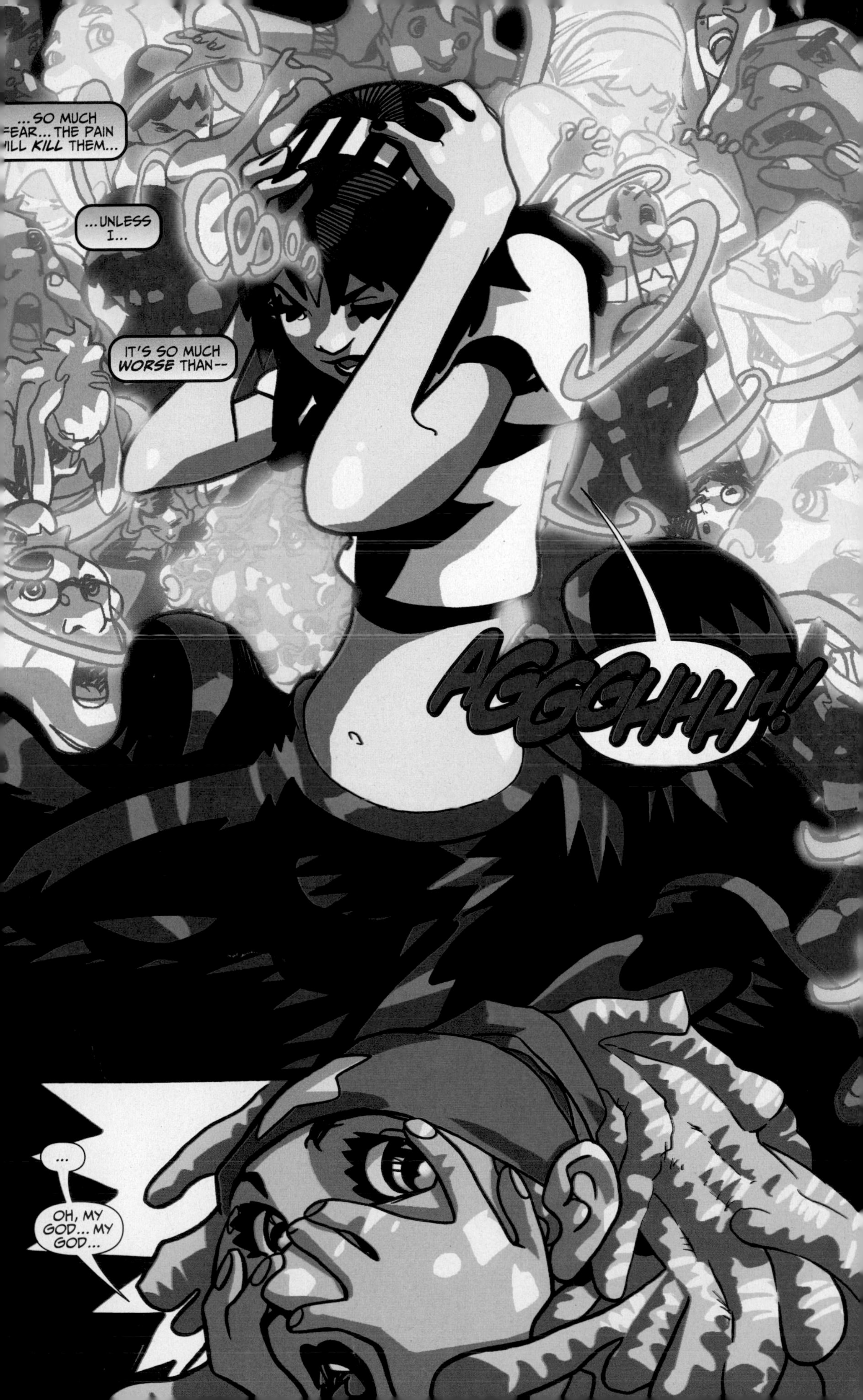
...SO MUCH FEAR... THE PAIN WILL KILL THEM...
...UNLESS I...
IT'S SO MUCH WORSE THAN--
AGGGHHHH!
...
OH, MY GOD... MY GOD...

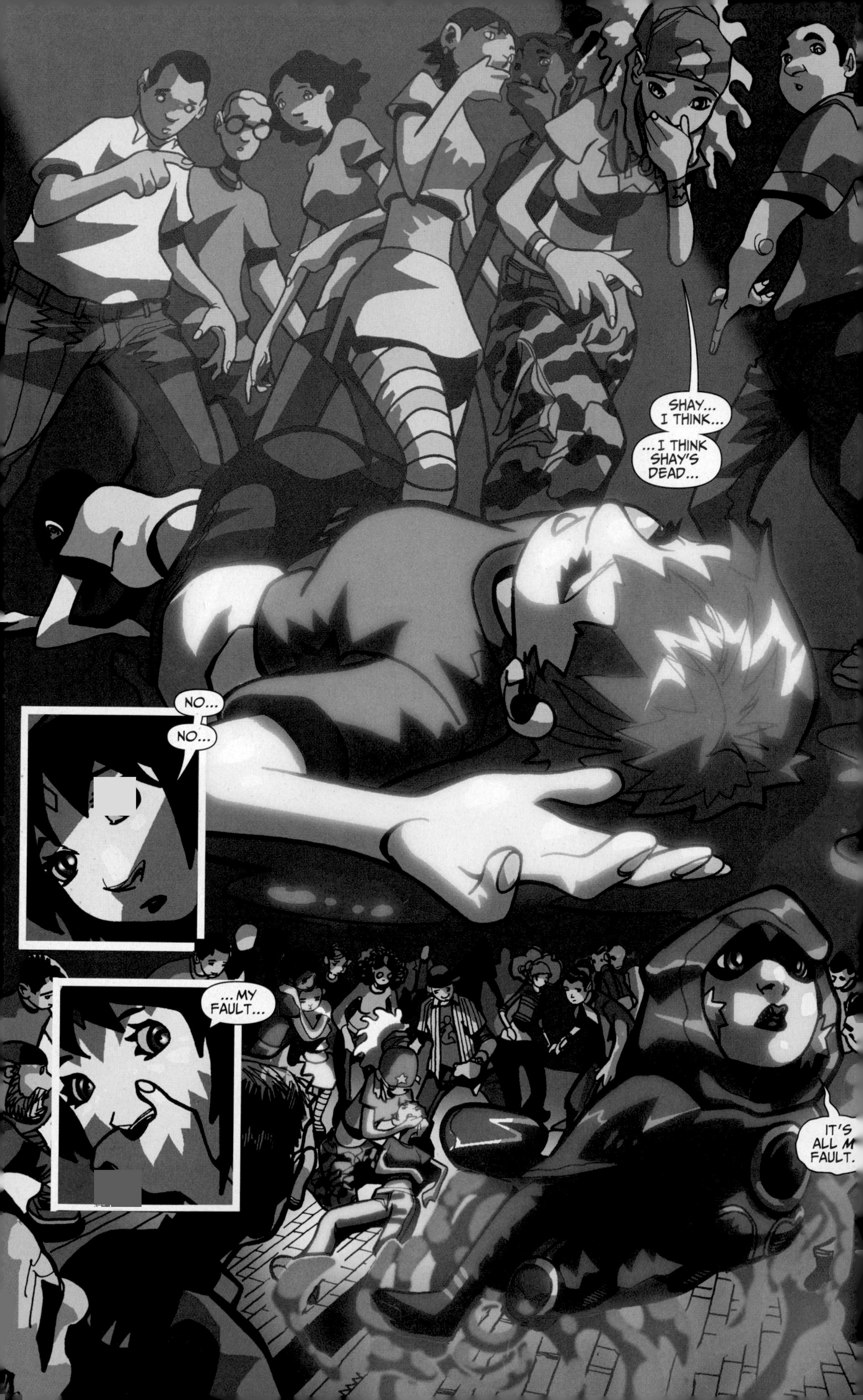
SHAY... I THINK...
...I THINK SHAY'S DEAD...
NO...
NO...
...MY FAULT...
IT'S ALL M FAULT.

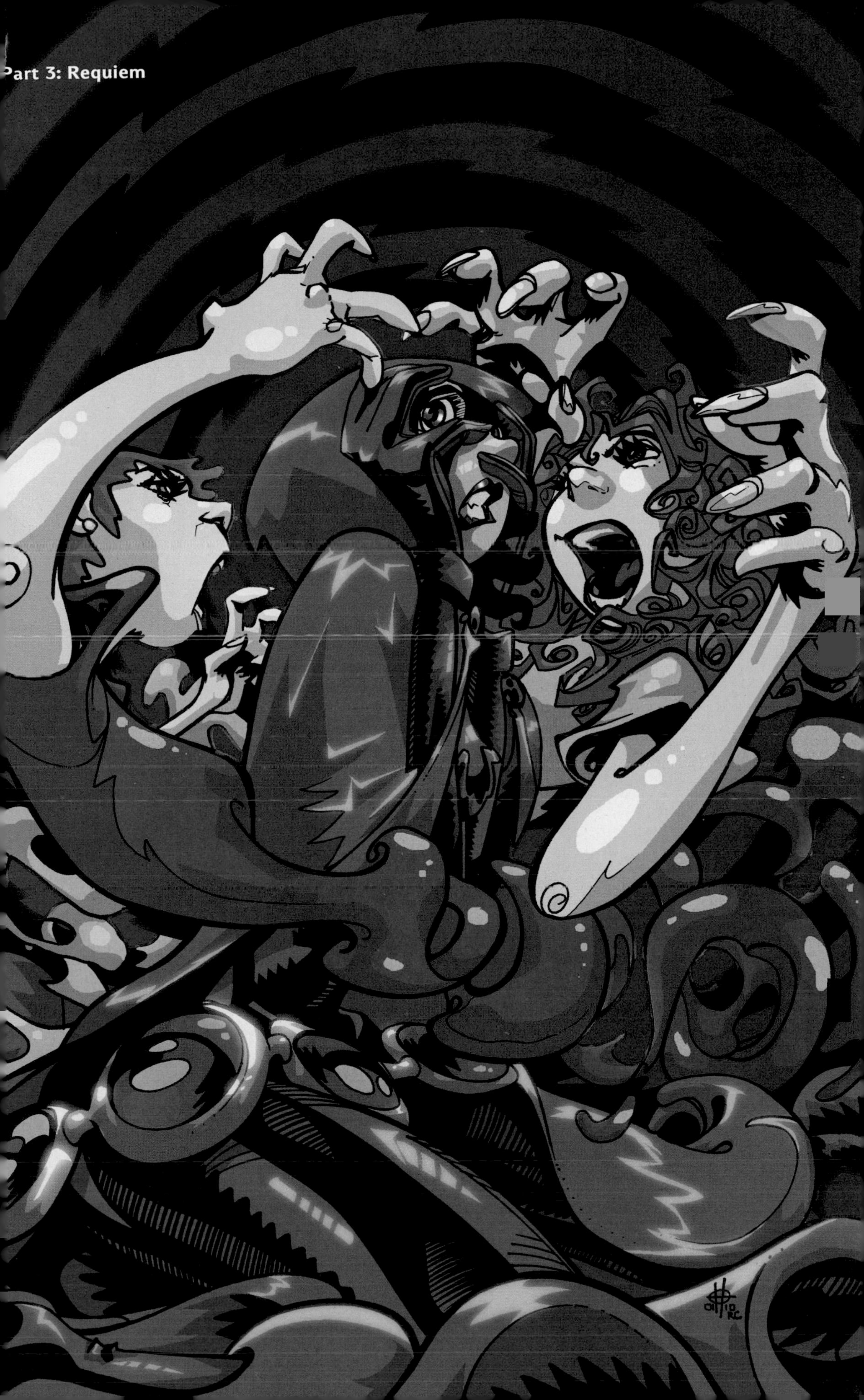

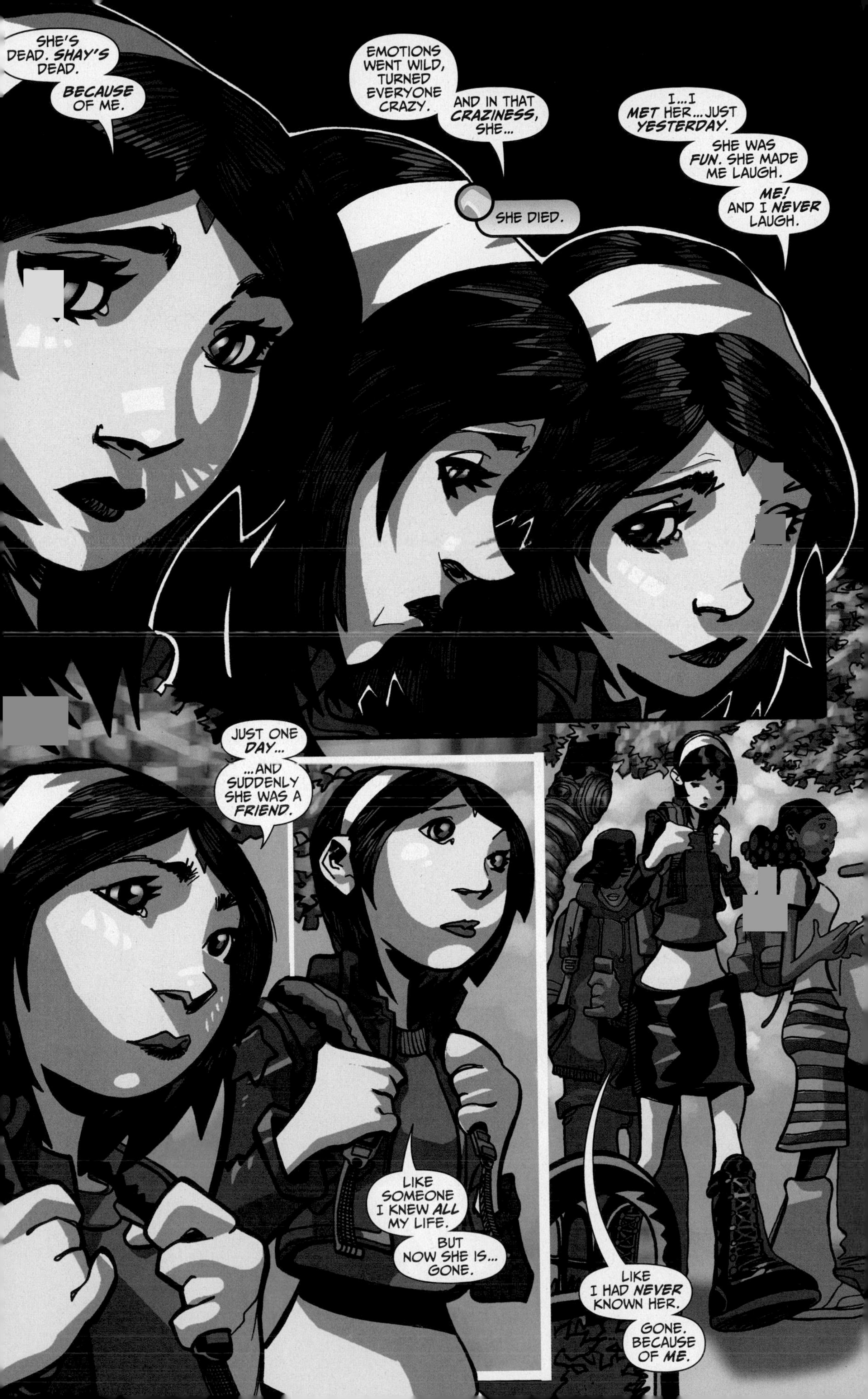
SHE'S DEAD. SHAY'S DEAD.
BECAUSE OF ME.
EMOTIONS WENT WILD, TURNED EVERYONE CRAZY.
AND IN THAT CRAZINESS, SHE...
SHE DIED.
I...I MET HER...JUST YESTERDAY.
SHE WAS FUN. SHE MADE ME LAUGH.
ME! AND I NEVER LAUGH.
JUST ONE DAY...
...AND SUDDENLY SHE WAS A FRIEND.
LIKE SOMEONE I KNEW ALL MY LIFE.
BUT NOW SHE IS... GONE.
LIKE I HAD NEVER KNOWN HER.
GONE. BECAUSE OF ME.

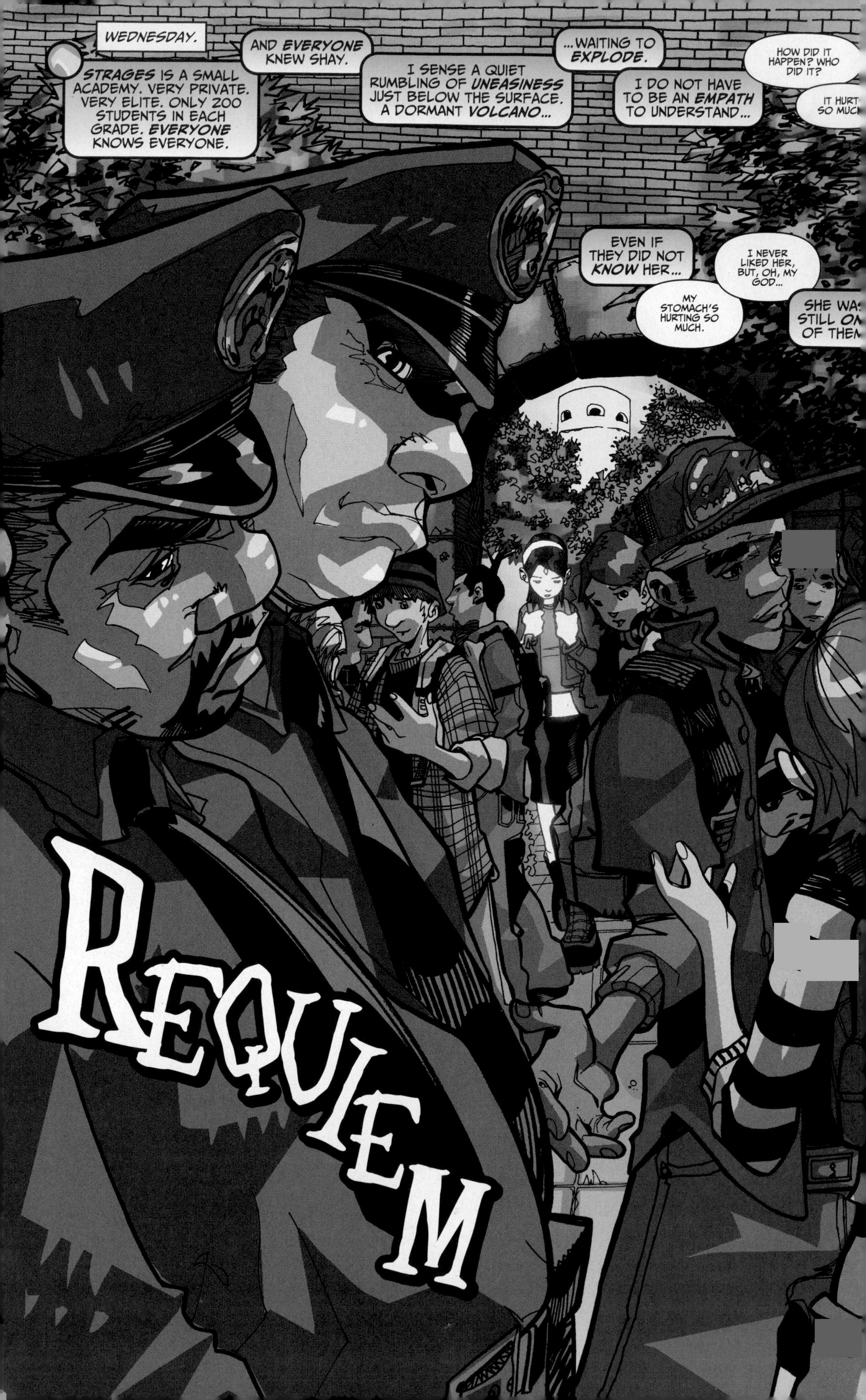

WEDNESDAY.
STRAGES IS A SMALL ACADEMY. VERY PRIVATE. VERY ELITE. ONLY 200 STUDENTS IN EACH GRADE. EVERYONE KNOWS EVERYONE.
AND EVERYONE KNEW SHAY.
I SENSE A QUIET RUMBLING OF UNEASINESS JUST BELOW THE SURFACE. A DORMANT VOLCANO...
...WAITING TO EXPLODE.
I DO NOT HAVE TO BE AN EMPATH TO UNDERSTAND...
HOW DID IT HAPPEN? WHO DID IT?
IT HURT SO MUC
EVEN IF THEY DID NOT KNOW HER...
I NEVER LIKED HER, BUT, OH, MY GOD...
MY STOMACH'S HURTING SO MUCH.
SHE WA STILL ON OF THEM
REQUIEM

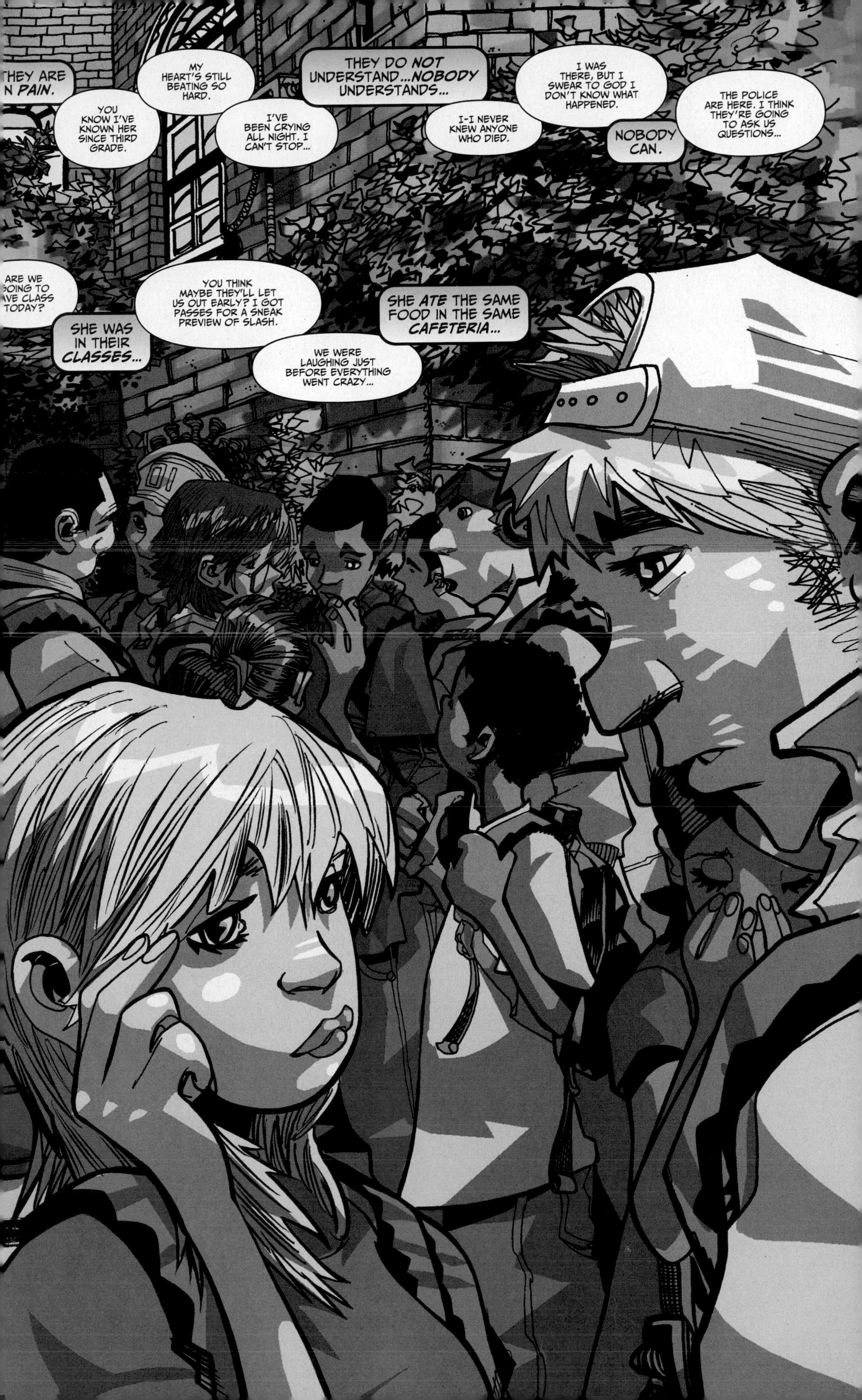
THEY ARE
N PAIN.
YOU KNOW I'VE KNOWN HER SINCE THIRD GRADE.
MY HEART'S STILL BEATING SO HARD.
I'VE BEEN CRYING ALL NIGHT. I CAN'T STOP...
THEY DO NOT UNDERSTAND...NOBODY UNDERSTANDS...
I-I NEVER KNEW ANYONE WHO DIED.
I WAS THERE, BUT I SWEAR TO GOD I DON'T KNOW WHAT HAPPENED.
NOBODY CAN.
THE POLICE ARE HERE. I THINK THEY'RE GOING TO ASK US QUESTIONS...
ARE WE
OING TO
AVE CLASS
TODAY?
YOU THINK MAYBE THEY'LL LET US OUT EARLY? I GOT PASSES FOR A SNEAK PREVIEW OF SLASH.
SHE WAS IN THEIR CLASSES...
SHE ATE THE SAME FOOD IN THE SAME CAFETERIA...
WE WERE LAUGHING JUST BEFORE EVERYTHING WENT CRAZY...

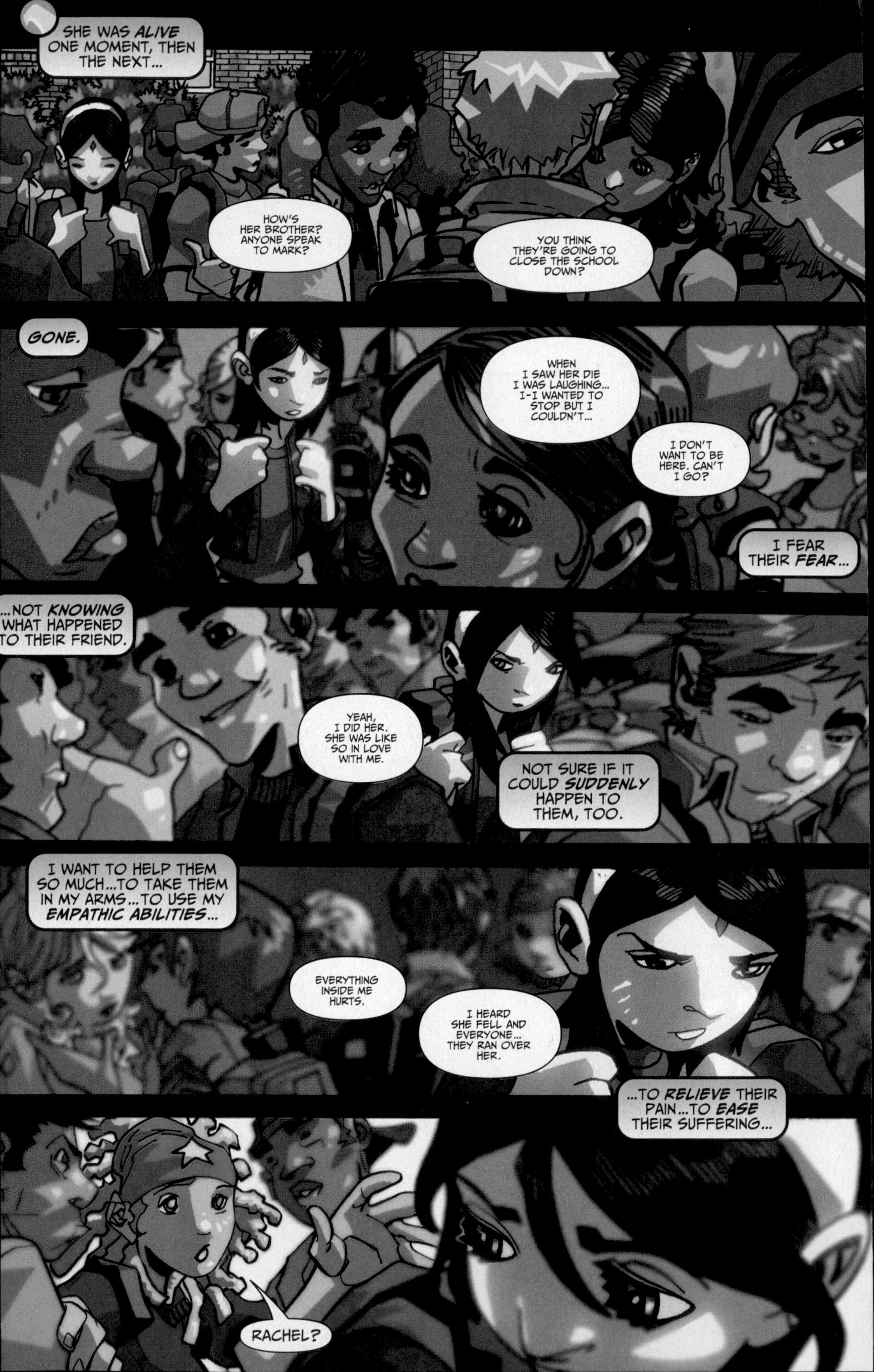
SHE WAS *ALIVE* ONE MOMENT, THEN THE NEXT...
HOW'S HER BROTHER? ANYONE SPEAK TO MARK?
YOU THINK THEY'RE GOING TO CLOSE THE SCHOOL DOWN?
GONE.
WHEN I SAW HER DIE I WAS LAUGHING... I-I WANTED TO STOP BUT I COULDN'T...
I DON'T WANT TO BE HERE. CAN'T I GO?
I FEAR THEIR *FEAR*...
...NOT *KNOWING* WHAT HAPPENED TO THEIR FRIEND.
YEAH, I DID HER. SHE WAS LIKE SO IN LOVE WITH ME.
NOT SURE IF IT COULD *SUDDENLY* HAPPEN TO THEM, TOO.
I WANT TO HELP THEM SO MUCH...TO TAKE THEM IN MY ARMS...TO USE MY *EMPATHIC ABILITIES*...
EVERYTHING INSIDE ME HURTS.
I HEARD SHE FELL AND EVERYONE... THEY RAN OVER HER.
...TO *RELIEVE* THEIR PAIN...TO *EASE* THEIR SUFFERING...
RACHEL?

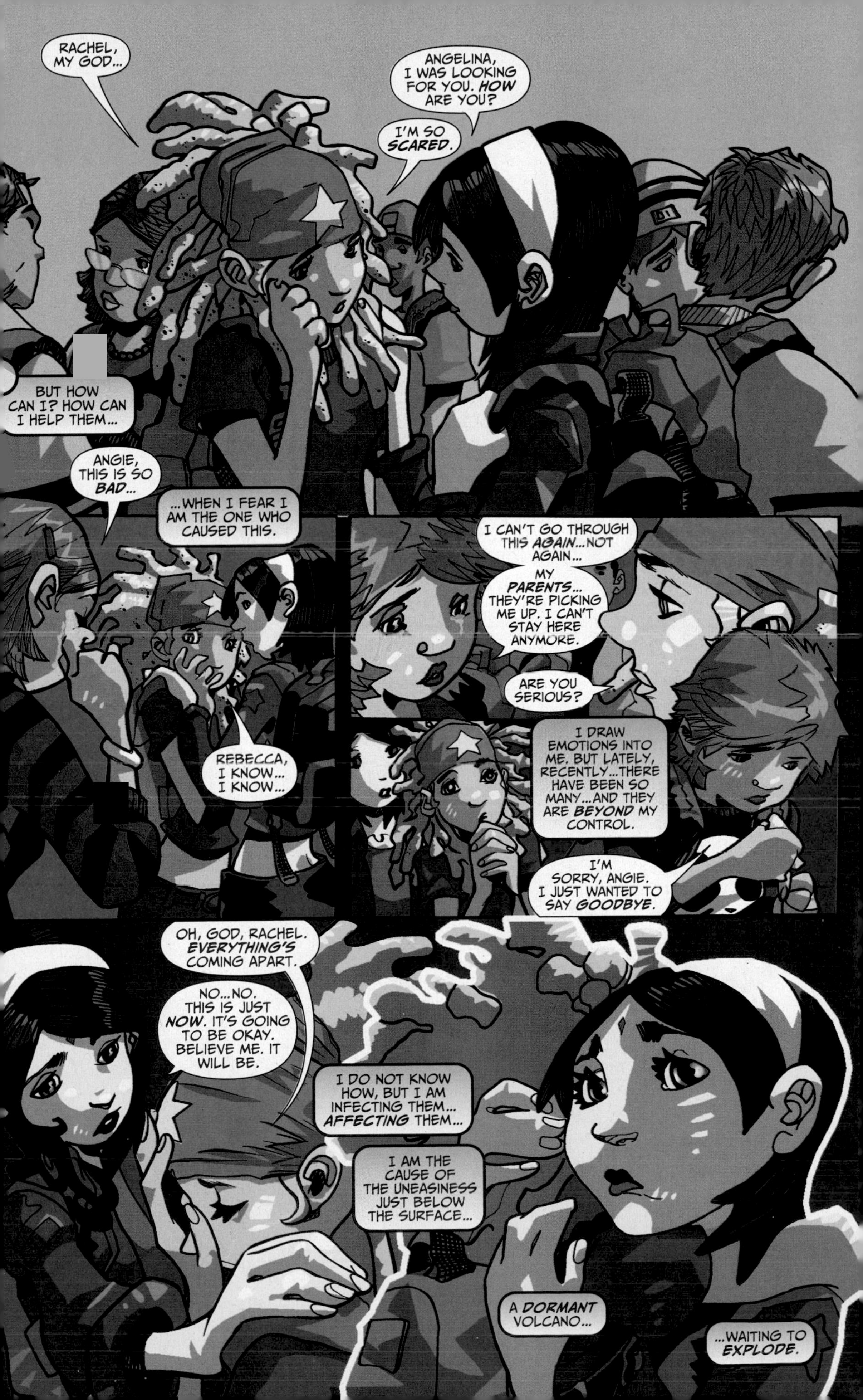

RACHEL, MY GOD...
ANGELINA, I WAS LOOKING FOR YOU. HOW ARE YOU?
I'M SO SCARED.
BUT HOW CAN I? HOW CAN I HELP THEM...
ANGIE, THIS IS SO BAD...
...WHEN I FEAR I AM THE ONE WHO CAUSED THIS.
REBECCA, I KNOW... I KNOW...
I CAN'T GO THROUGH THIS AGAIN...NOT AGAIN...
MY PARENTS... THEY'RE PICKING ME UP. I CAN'T STAY HERE ANYMORE.
ARE YOU SERIOUS?
I DRAW EMOTIONS INTO ME. BUT LATELY, RECENTLY...THERE HAVE BEEN SO MANY...AND THEY ARE BEYOND MY CONTROL.
I'M SORRY, ANGIE. I JUST WANTED TO SAY GOODBYE.
OH, GOD, RACHEL. EVERYTHING'S COMING APART.
NO...NO. THIS IS JUST NOW. IT'S GOING TO BE OKAY. BELIEVE ME. IT WILL BE.
I DO NOT KNOW HOW, BUT I AM INFECTING THEM... AFFECTING THEM...
I AM THE CAUSE OF THE UNEASINESS JUST BELOW THE SURFACE...
A DORMANT VOLCANO...
...WAITING TO EXPLODE.

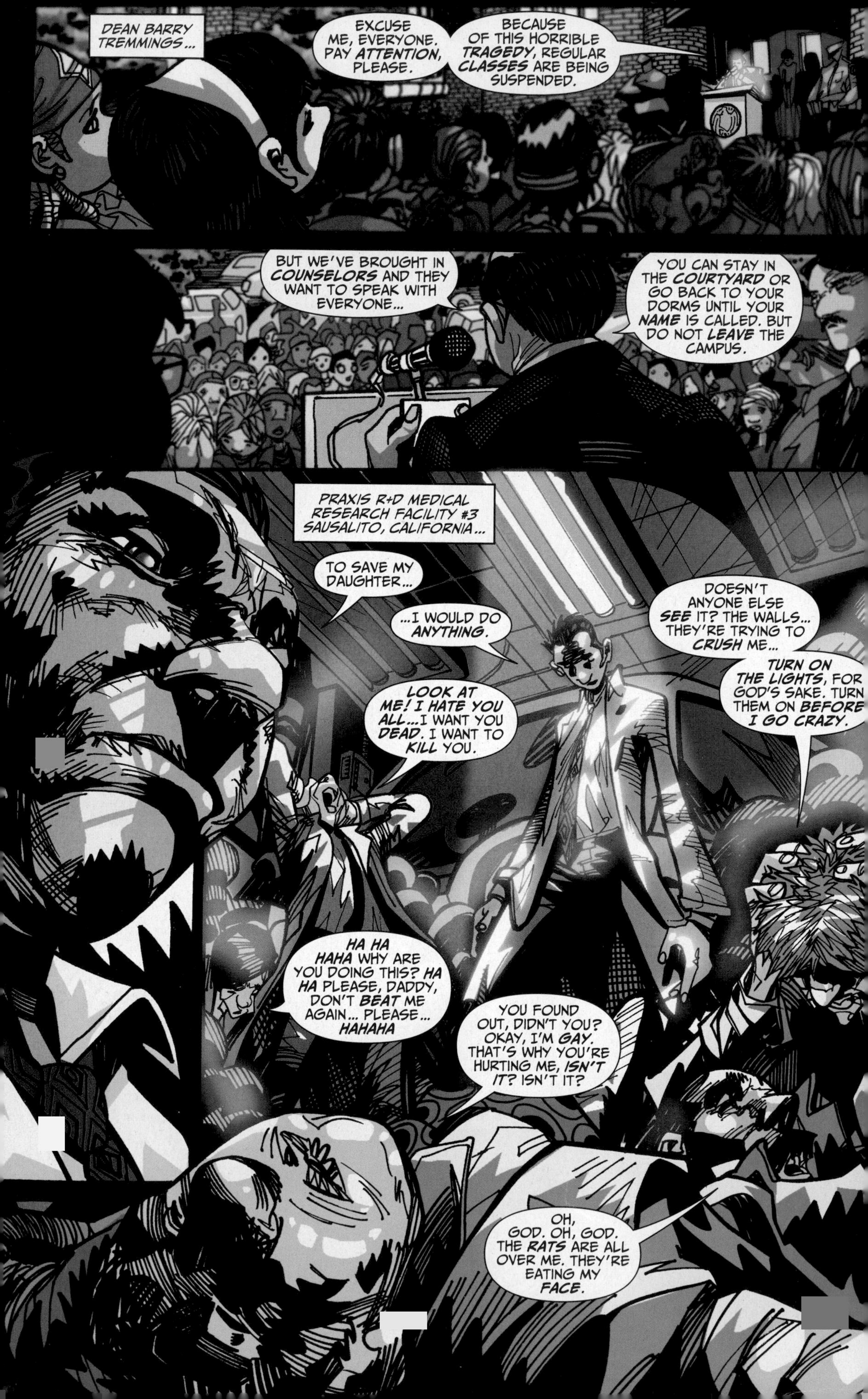
DEAN BARRY TREMMINGS...
EXCUSE ME, EVERYONE. PAY ATTENTION, PLEASE.
BECAUSE OF THIS HORRIBLE TRAGEDY, REGULAR CLASSES ARE BEING SUSPENDED.
BUT WE'VE BROUGHT IN COUNSELORS AND THEY WANT TO SPEAK WITH EVERYONE...
YOU CAN STAY IN THE COURTYARD OR GO BACK TO YOUR DORMS UNTIL YOUR NAME IS CALLED. BUT DO NOT LEAVE THE CAMPUS.
PRAXIS R+D MEDICAL RESEARCH FACILITY #3 SAUSALITO, CALIFORNIA...
TO SAVE MY DAUGHTER...
...I WOULD DO ANYTHING.
DOESN'T ANYONE ELSE SEE IT? THE WALLS... THEY'RE TRYING TO CRUSH ME...
TURN ON THE LIGHTS, FOR GOD'S SAKE. TURN THEM ON BEFORE I GO CRAZY.
LOOK AT ME! I HATE YOU ALL...I WANT YOU DEAD. I WANT TO KILL YOU.
HA HA HAHA WHY ARE YOU DOING THIS? HA HA PLEASE, DADDY, DON'T BEAT ME AGAIN... PLEASE... HAHAHA
YOU FOUND OUT, DIDN'T YOU? OKAY, I'M GAY. THAT'S WHY YOU'RE HURTING ME, ISN'T IT? ISN'T IT?
OH, GOD. OH, GOD. THE RATS ARE ALL OVER ME. THEY'RE EATING MY FACE.

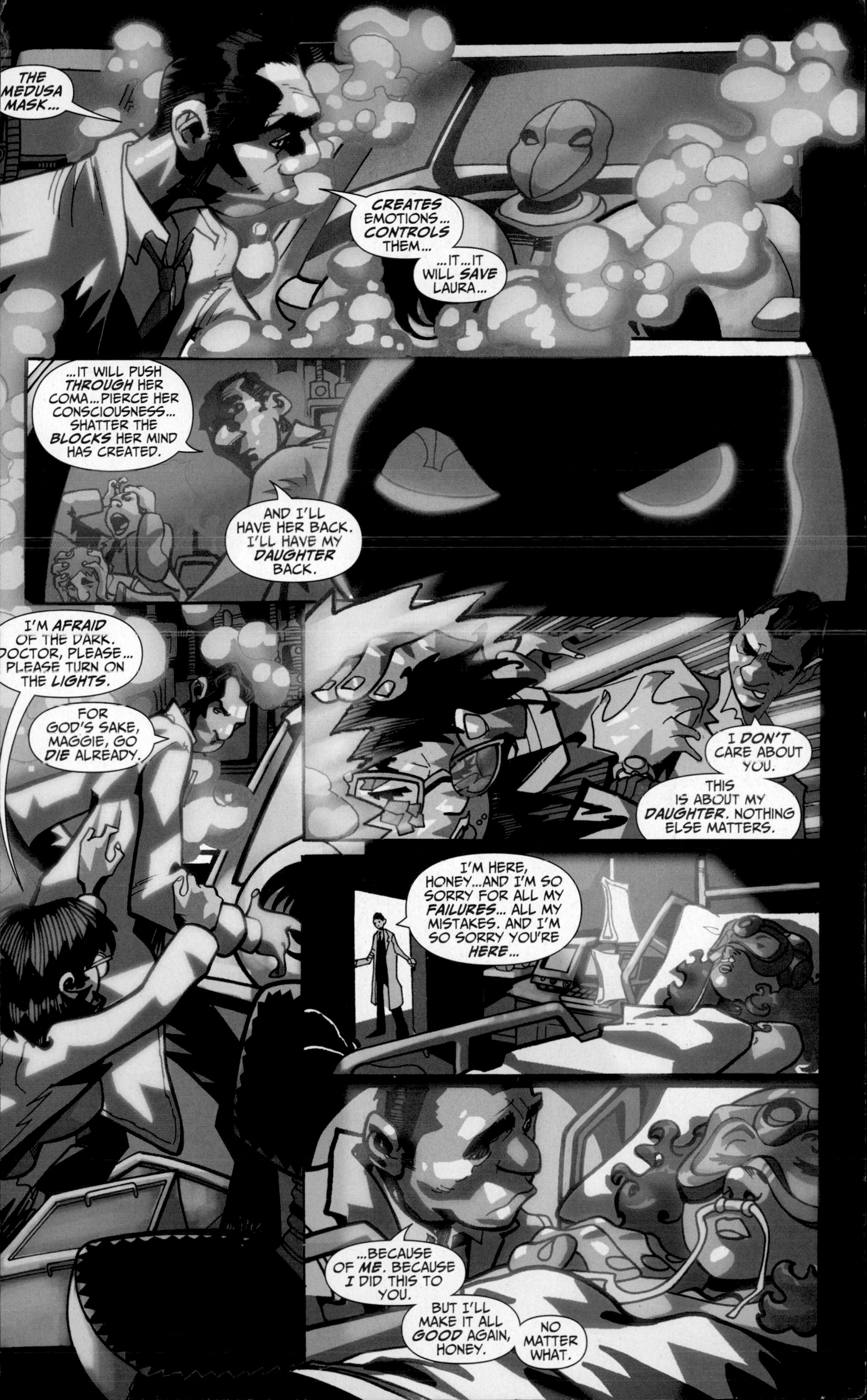

THE MEDUSA MASK...
CREATES EMOTIONS... CONTROLS THEM...
...IT...IT WILL SAVE LAURA...
...IT WILL PUSH THROUGH HER COMA...PIERCE HER CONSCIOUSNESS... SHATTER THE BLOCKS HER MIND HAS CREATED.
AND I'LL HAVE HER BACK. I'LL HAVE MY DAUGHTER BACK.
I'M AFRAID OF THE DARK. DOCTOR, PLEASE... PLEASE TURN ON THE LIGHTS.
FOR GOD'S SAKE, MAGGIE, GO DIE ALREADY.
I DON'T CARE ABOUT YOU.
THIS IS ABOUT MY DAUGHTER. NOTHING ELSE MATTERS.
I'M HERE, HONEY...AND I'M SO SORRY FOR ALL MY FAILURES... ALL MY MISTAKES. AND I'M SO SORRY YOU'RE HERE...
...BECAUSE OF ME. BECAUSE I DID THIS TO YOU.
BUT I'LL MAKE IT ALL GOOD AGAIN, HONEY.
NO MATTER WHAT.

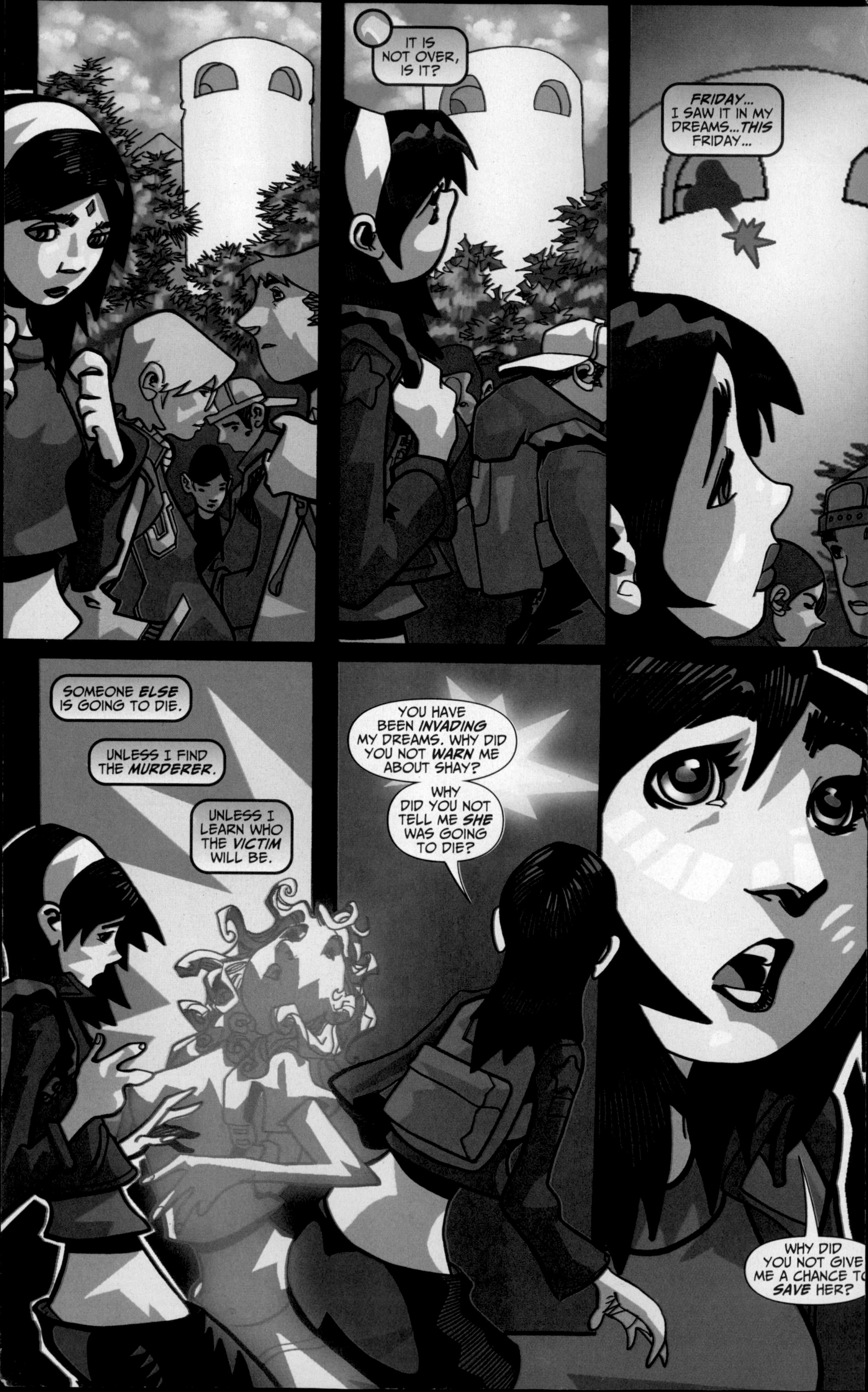
IT IS NOT OVER, IS IT?
FRIDAY... I SAW IT IN MY DREAMS...THIS FRIDAY...
SOMEONE ELSE IS GOING TO DIE.
UNLESS I FIND THE MURDERER.
UNLESS I LEARN WHO THE VICTIM WILL BE.
YOU HAVE BEEN INVADING MY DREAMS. WHY DID YOU NOT WARN ME ABOUT SHAY?
WHY DID YOU NOT TELL ME SHE WAS GOING TO DIE?
WHY DID YOU NOT GIVE ME A CHANCE TO SAVE HER?

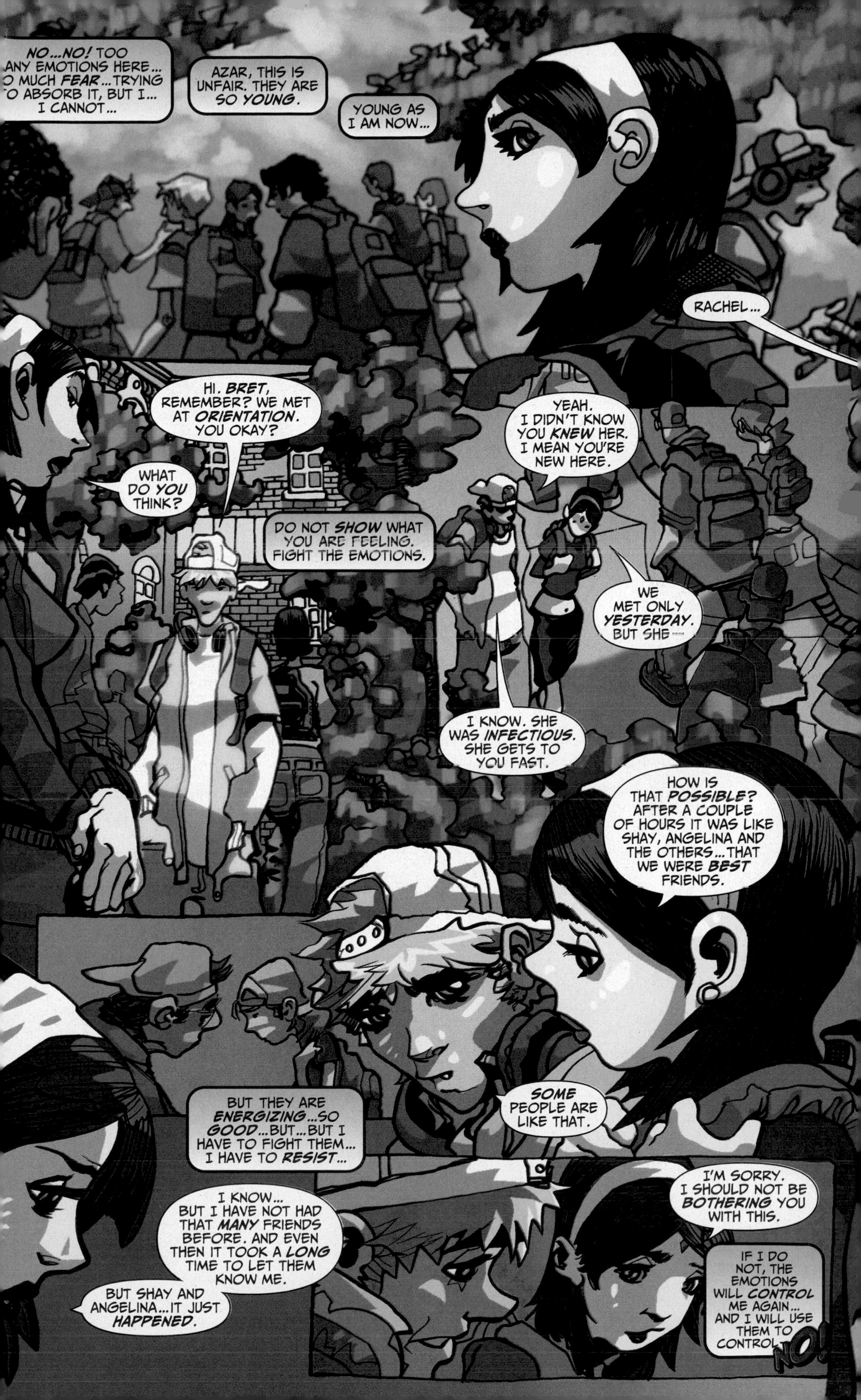

NO...NO! TOO ANY EMOTIONS HERE... O MUCH FEAR...TRYING O ABSORB IT, BUT I... I CANNOT...
AZAR, THIS IS UNFAIR. THEY ARE SO YOUNG.
YOUNG AS I AM NOW...
RACHEL...
HI. BRET, REMEMBER? WE MET AT ORIENTATION. YOU OKAY?
WHAT DO YOU THINK?
DO NOT SHOW WHAT YOU ARE FEELING. FIGHT THE EMOTIONS.
YEAH. I DIDN'T KNOW YOU KNEW HER. I MEAN YOU'RE NEW HERE.
WE MET ONLY YESTERDAY. BUT SHE--
I KNOW. SHE WAS INFECTIOUS. SHE GETS TO YOU FAST.
HOW IS THAT POSSIBLE? AFTER A COUPLE OF HOURS IT WAS LIKE SHAY, ANGELINA AND THE OTHERS...THAT WE WERE BEST FRIENDS.
BUT THEY ARE ENERGIZING...SO GOOD...BUT...BUT I HAVE TO FIGHT THEM... I HAVE TO RESIST...
SOME PEOPLE ARE LIKE THAT.
I KNOW... BUT I HAVE NOT HAD THAT MANY FRIENDS BEFORE. AND EVEN THEN IT TOOK A LONG TIME TO LET THEM KNOW ME.
BUT SHAY AND ANGELINA...IT JUST HAPPENED.
I'M SORRY. I SHOULD NOT BE BOTHERING YOU WITH THIS.
IF I DO NOT, THE EMOTIONS WILL CONTROL ME AGAIN... AND I WILL USE THEM TO CONTROL--
NO!

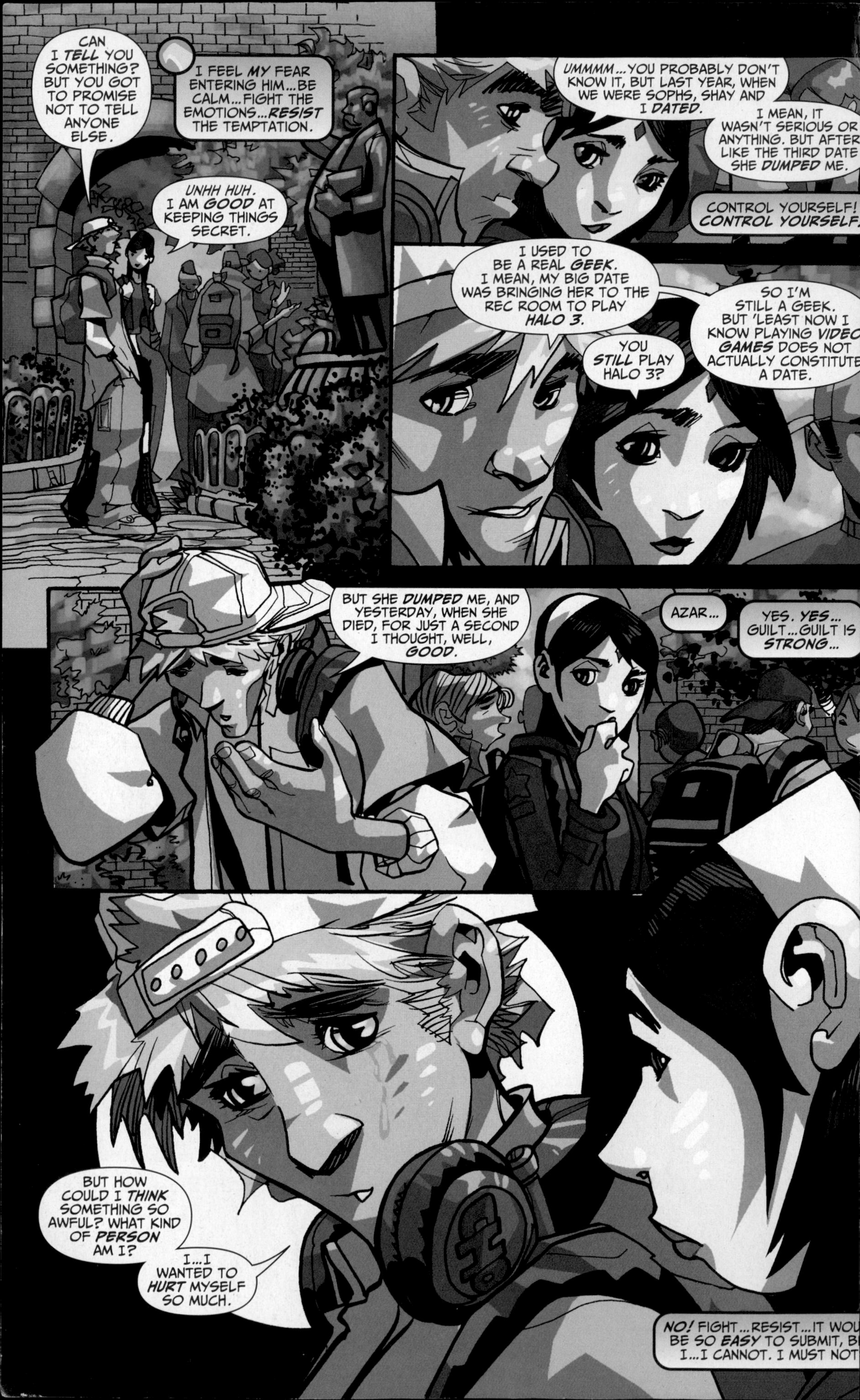
CAN I TELL YOU SOMETHING? BUT YOU GOT TO PROMISE NOT TO TELL ANYONE ELSE.
I FEEL MY FEAR ENTERING HIM...BE CALM...FIGHT THE EMOTIONS...RESIST THE TEMPTATION.
UNHH HUH. I AM GOOD AT KEEPING THINGS SECRET.
UMMMM...YOU PROBABLY DON'T KNOW IT, BUT LAST YEAR, WHEN WE WERE SOPHS, SHAY AND I DATED.
I MEAN, IT WASN'T SERIOUS OR ANYTHING. BUT AFTER LIKE THE THIRD DATE SHE DUMPED ME.
CONTROL YOURSELF! CONTROL YOURSELF!
I USED TO BE A REAL GEEK. I MEAN, MY BIG DATE WAS BRINGING HER TO THE REC ROOM TO PLAY HALO 3.
YOU STILL PLAY HALO 3?
SO I'M STILL A GEEK. BUT 'LEAST NOW I KNOW PLAYING VIDEO GAMES DOES NOT ACTUALLY CONSTITUTE A DATE.
BUT SHE DUMPED ME, AND YESTERDAY, WHEN SHE DIED, FOR JUST A SECOND I THOUGHT, WELL, GOOD.
AZAR...
YES. YES... GUILT...GUILT IS STRONG...
BUT HOW COULD I THINK SOMETHING SO AWFUL? WHAT KIND OF PERSON AM I?
I...I WANTED TO HURT MYSELF SO MUCH.
NO! FIGHT...RESIST...IT WOU BE SO EASY TO SUBMIT, B I...I CANNOT. I MUST NOT

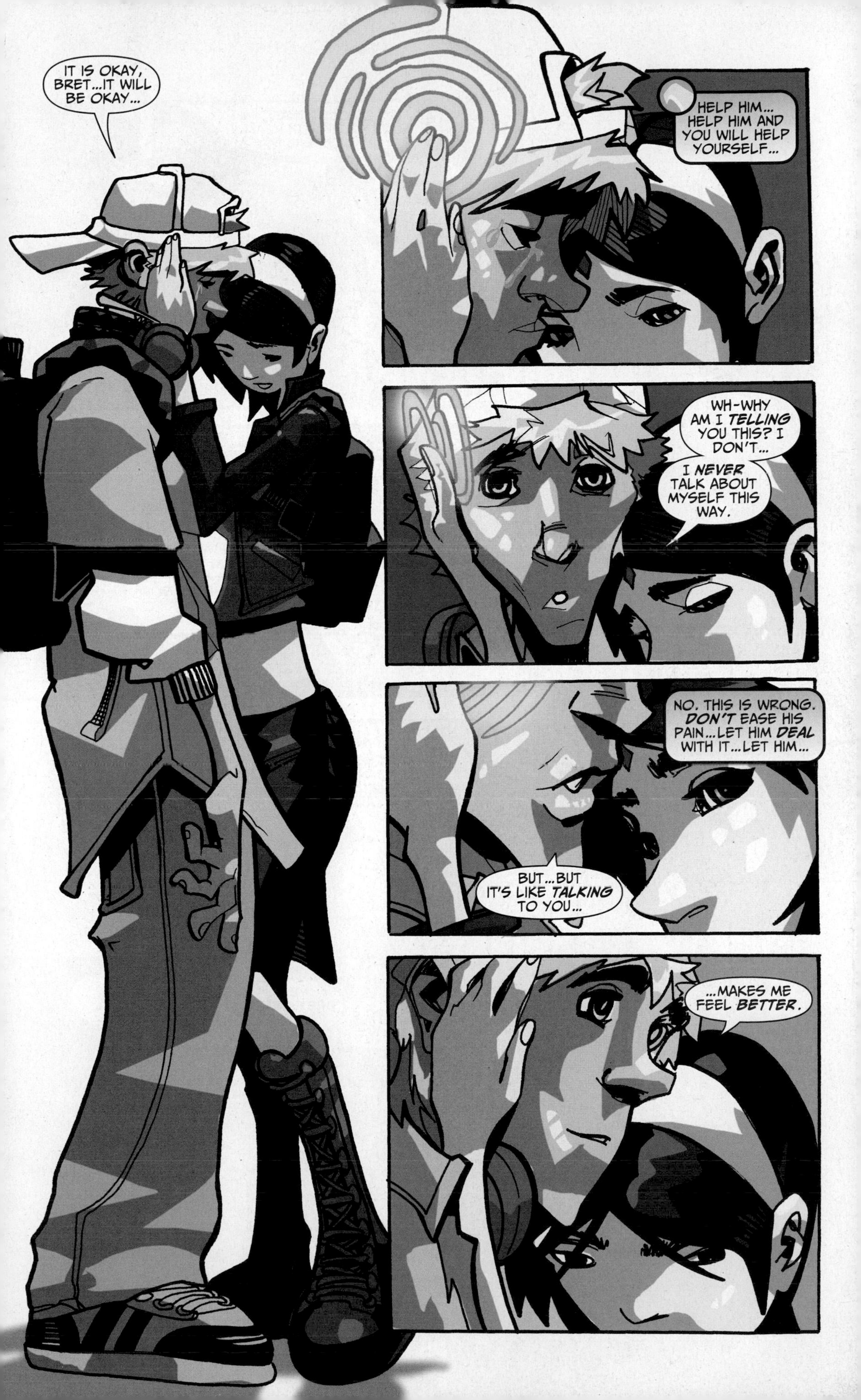
IT IS OKAY, BRET...IT WILL BE OKAY...
HELP HIM... HELP HIM AND YOU WILL HELP YOURSELF...
WH-WHY AM I *TELLING* YOU THIS? I DON'T...
I *NEVER* TALK ABOUT MYSELF THIS WAY.
NO. THIS IS WRONG. *DON'T* EASE HIS PAIN...LET HIM *DEAL* WITH IT...LET HIM...
BUT...BUT IT'S LIKE *TALKING* TO YOU...
...MAKES ME FEEL *BETTER*.

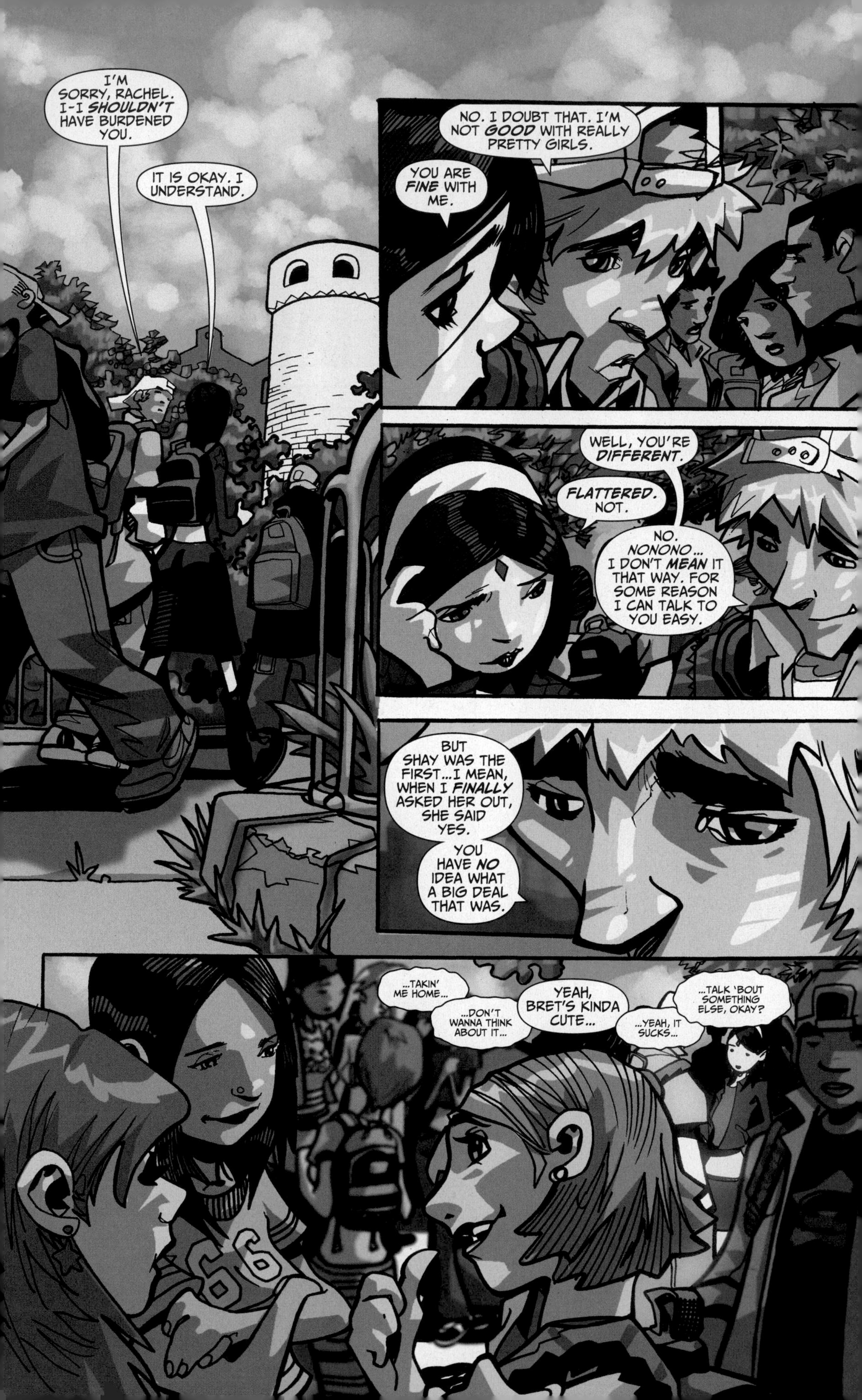
I'M SORRY, RACHEL. I-I SHOULDN'T HAVE BURDENED YOU.
IT IS OKAY. I UNDERSTAND.
NO. I DOUBT THAT. I'M NOT GOOD WITH REALLY PRETTY GIRLS.
YOU ARE FINE WITH ME.
WELL, YOU'RE DIFFERENT.
FLATTERED. NOT.
NO. NONONO... I DON'T MEAN IT THAT WAY. FOR SOME REASON I CAN TALK TO YOU EASY.
BUT SHAY WAS THE FIRST...I MEAN, WHEN I FINALLY ASKED HER OUT, SHE SAID YES.
YOU HAVE NO IDEA WHAT A BIG DEAL THAT WAS.
...TAKIN' ME HOME...
...DON'T WANNA THINK ABOUT IT...
YEAH, BRET'S KINDA CUTE...
...YEAH, IT SUCKS...
...TALK 'BOUT SOMETHING ELSE, OKAY?

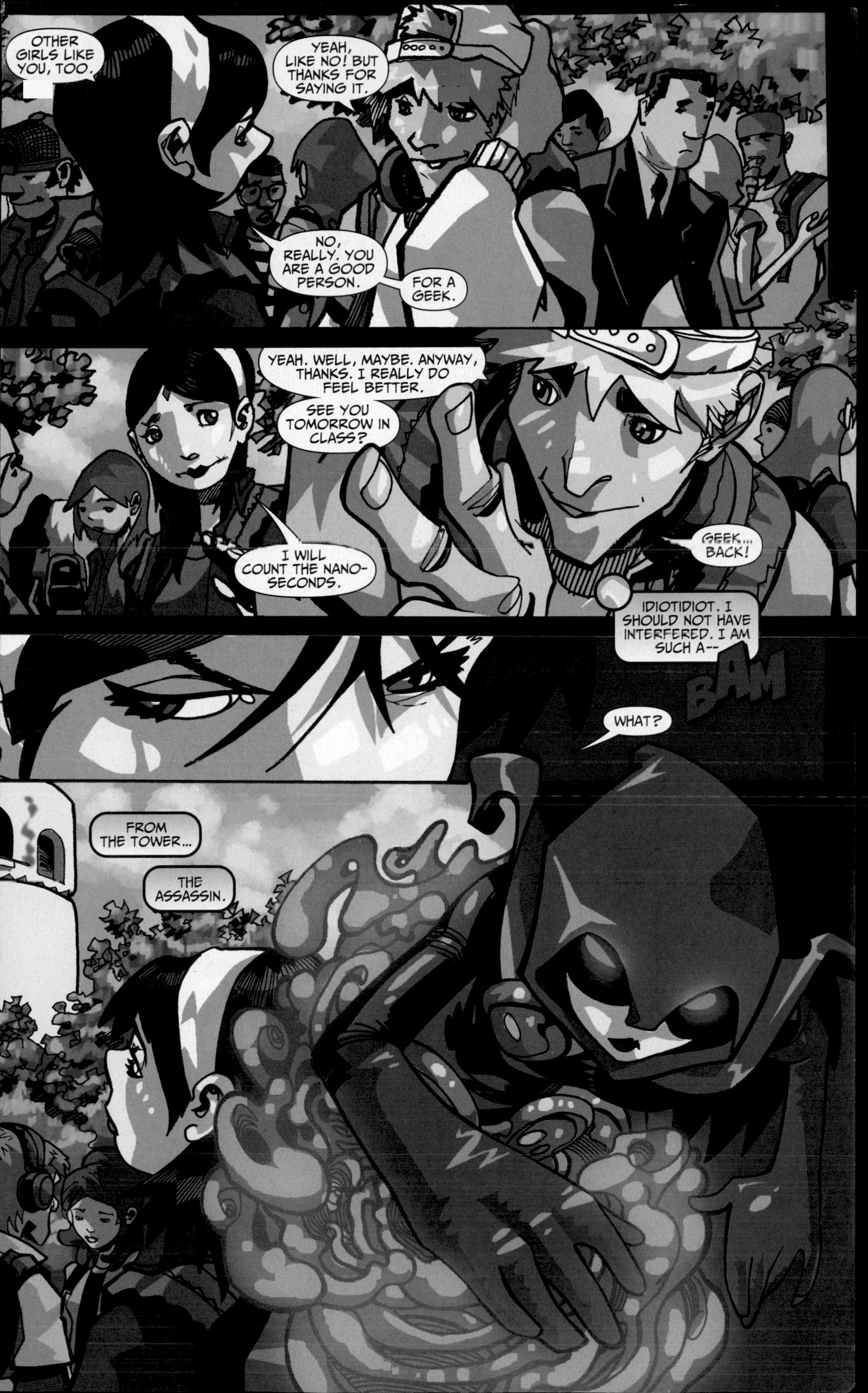
OTHER GIRLS LIKE YOU, TOO.
YEAH, LIKE NO! BUT THANKS FOR SAYING IT.
NO, REALLY. YOU ARE A GOOD PERSON.
FOR A GEEK.
YEAH. WELL, MAYBE. ANYWAY, THANKS. I REALLY DO FEEL BETTER.
SEE YOU TOMORROW IN CLASS?
I WILL COUNT THE NANO-SECONDS.
GEEK... BACK!
IDIOTIDIOT. I SHOULD NOT HAVE INTERFERED. I AM SUCH A--
BAM
WHAT?
FROM THE TOWER...
THE ASSASSIN.

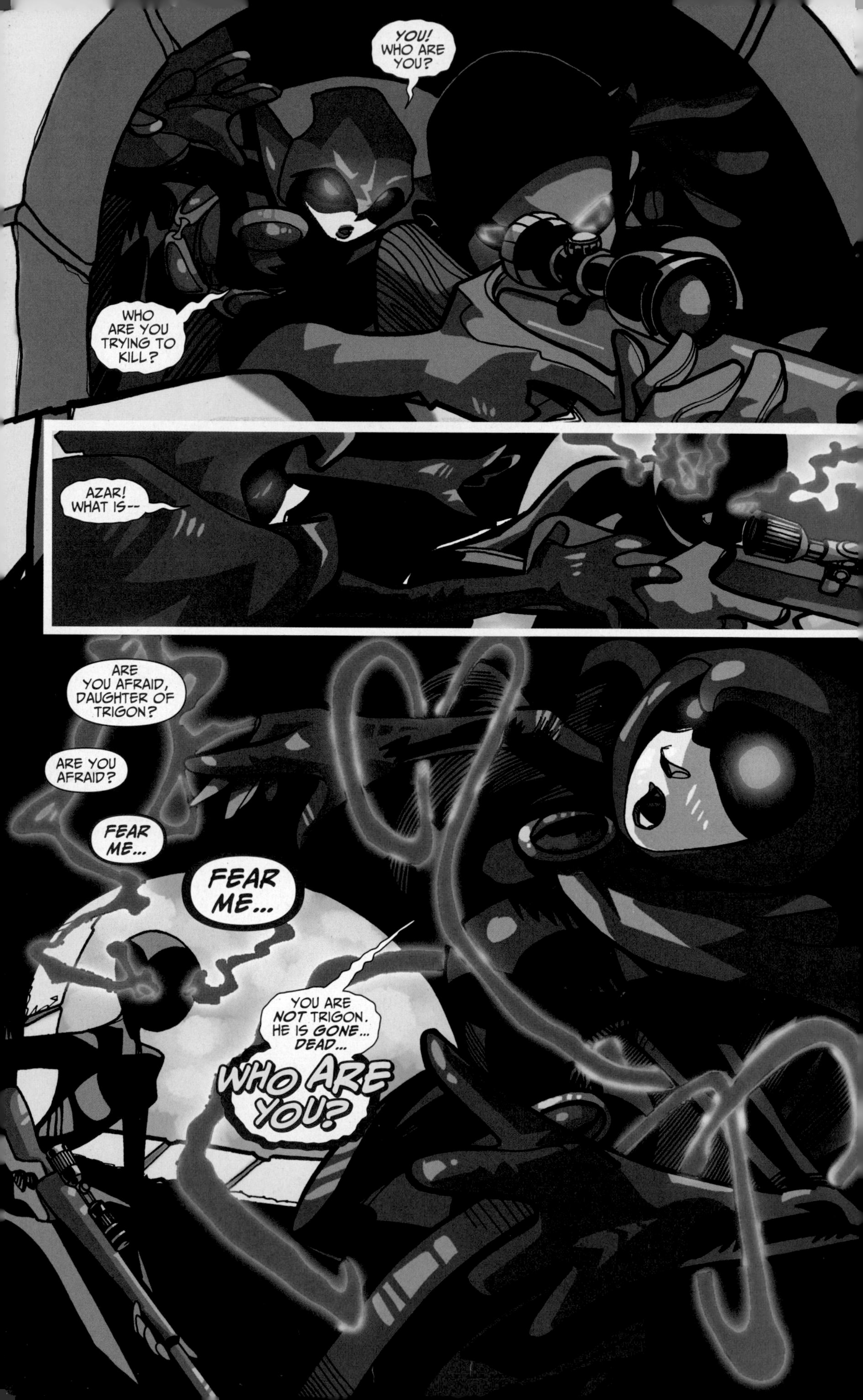
YOU! WHO ARE YOU?
WHO ARE YOU TRYING TO KILL?
AZAR! WHAT IS--
ARE YOU AFRAID, DAUGHTER OF TRIGON?
ARE YOU AFRAID?
FEAR ME...
FEAR ME...
YOU ARE NOT TRIGON. HE IS GONE... DEAD...
WHO ARE YOU?

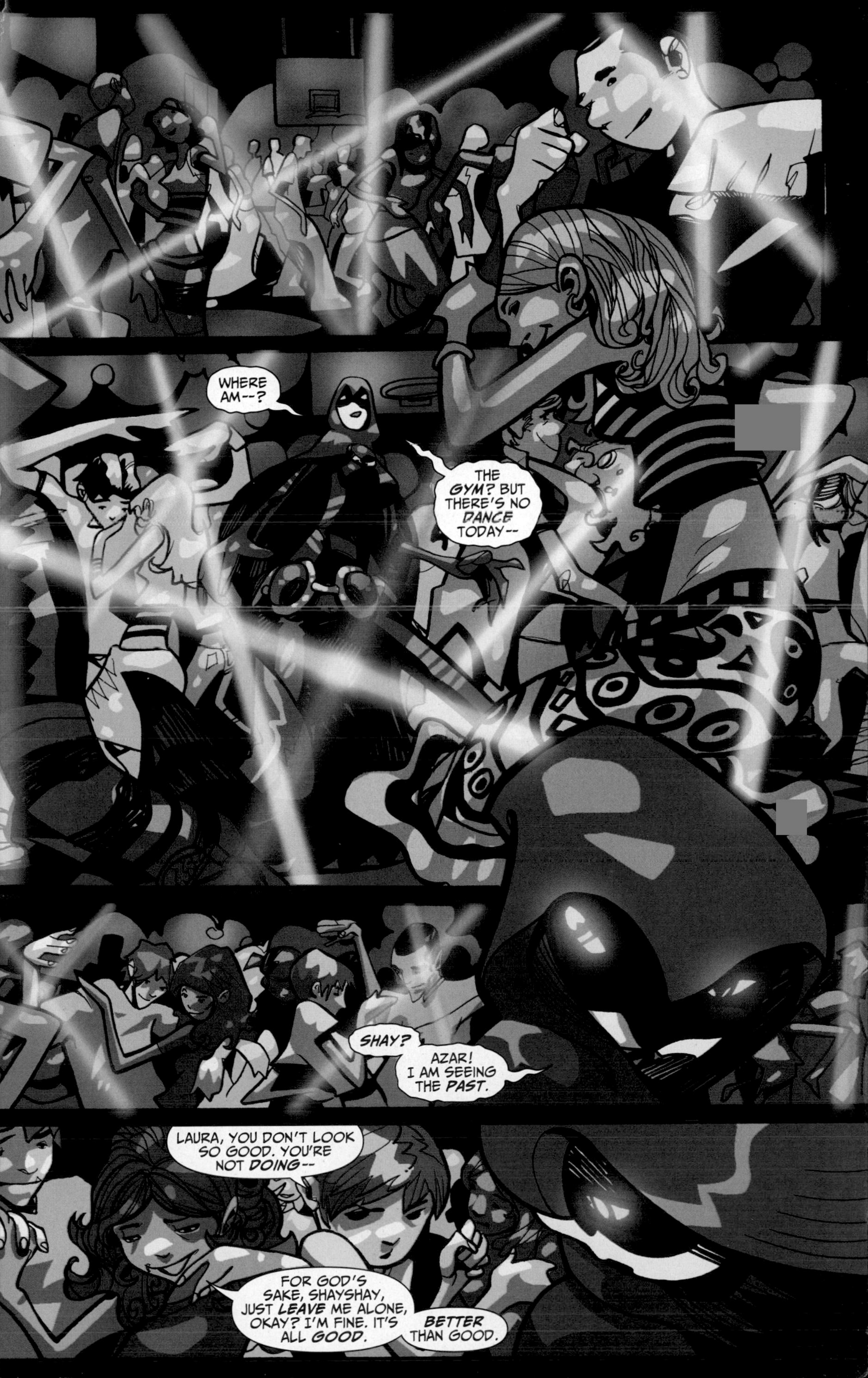
WHERE AM--?
THE GYM? BUT THERE'S NO DANCE TODAY--
SHAY?
AZAR! I AM SEEING THE PAST.
LAURA, YOU DON'T LOOK SO GOOD. YOU'RE NOT DOING--
FOR GOD'S SAKE, SHAYSHAY, JUST LEAVE ME ALONE, OKAY? I'M FINE. IT'S ALL GOOD.
BETTER THAN GOOD.

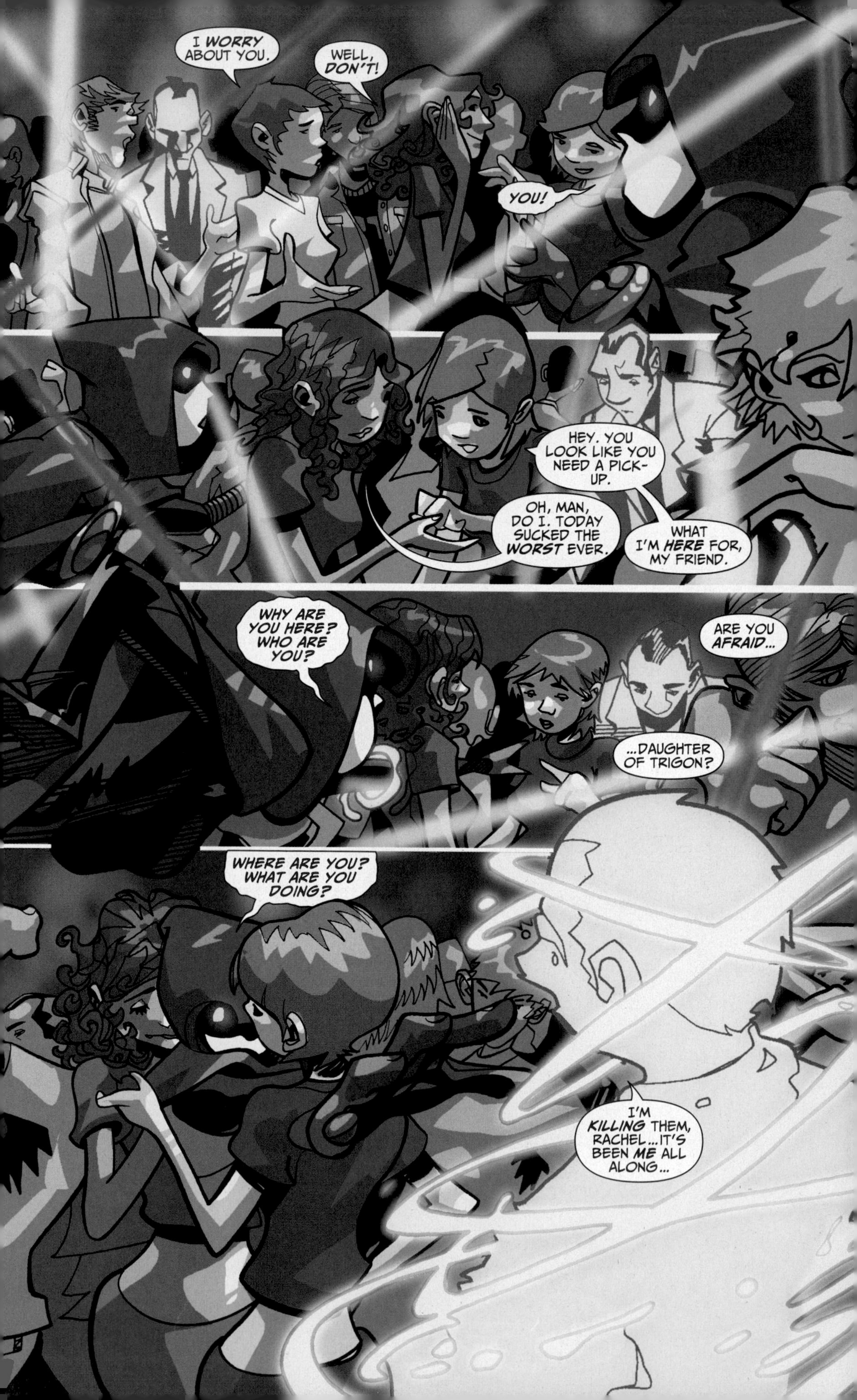
I WORRY ABOUT YOU.
WELL, DON'T!
YOU!
HEY. YOU LOOK LIKE YOU NEED A PICK-UP.
OH, MAN, DO I. TODAY SUCKED THE WORST EVER.
WHAT I'M HERE FOR, MY FRIEND.
WHY ARE YOU HERE? WHO ARE YOU?
ARE YOU AFRAID...
...DAUGHTER OF TRIGON?
WHERE ARE YOU? WHAT ARE YOU DOING?
I'M KILLING THEM, RACHEL...IT'S BEEN ME ALL ALONG...

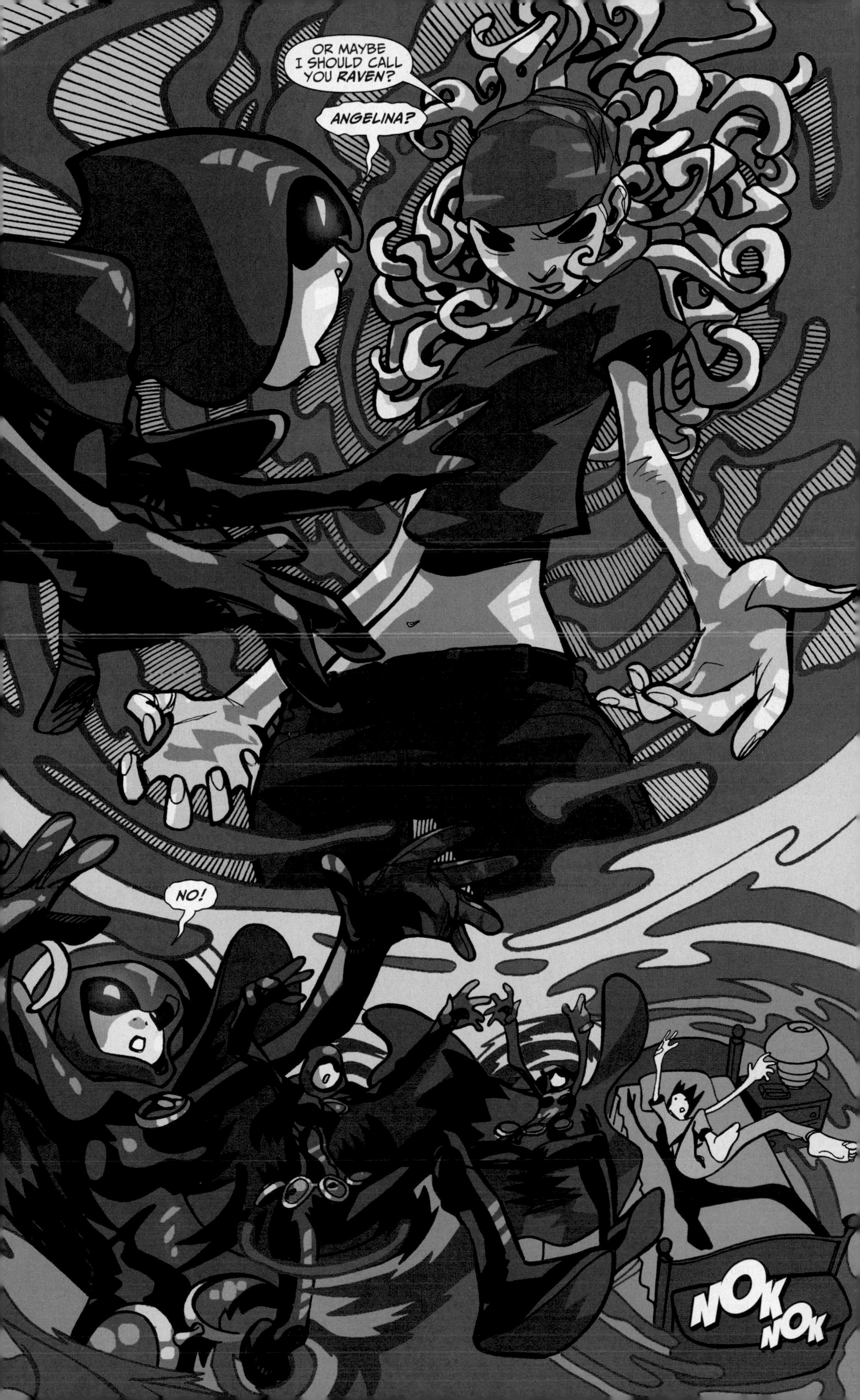
OR MAYBE I SHOULD CALL YOU RAVEN?
ANGELINA?
NO!
NOK NOK

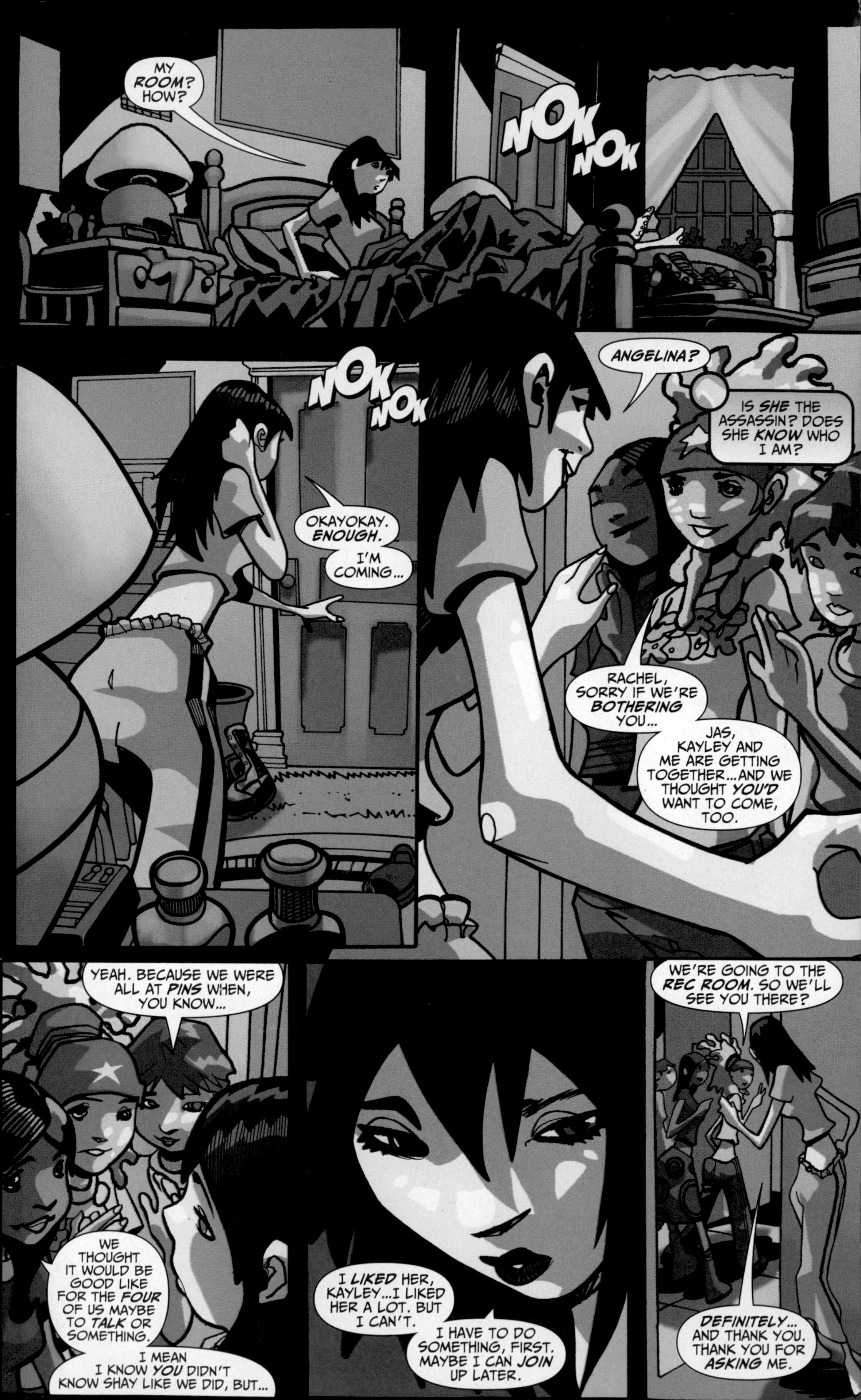
MY ROOM? HOW?
NOK NOK
NOK NOK
OKAYOKAY. ENOUGH.
I'M COMING...
ANGELINA?
IS SHE THE ASSASSIN? DOES SHE KNOW WHO I AM?
RACHEL, SORRY IF WE'RE BOTHERING YOU...
JAS, KAYLEY AND ME ARE GETTING TOGETHER...AND WE THOUGHT YOU'D WANT TO COME, TOO.
YEAH. BECAUSE WE WERE ALL AT PINS WHEN, YOU KNOW...
WE THOUGHT IT WOULD BE GOOD LIKE FOR THE FOUR OF US MAYBE TO TALK OR SOMETHING.
I MEAN I KNOW YOU DIDN'T KNOW SHAY LIKE WE DID, BUT...
I LIKED HER, KAYLEY...I LIKED HER A LOT. BUT I CAN'T.
I HAVE TO DO SOMETHING, FIRST. MAYBE I CAN JOIN UP LATER.
WE'RE GOING TO THE REC ROOM. SO WE'LL SEE YOU THERE?
DEFINITELY... AND THANK YOU. THANK YOU FOR ASKING ME.

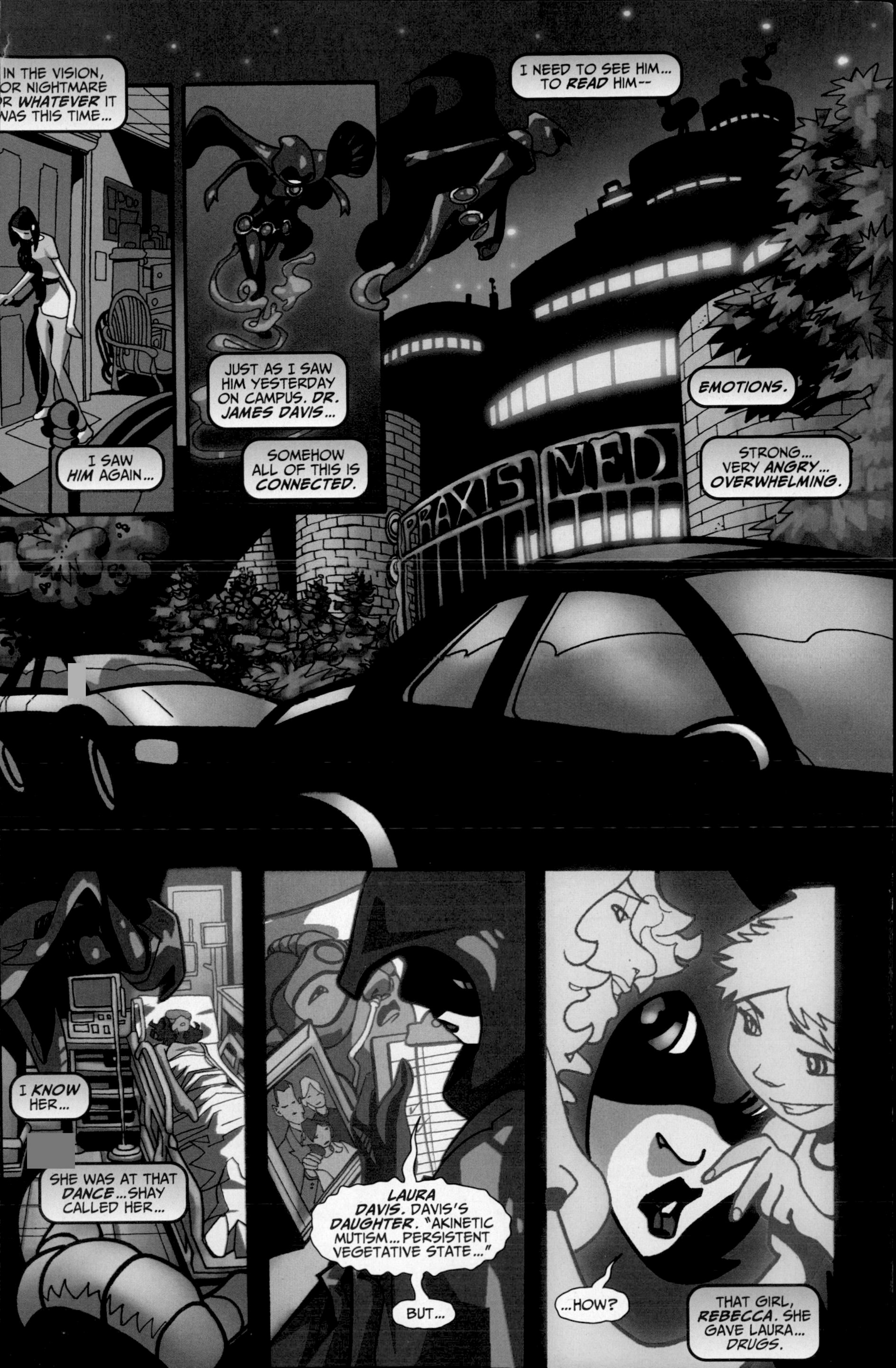
IN THE VISION, OR NIGHTMARE OR WHATEVER IT WAS THIS TIME...
I SAW HIM AGAIN...
JUST AS I SAW HIM YESTERDAY ON CAMPUS. DR. JAMES DAVIS...
SOMEHOW ALL OF THIS IS CONNECTED.
I NEED TO SEE HIM... TO READ HIM--
PRAXIS MED
EMOTIONS.
STRONG... VERY ANGRY... OVERWHELMING.
I KNOW HER...
SHE WAS AT THAT DANCE...SHAY CALLED HER...
LAURA DAVIS. DAVIS'S DAUGHTER. "AKINETIC MUTISM... PERSISTENT VEGETATIVE STATE..."
BUT...
...HOW?
THAT GIRL, REBECCA. SHE GAVE LAURA... DRUGS.

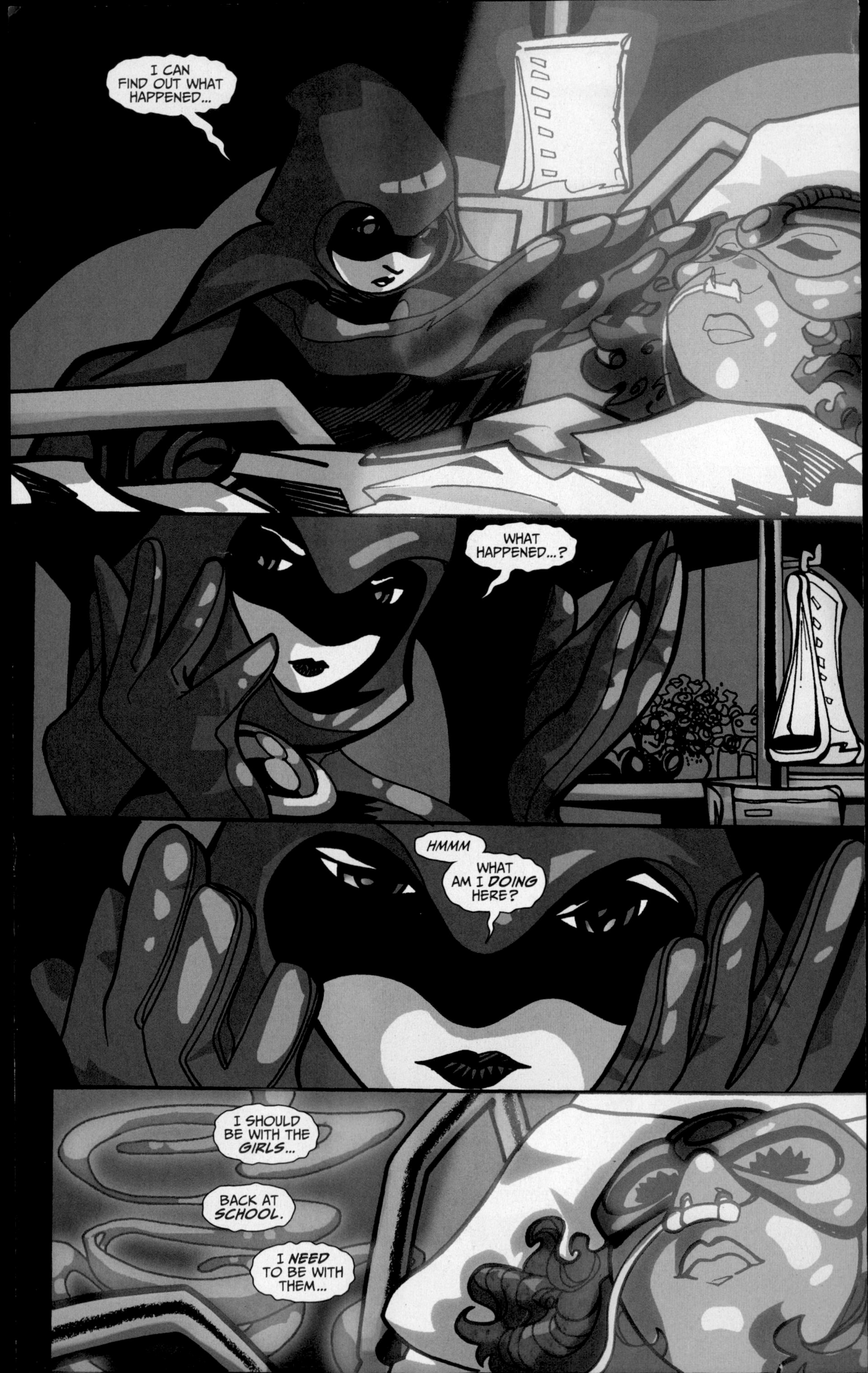
I CAN FIND OUT WHAT HAPPENED...
WHAT HAPPENED...?
HMMM
WHAT AM I *DOING* HERE?
I SHOULD BE WITH THE *GIRLS*...
BACK AT *SCHOOL*.
I *NEED* TO BE WITH THEM...

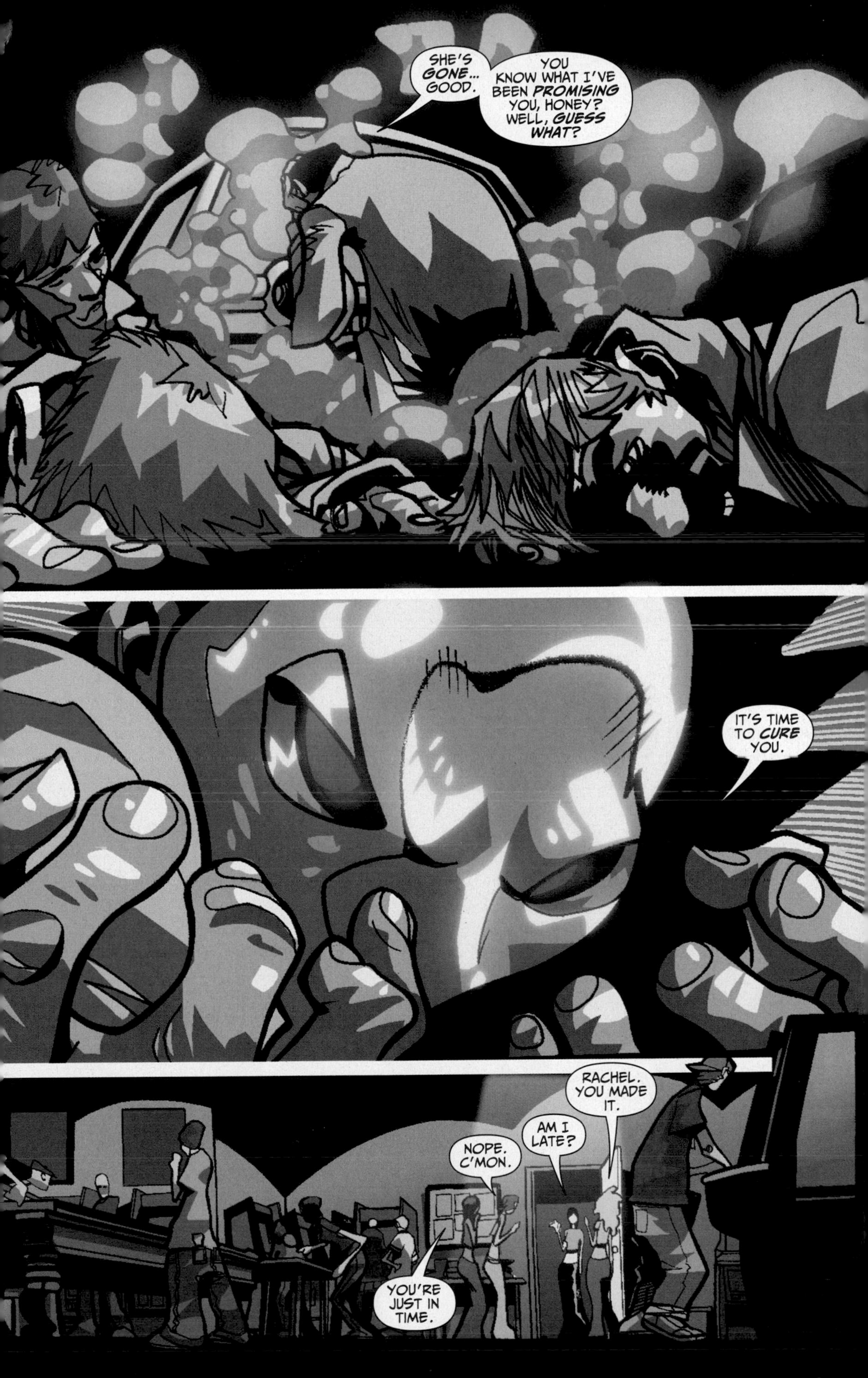
SHE'S GONE... GOOD.
YOU KNOW WHAT I'VE BEEN PROMISING YOU, HONEY? WELL, GUESS WHAT?
IT'S TIME TO CURE YOU.
RACHEL. YOU MADE IT.
AM I LATE?
NOPE. C'MON.
YOU'RE JUST IN TIME.

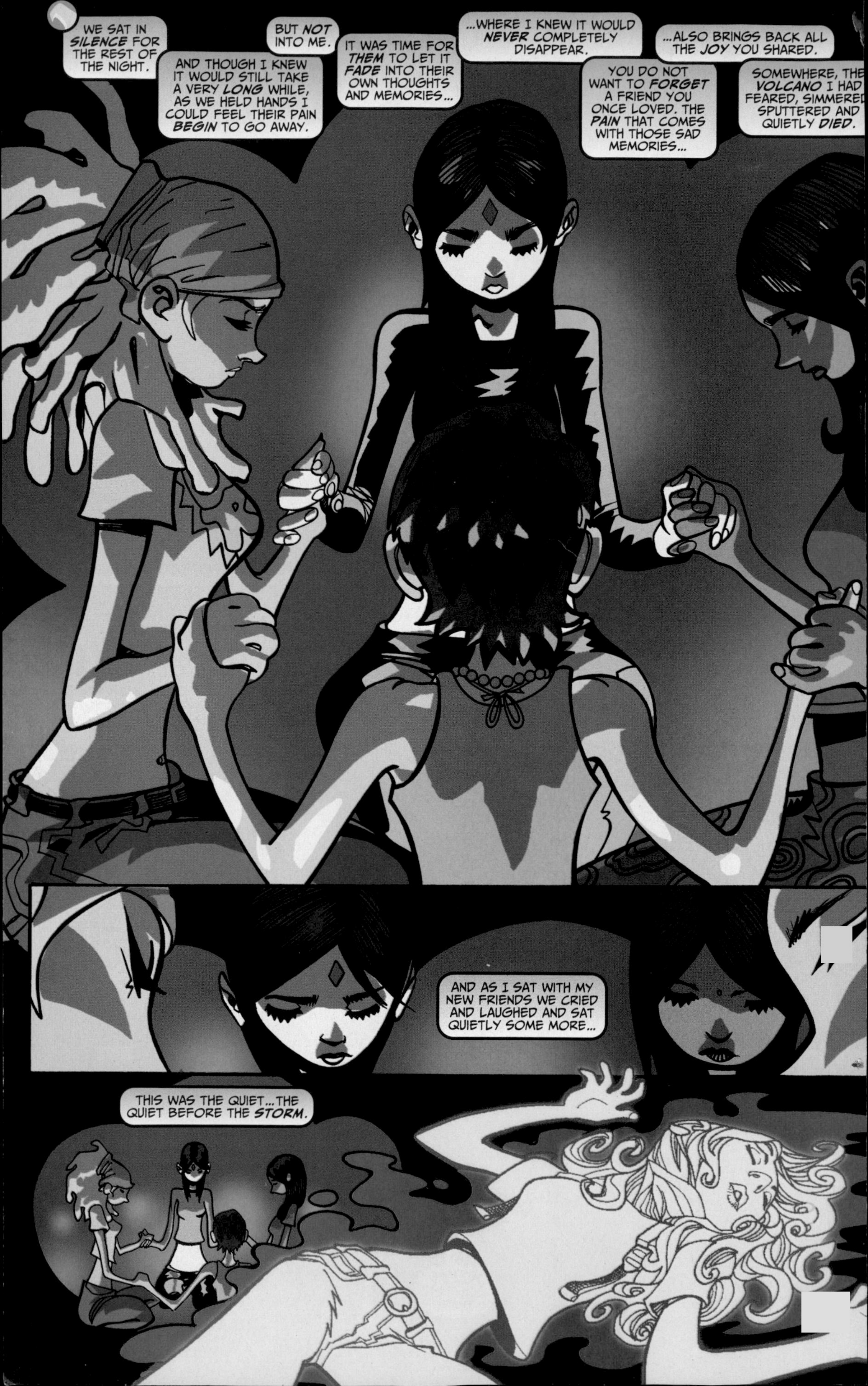
WE SAT IN SILENCE FOR THE REST OF THE NIGHT.
AND THOUGH I KNEW IT WOULD STILL TAKE A VERY LONG WHILE, AS WE HELD HANDS I COULD FEEL THEIR PAIN BEGIN TO GO AWAY.
BUT NOT INTO ME.
IT WAS TIME FOR THEM TO LET IT FADE INTO THEIR OWN THOUGHTS AND MEMORIES...
...WHERE I KNEW IT WOULD NEVER COMPLETELY DISAPPEAR.
YOU DO NOT WANT TO FORGET A FRIEND YOU ONCE LOVED. THE PAIN THAT COMES WITH THOSE SAD MEMORIES...
...ALSO BRINGS BACK ALL THE JOY YOU SHARED.
SOMEWHERE, THE VOLCANO I HAD FEARED, SIMMERED, SPUTTERED AND QUIETLY DIED.
AND AS I SAT WITH MY NEW FRIENDS WE CRIED AND LAUGHED AND SAT QUIETLY SOME MORE...
THIS WAS THE QUIET...THE QUIET BEFORE THE STORM.

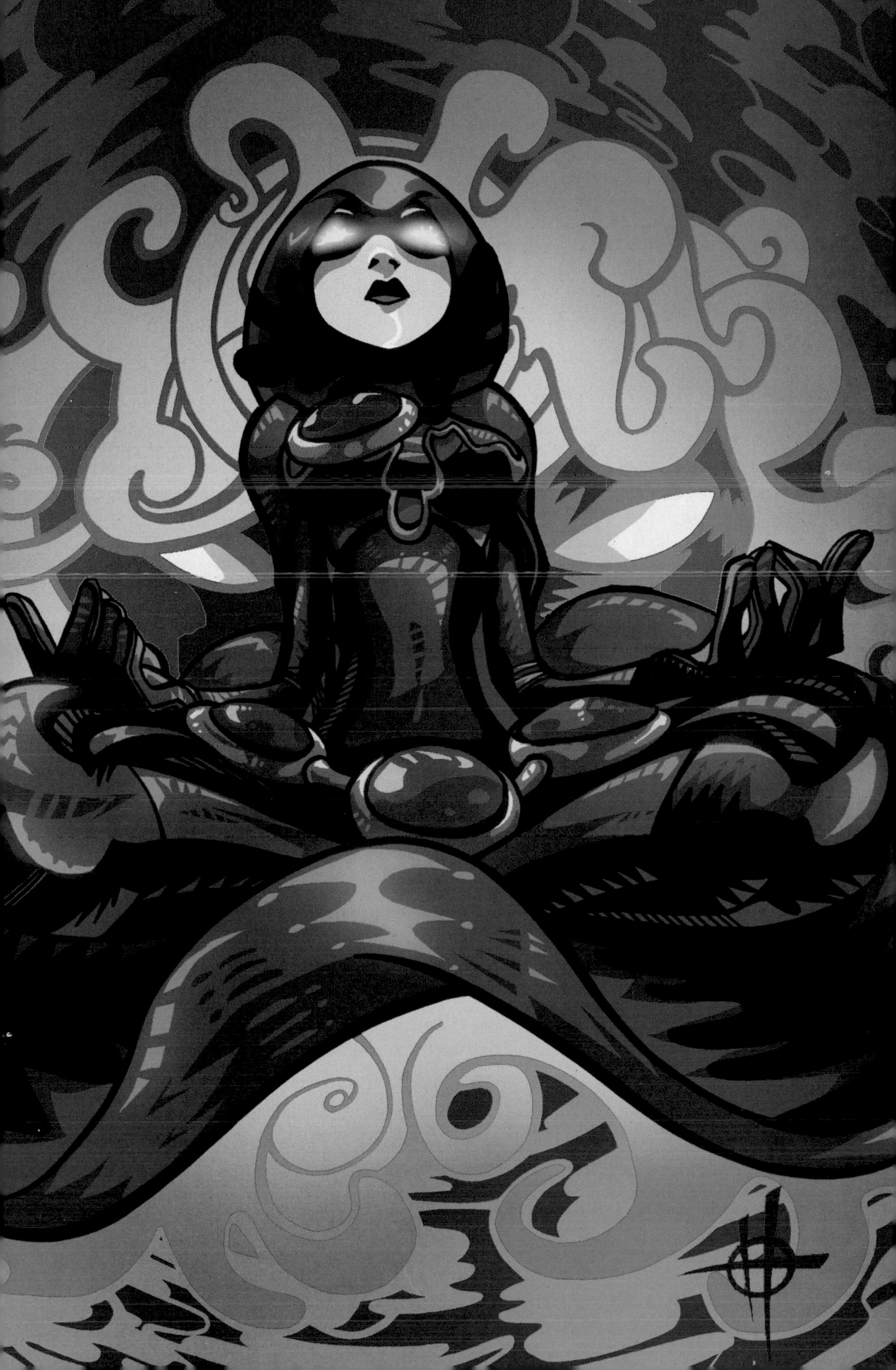

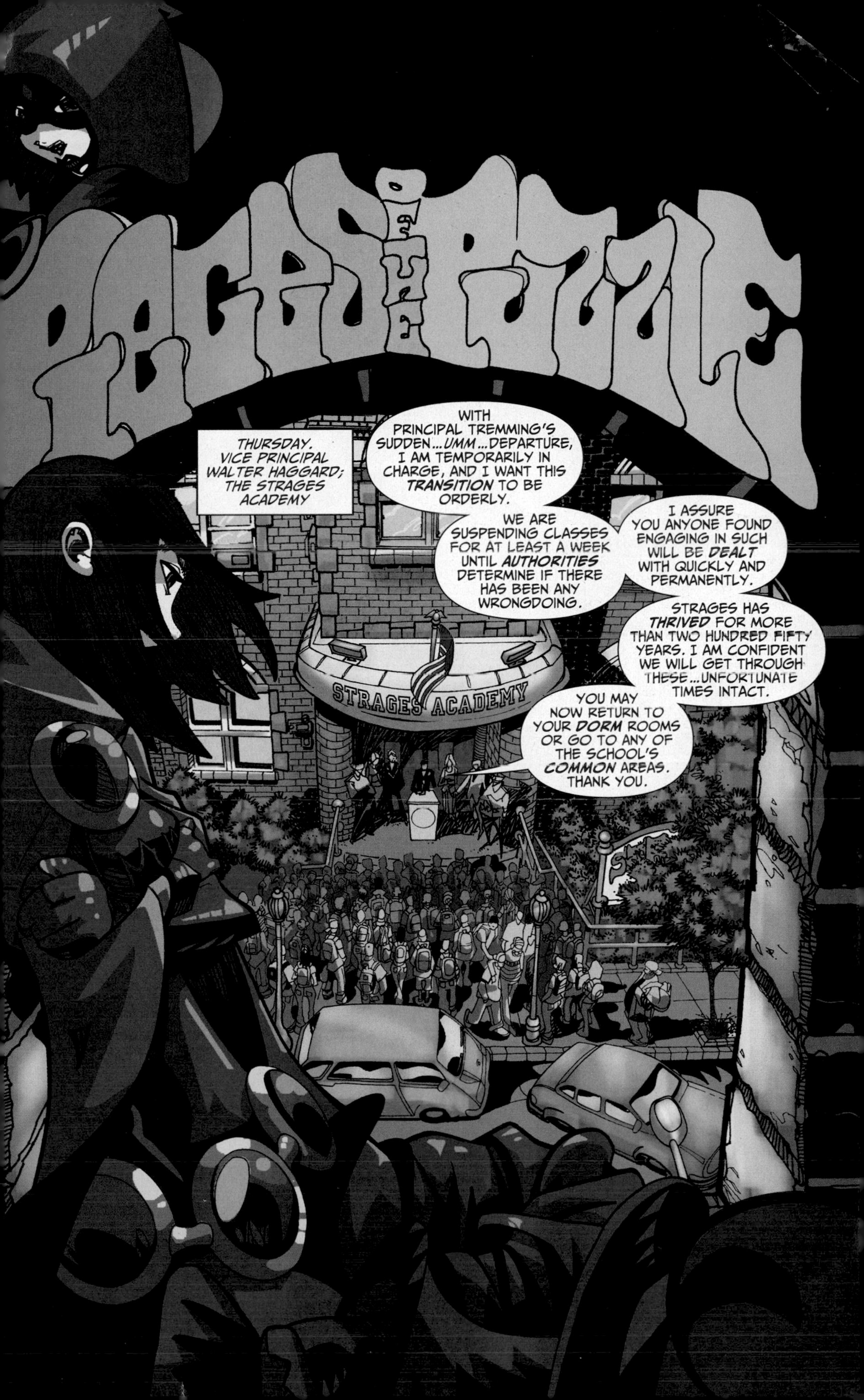

THURSDAY. VICE PRINCIPAL WALTER HAGGARD; THE STRAGES ACADEMY
WITH PRINCIPAL TREMMING'S SUDDEN...UMM...DEPARTURE, I AM TEMPORARILY IN CHARGE, AND I WANT THIS TRANSITION TO BE ORDERLY.
WE ARE SUSPENDING CLASSES FOR AT LEAST A WEEK UNTIL AUTHORITIES DETERMINE IF THERE HAS BEEN ANY WRONGDOING.
I ASSURE YOU ANYONE FOUND ENGAGING IN SUCH WILL BE DEALT WITH QUICKLY AND PERMANENTLY.
STRAGES HAS THRIVED FOR MORE THAN TWO HUNDRED FIFTY YEARS. I AM CONFIDENT WE WILL GET THROUGH THESE...UNFORTUNATE TIMES INTACT.
STRAGES ACADEMY
YOU MAY NOW RETURN TO YOUR DORM ROOMS OR GO TO ANY OF THE SCHOOL'S COMMON AREAS. THANK YOU.

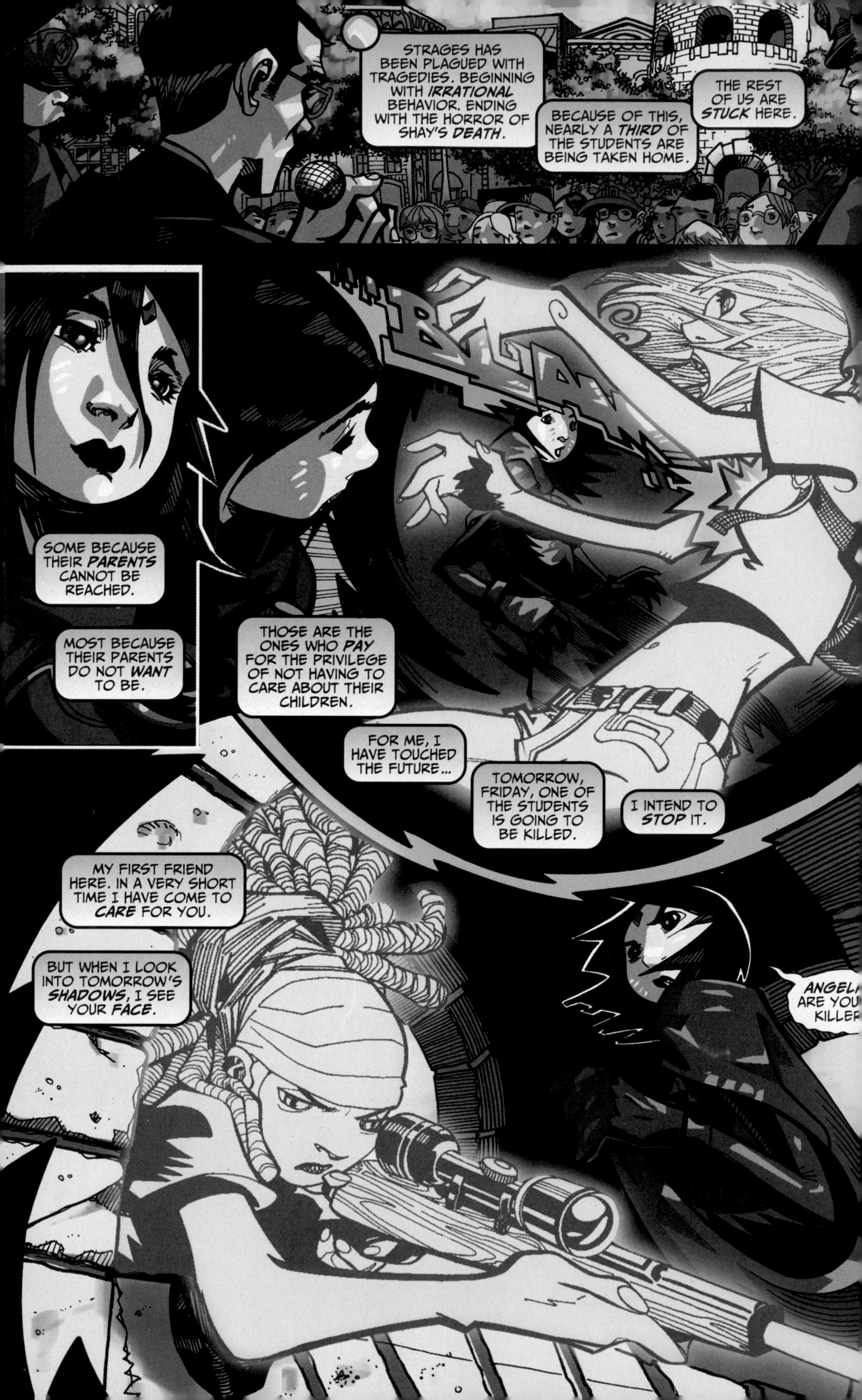
STRAGES HAS BEEN PLAGUED WITH TRAGEDIES. BEGINNING WITH IRRATIONAL BEHAVIOR. ENDING WITH THE HORROR OF SHAY'S DEATH.
BECAUSE OF THIS, NEARLY A THIRD OF THE STUDENTS ARE BEING TAKEN HOME.
THE REST OF US ARE STUCK HERE.
SOME BECAUSE THEIR PARENTS CANNOT BE REACHED.
MOST BECAUSE THEIR PARENTS DO NOT WANT TO BE.
THOSE ARE THE ONES WHO PAY FOR THE PRIVILEGE OF NOT HAVING TO CARE ABOUT THEIR CHILDREN.
FOR ME, I HAVE TOUCHED THE FUTURE...
TOMORROW, FRIDAY, ONE OF THE STUDENTS IS GOING TO BE KILLED.
I INTEND TO STOP IT.
MY FIRST FRIEND HERE. IN A VERY SHORT TIME I HAVE COME TO CARE FOR YOU.
BUT WHEN I LOOK INTO TOMORROW'S SHADOWS, I SEE YOUR FACE.

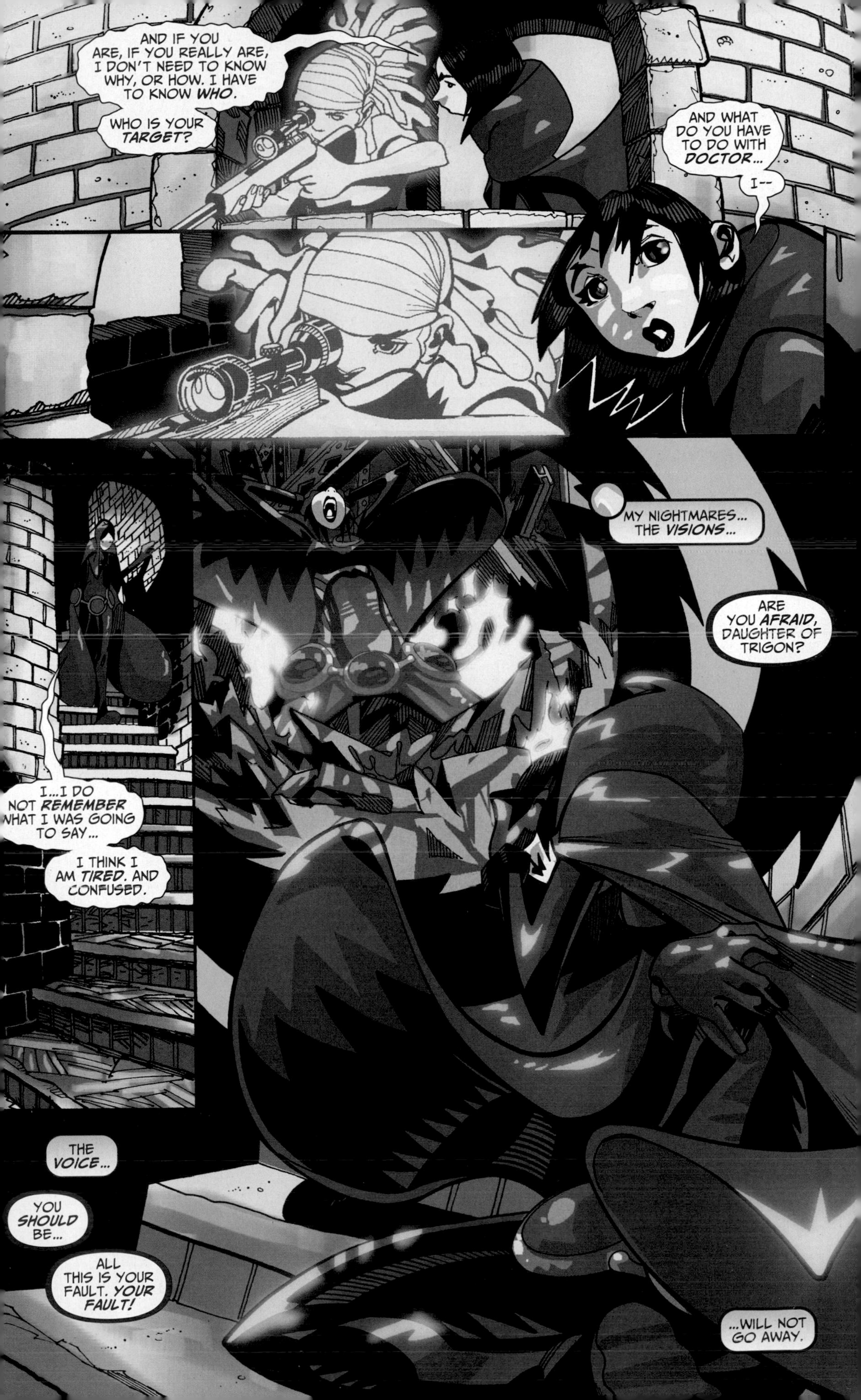
AND IF YOU ARE, IF YOU REALLY ARE, I DON'T NEED TO KNOW WHY, OR HOW. I HAVE TO KNOW WHO.
WHO IS YOUR TARGET?
AND WHAT DO YOU HAVE TO DO WITH DOCTOR...
I--
MY NIGHTMARES... THE VISIONS...
ARE YOU AFRAID, DAUGHTER OF TRIGON?
I...I DO NOT REMEMBER WHAT I WAS GOING TO SAY...
I THINK I AM TIRED. AND CONFUSED.
THE VOICE...
YOU SHOULD BE...
ALL THIS IS YOUR FAULT. YOUR FAULT!
...WILL NOT GO AWAY.

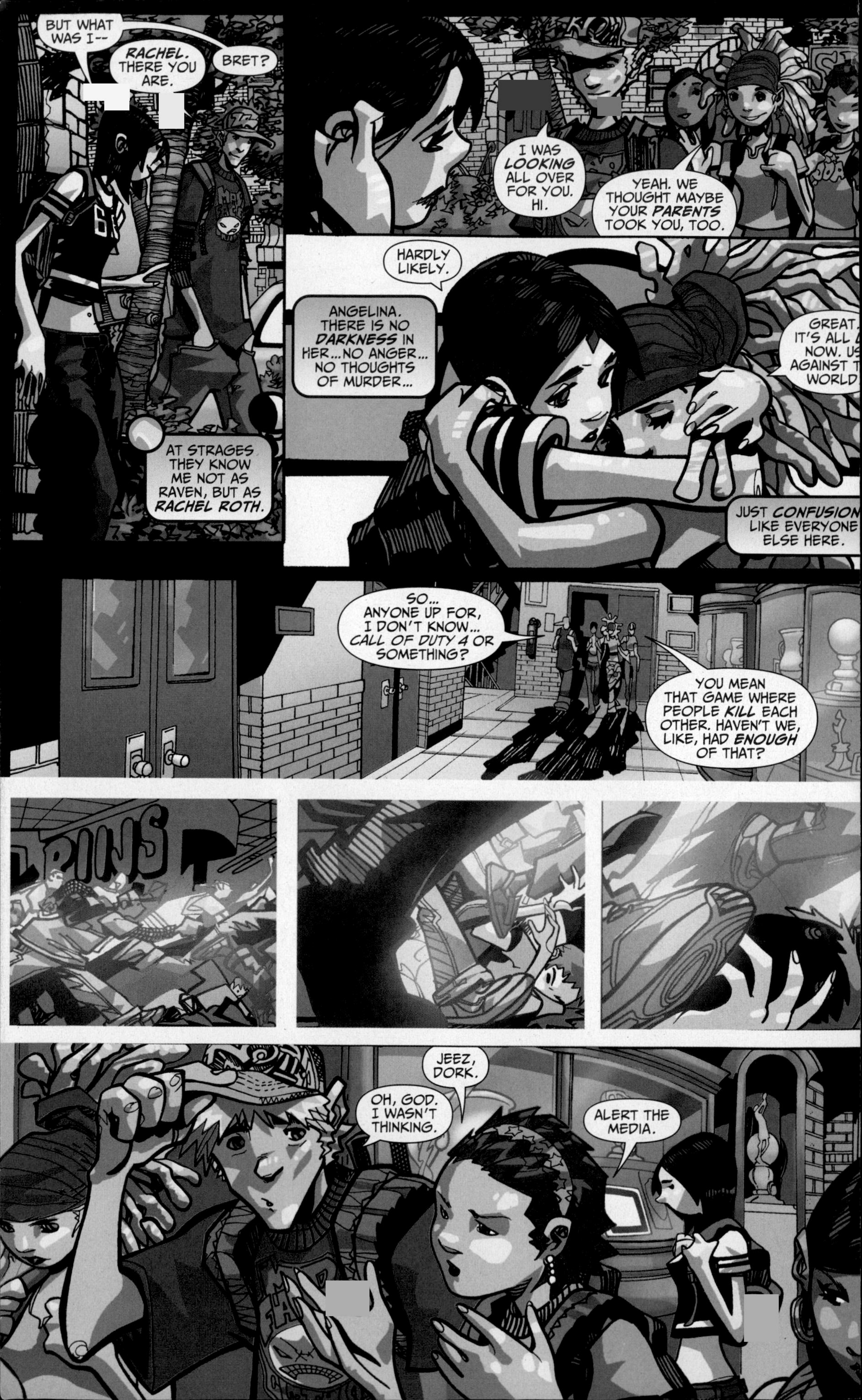

BUT WHAT WAS I--
RACHEL. THERE YOU ARE.
BRET?
AT STRAGES THEY KNOW ME NOT AS RAVEN, BUT AS RACHEL ROTH.
I WAS LOOKING ALL OVER FOR YOU. HI.
YEAH. WE THOUGHT MAYBE YOUR PARENTS TOOK YOU, TOO.
HARDLY LIKELY.
ANGELINA. THERE IS NO DARKNESS IN HER...NO ANGER... NO THOUGHTS OF MURDER...
GREAT. IT'S ALL NOW. AGAINST WORLD
JUST CONFUSION LIKE EVERYONE ELSE HERE.
SO... ANYONE UP FOR, I DON'T KNOW... CALL OF DUTY 4 OR SOMETHING?
YOU MEAN THAT GAME WHERE PEOPLE KILL EACH OTHER. HAVEN'T WE, LIKE, HAD ENOUGH OF THAT?
OH, GOD. I WASN'T THINKING.
JEEZ, DORK.
ALERT THE MEDIA.

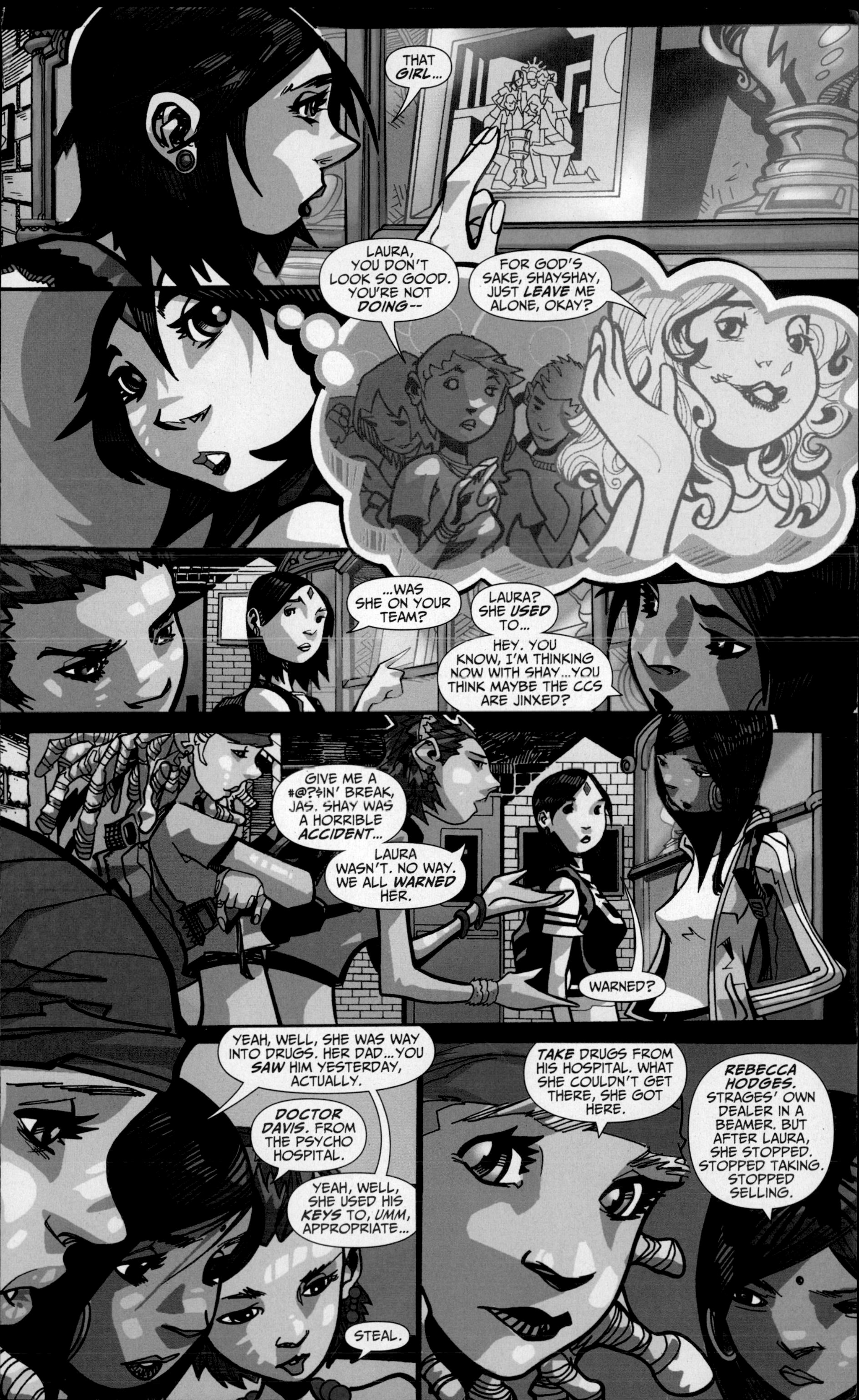
THAT GIRL...
LAURA, YOU DON'T LOOK SO GOOD. YOU'RE NOT DOING--
FOR GOD'S SAKE, SHAYSHAY, JUST LEAVE ME ALONE, OKAY?
...WAS SHE ON YOUR TEAM?
LAURA? SHE USED TO...
HEY. YOU KNOW, I'M THINKING NOW WITH SHAY...YOU THINK MAYBE THE CCS ARE JINXED?
GIVE ME A #@?$IN' BREAK, JAS. SHAY WAS A HORRIBLE ACCIDENT...
LAURA WASN'T. NO WAY. WE ALL WARNED HER.
WARNED?
YEAH, WELL, SHE WAS WAY INTO DRUGS. HER DAD...YOU SAW HIM YESTERDAY, ACTUALLY.
DOCTOR DAVIS. FROM THE PSYCHO HOSPITAL.
YEAH, WELL, SHE USED HIS KEYS TO, UMM, APPROPRIATE...
STEAL.
TAKE DRUGS FROM HIS HOSPITAL. WHAT SHE COULDN'T GET THERE, SHE GOT HERE.
REBECCA HODGES. STRAGES' OWN DEALER IN A BEAMER. BUT AFTER LAURA, SHE STOPPED. STOPPED TAKING. STOPPED SELLING.

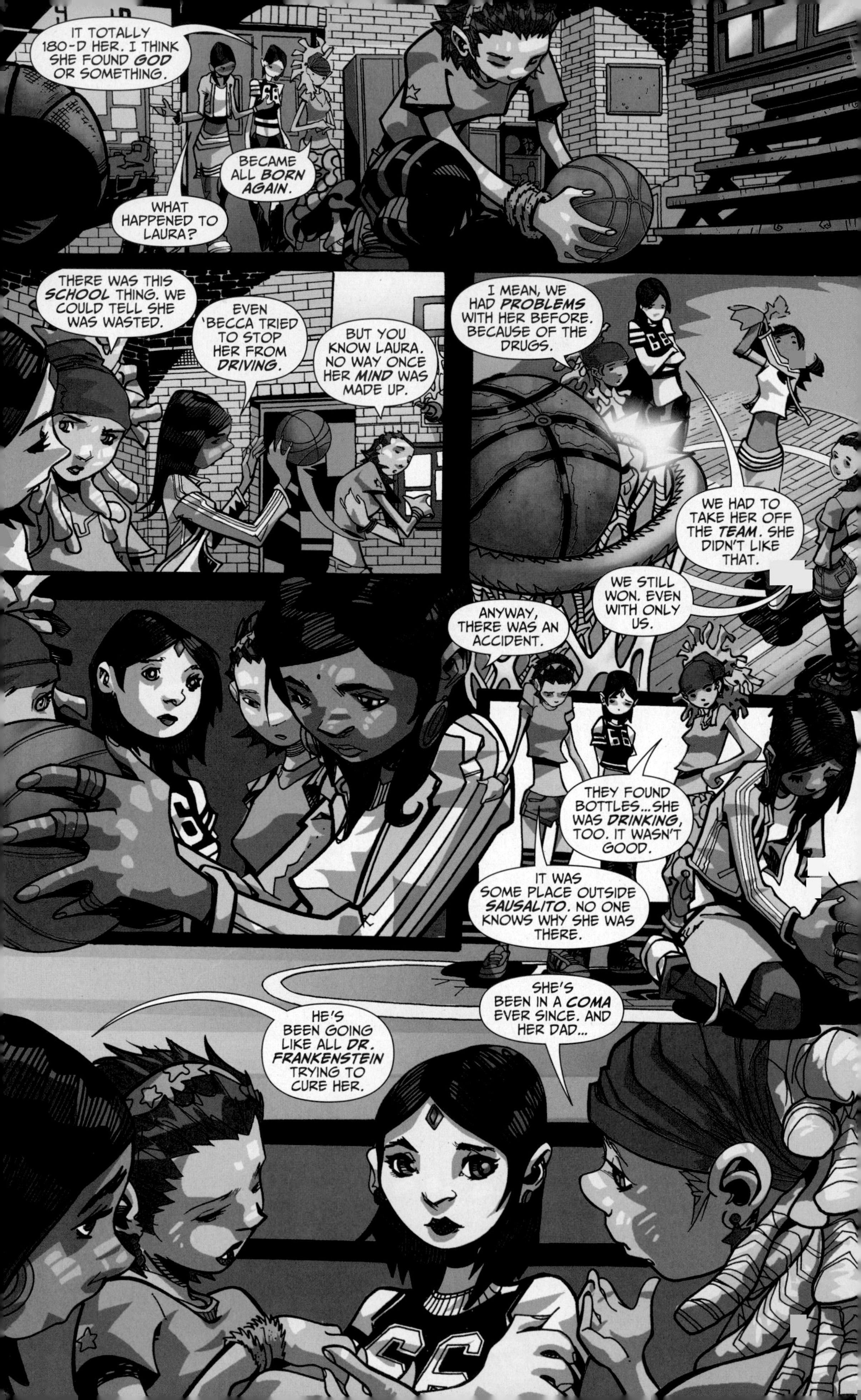

IT TOTALLY 180-D HER. I THINK SHE FOUND GOD OR SOMETHING.
BECAME ALL BORN AGAIN.
WHAT HAPPENED TO LAURA?
THERE WAS THIS SCHOOL THING. WE COULD TELL SHE WAS WASTED.
EVEN 'BECCA TRIED TO STOP HER FROM DRIVING.
BUT YOU KNOW LAURA. NO WAY ONCE HER MIND WAS MADE UP.
I MEAN, WE HAD PROBLEMS WITH HER BEFORE. BECAUSE OF THE DRUGS.
WE HAD TO TAKE HER OFF THE TEAM. SHE DIDN'T LIKE THAT.
WE STILL WON. EVEN WITH ONLY US.
ANYWAY, THERE WAS AN ACCIDENT.
THEY FOUND BOTTLES...SHE WAS DRINKING, TOO. IT WASN'T GOOD.
IT WAS SOME PLACE OUTSIDE SAUSALITO. NO ONE KNOWS WHY SHE WAS THERE.
SHE'S BEEN IN A COMA EVER SINCE. AND HER DAD...
HE'S BEEN GOING LIKE ALL DR. FRANKENSTEIN TRYING TO CURE HER.

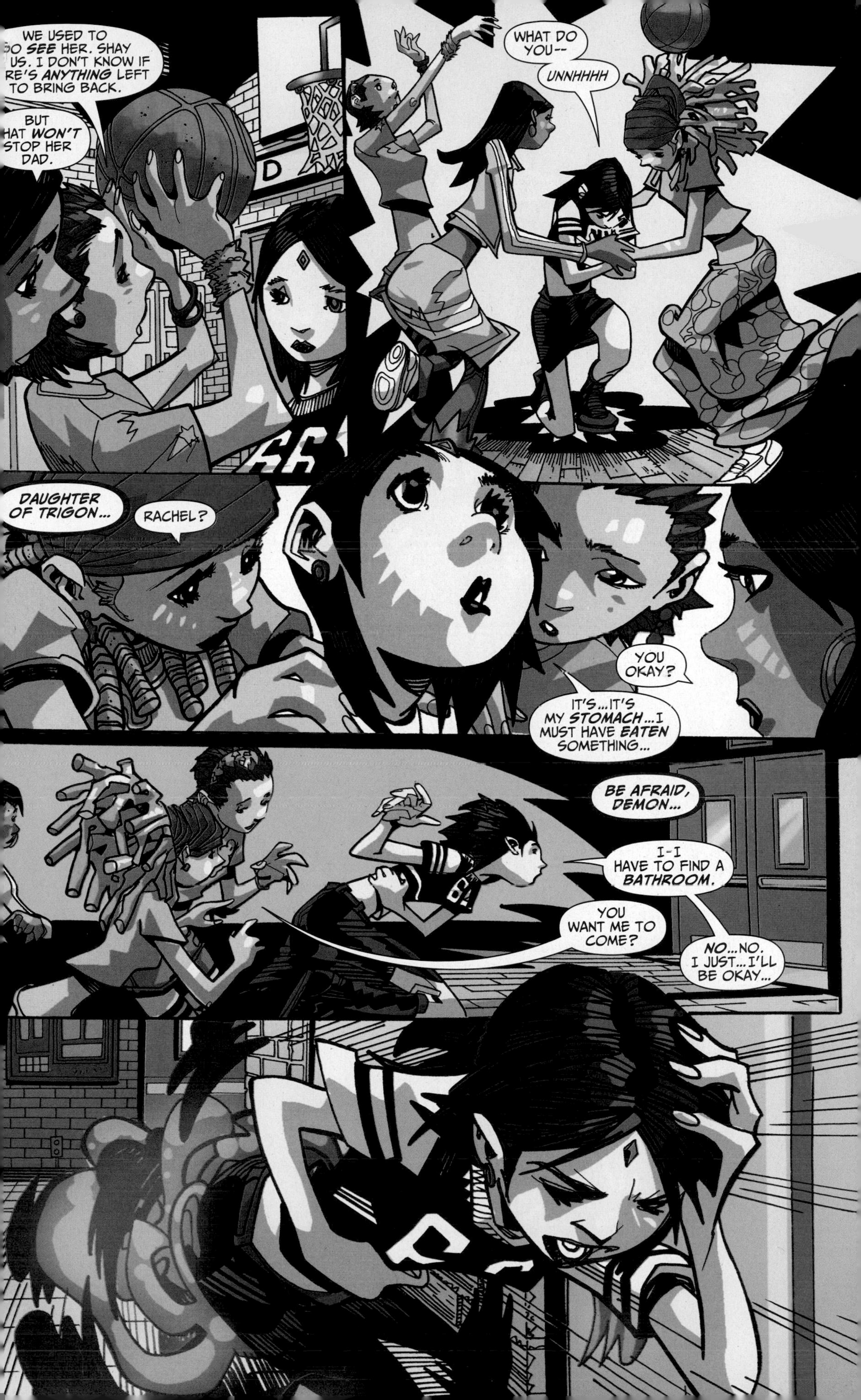
WE USED TO GO SEE HER. SHAY US. I DON'T KNOW IF RE'S ANYTHING LEFT TO BRING BACK.
BUT HAT WON'T STOP HER DAD.
WHAT DO YOU--
UNNHHHH
DAUGHTER OF TRIGON...
RACHEL?
YOU OKAY?
IT'S...IT'S MY STOMACH...I MUST HAVE EATEN SOMETHING...
BE AFRAID, DEMON...
I-I HAVE TO FIND A BATHROOM.
YOU WANT ME TO COME?
NO...NO. I JUST...I'LL BE OKAY...

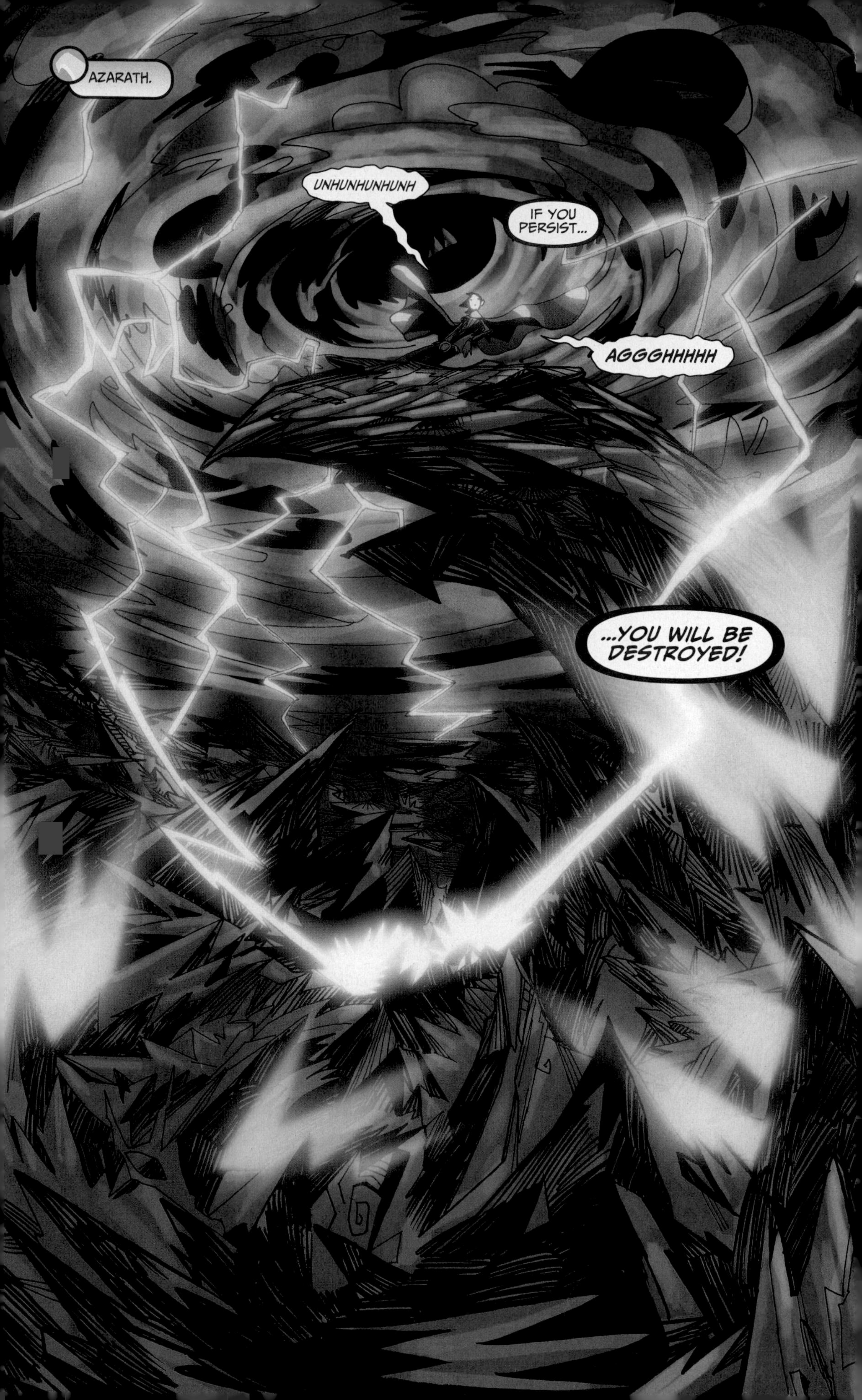
AZARATH.
UNHUNHUNHUNH
IF YOU PERSIST...
AGGGHHHHH
...YOU WILL BE DESTROYED!

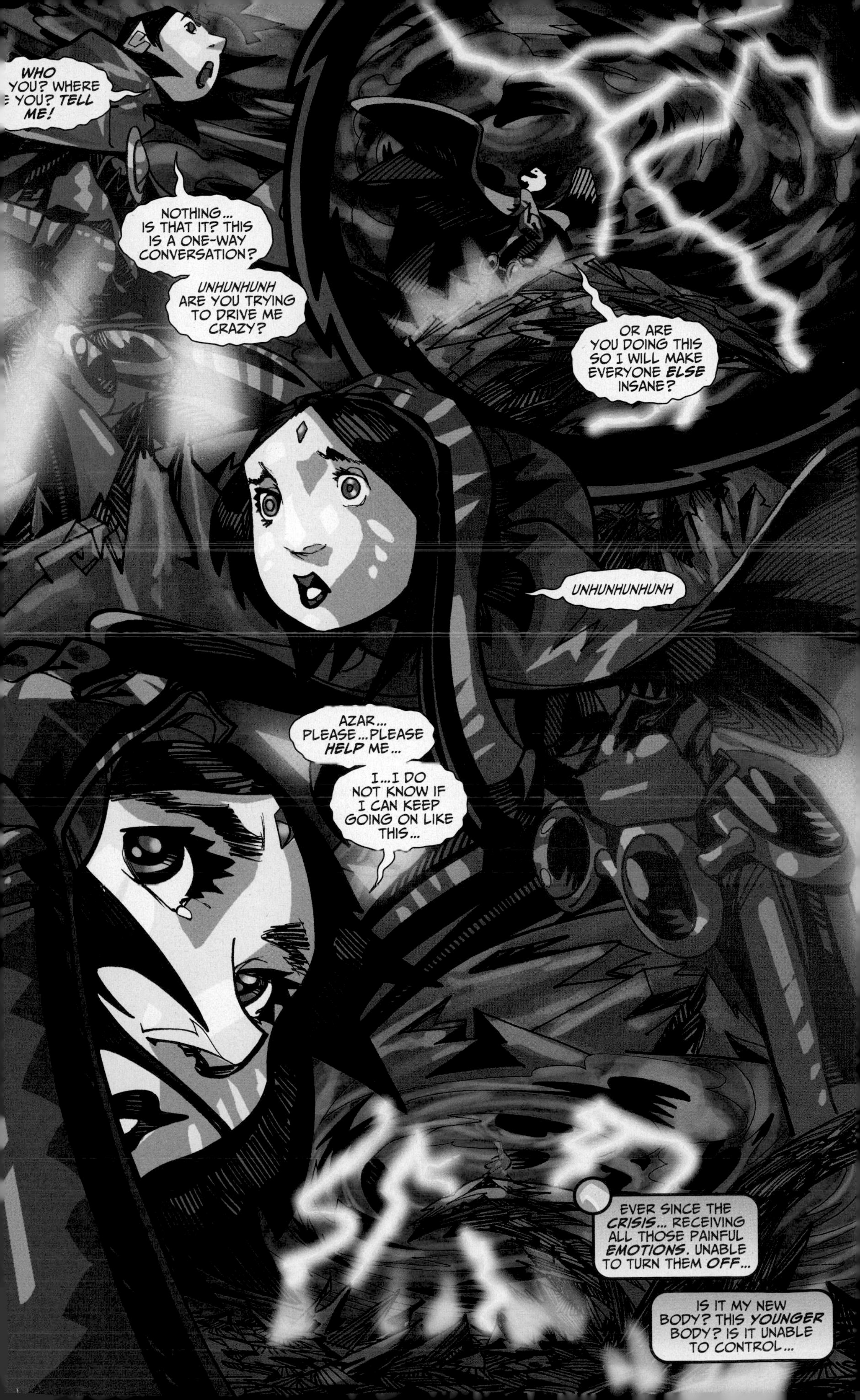
WHO
YOU? WHERE
E YOU? TELL
ME!
NOTHING... IS THAT IT? THIS IS A ONE-WAY CONVERSATION?
UNHUNHUNH ARE YOU TRYING TO DRIVE ME CRAZY?
OR ARE YOU DOING THIS SO I WILL MAKE EVERYONE ELSE INSANE?
UNHUNHUNHUNH
AZAR... PLEASE...PLEASE HELP ME...
I...I DO NOT KNOW IF I CAN KEEP GOING ON LIKE THIS...
EVER SINCE THE CRISIS... RECEIVING ALL THOSE PAINFUL EMOTIONS. UNABLE TO TURN THEM OFF...
IS IT MY NEW BODY? THIS YOUNGER BODY? IS IT UNABLE TO CONTROL...

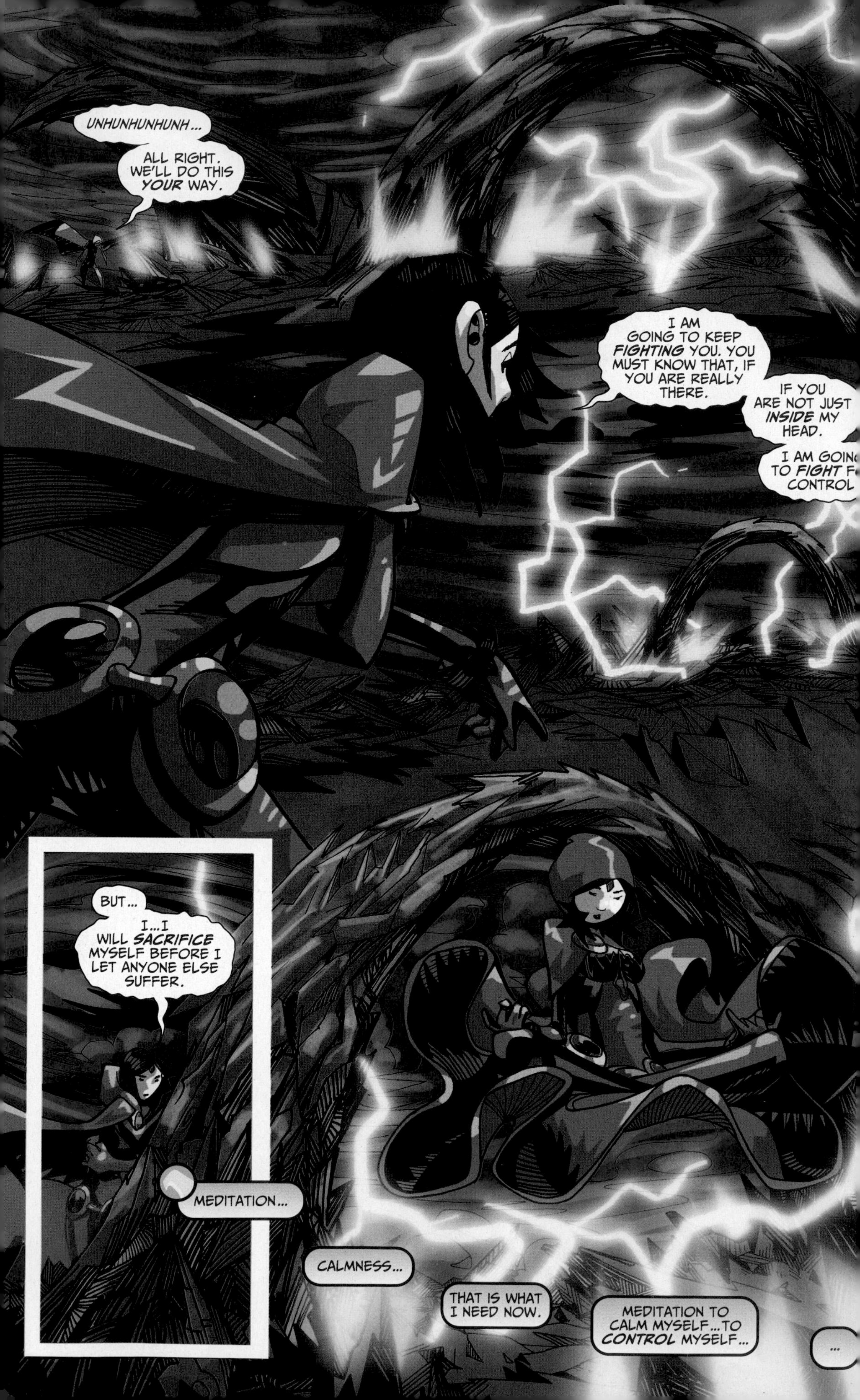
UNHUNHUNHUNH...
ALL RIGHT. WE'LL DO THIS YOUR WAY.
I AM GOING TO KEEP FIGHTING YOU. YOU MUST KNOW THAT, IF YOU ARE REALLY THERE.
IF YOU ARE NOT JUST INSIDE MY HEAD.
I AM GOIN TO FIGHT F CONTROL
BUT...
I...I WILL SACRIFICE MYSELF BEFORE I LET ANYONE ELSE SUFFER.
MEDITATION...
CALMNESS...
THAT IS WHAT I NEED NOW.
MEDITATION TO CALM MYSELF...TO CONTROL MYSELF...
...

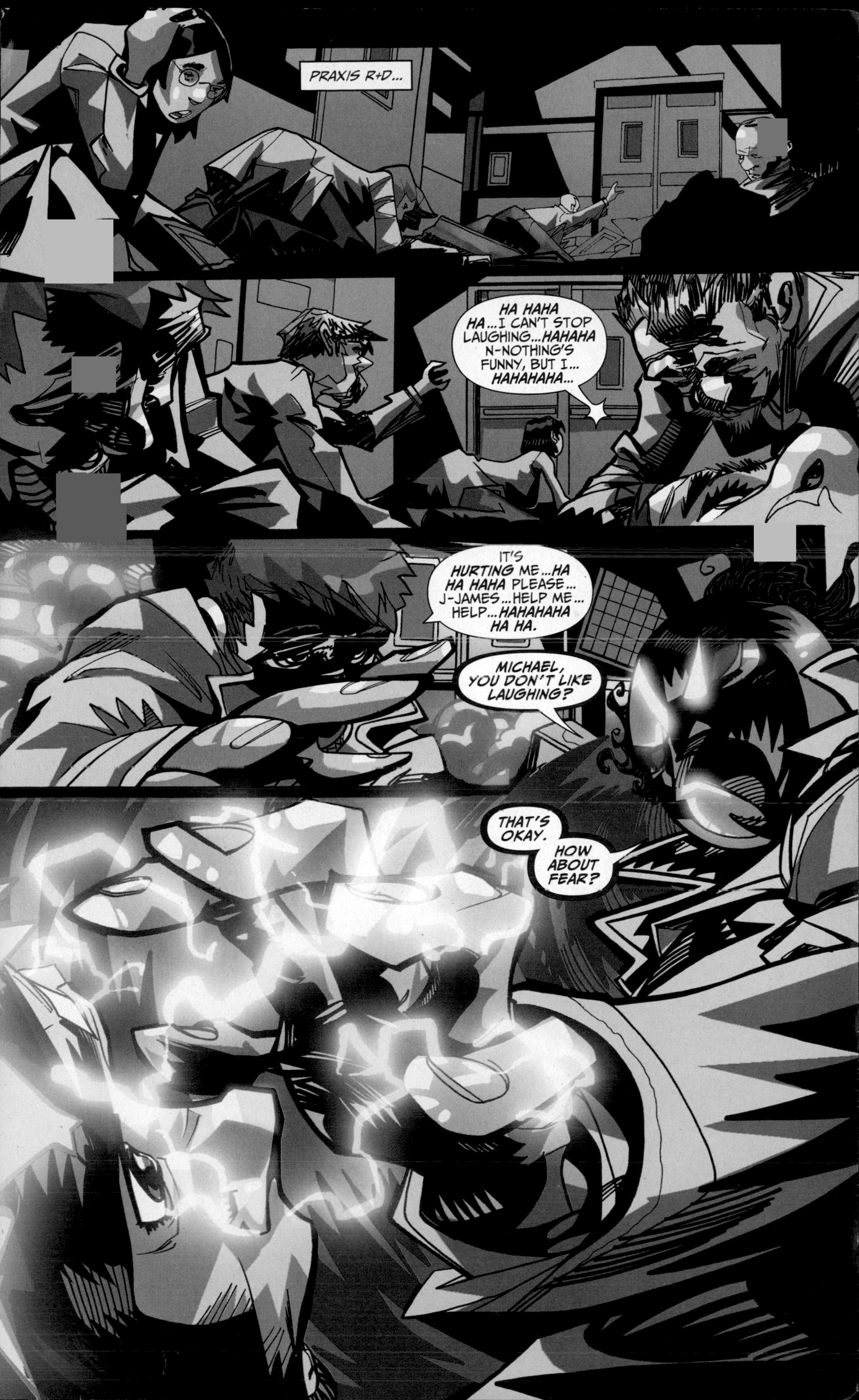
PRAXIS R+D...
HA HAHA HA...I CAN'T STOP LAUGHING...HAHAHA N-NOTHING'S FUNNY, BUT I... HAHAHAHA...
IT'S HURTING ME...HA HA HA HAHA PLEASE... J-JAMES...HELP ME... HELP...HAHAHAHA HA HA.
MICHAEL, YOU DON'T LIKE LAUGHING?
THAT'S OKAY.
HOW ABOUT FEAR?

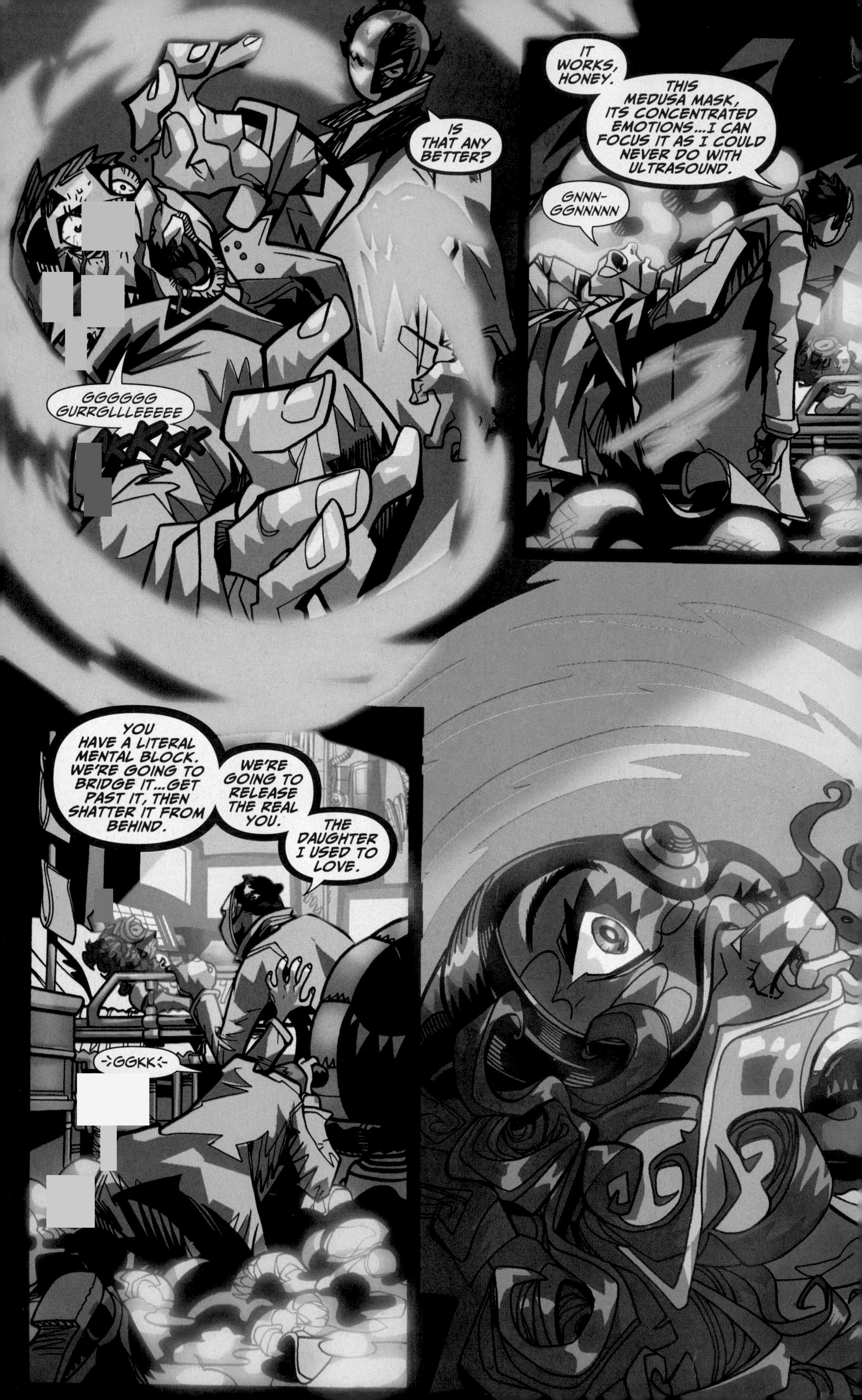
IS THAT ANY BETTER?
GGGGGG GURRGLLLEEEEE
AKKKK
IT WORKS, HONEY.
THIS MEDUSA MASK, ITS CONCENTRATED EMOTIONS...I CAN FOCUS IT AS I COULD NEVER DO WITH ULTRASOUND.
GNNN-GGNNNNN
YOU HAVE A LITERAL MENTAL BLOCK. WE'RE GOING TO BRIDGE IT...GET PAST IT, THEN SHATTER IT FROM BEHIND.
WE'RE GOING TO RELEASE THE REAL YOU.
THE DAUGHTER I USED TO LOVE.
GGKK

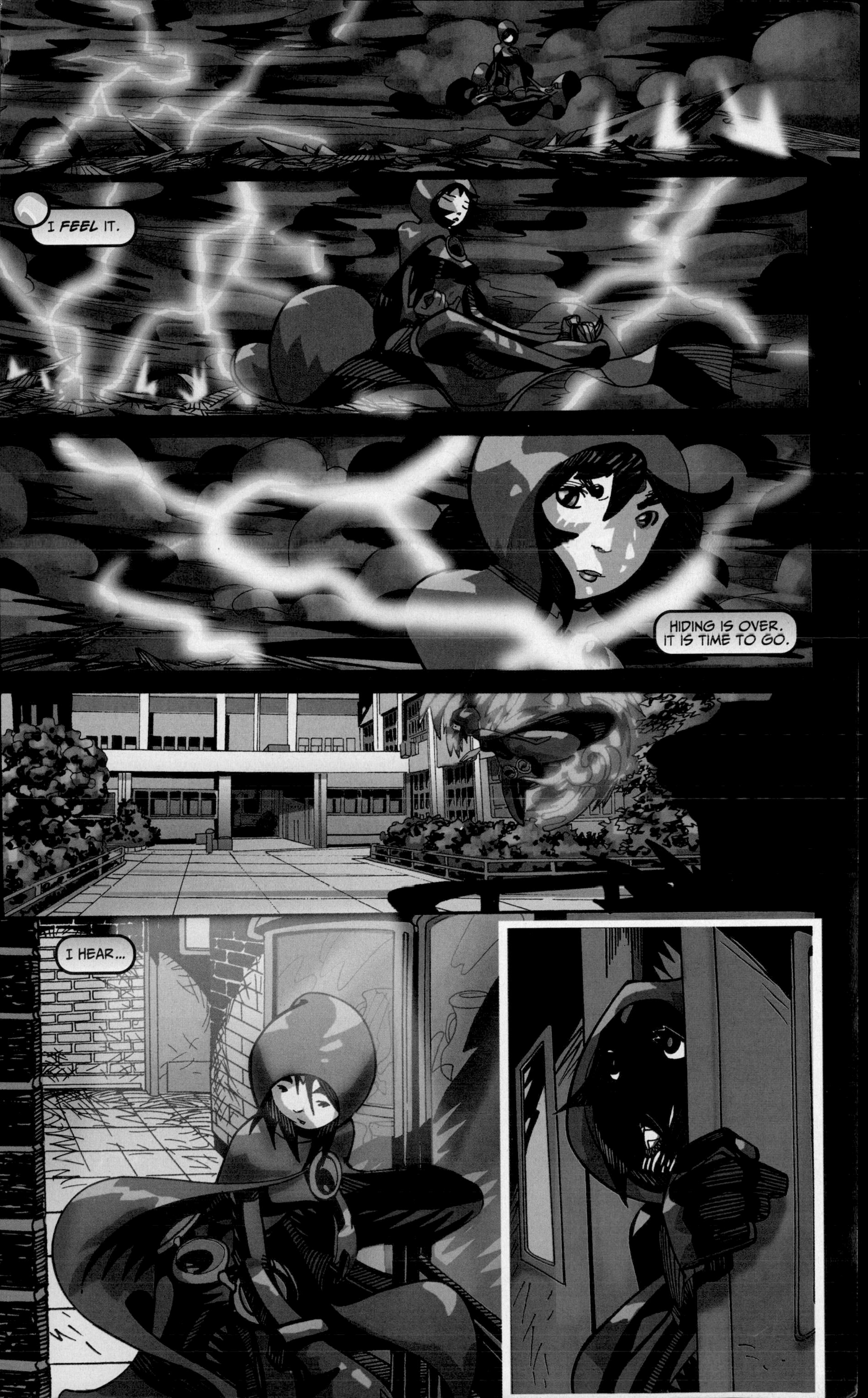
I FEEL IT.
HIDING IS OVER. IT IS TIME TO GO.
I HEAR...

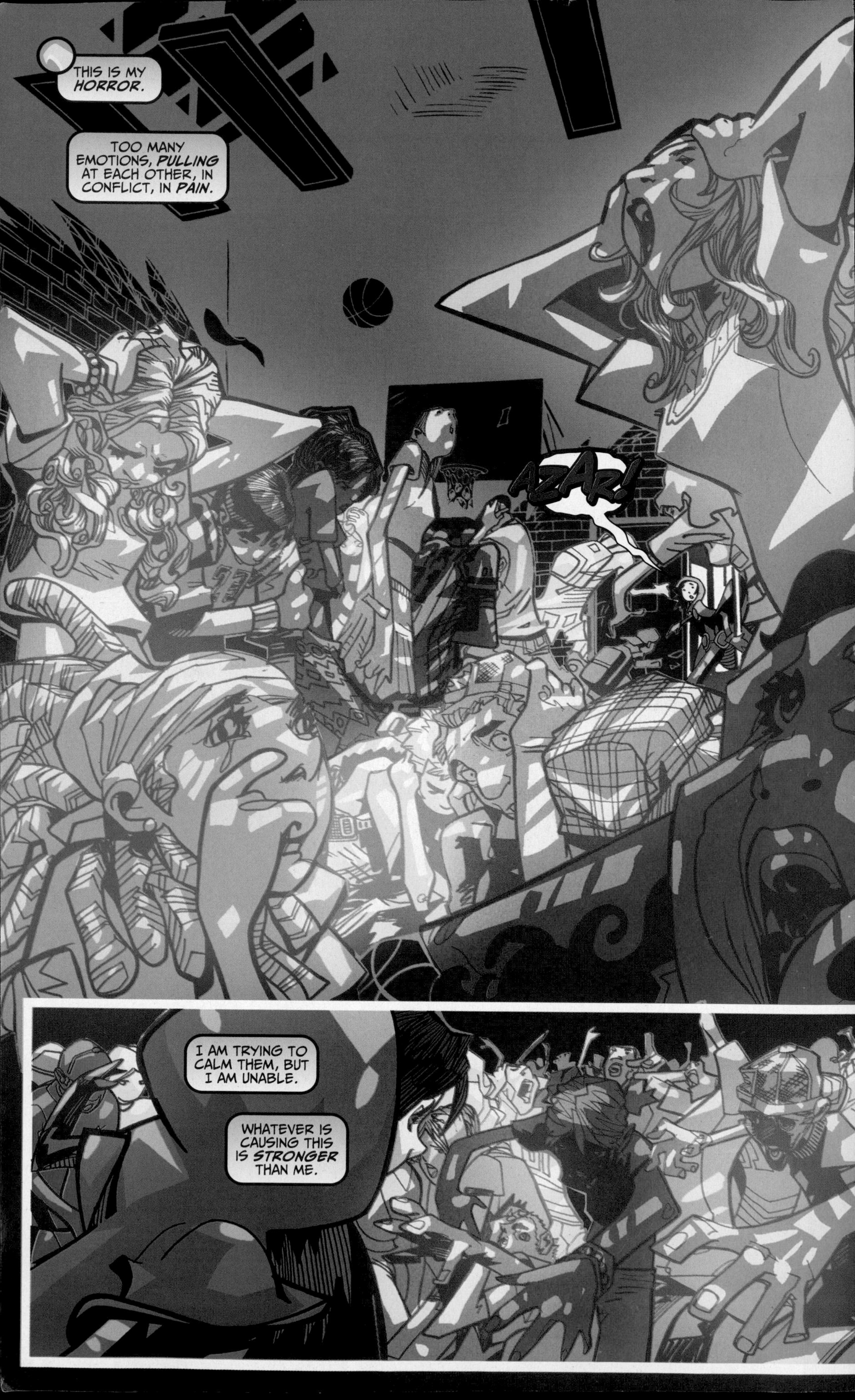
THIS IS MY HORROR.
TOO MANY EMOTIONS, PULLING AT EACH OTHER, IN CONFLICT, IN PAIN.
AZAR!
I AM TRYING TO CALM THEM, BUT I AM UNABLE.
WHATEVER IS CAUSING THIS IS STRONGER THAN ME.

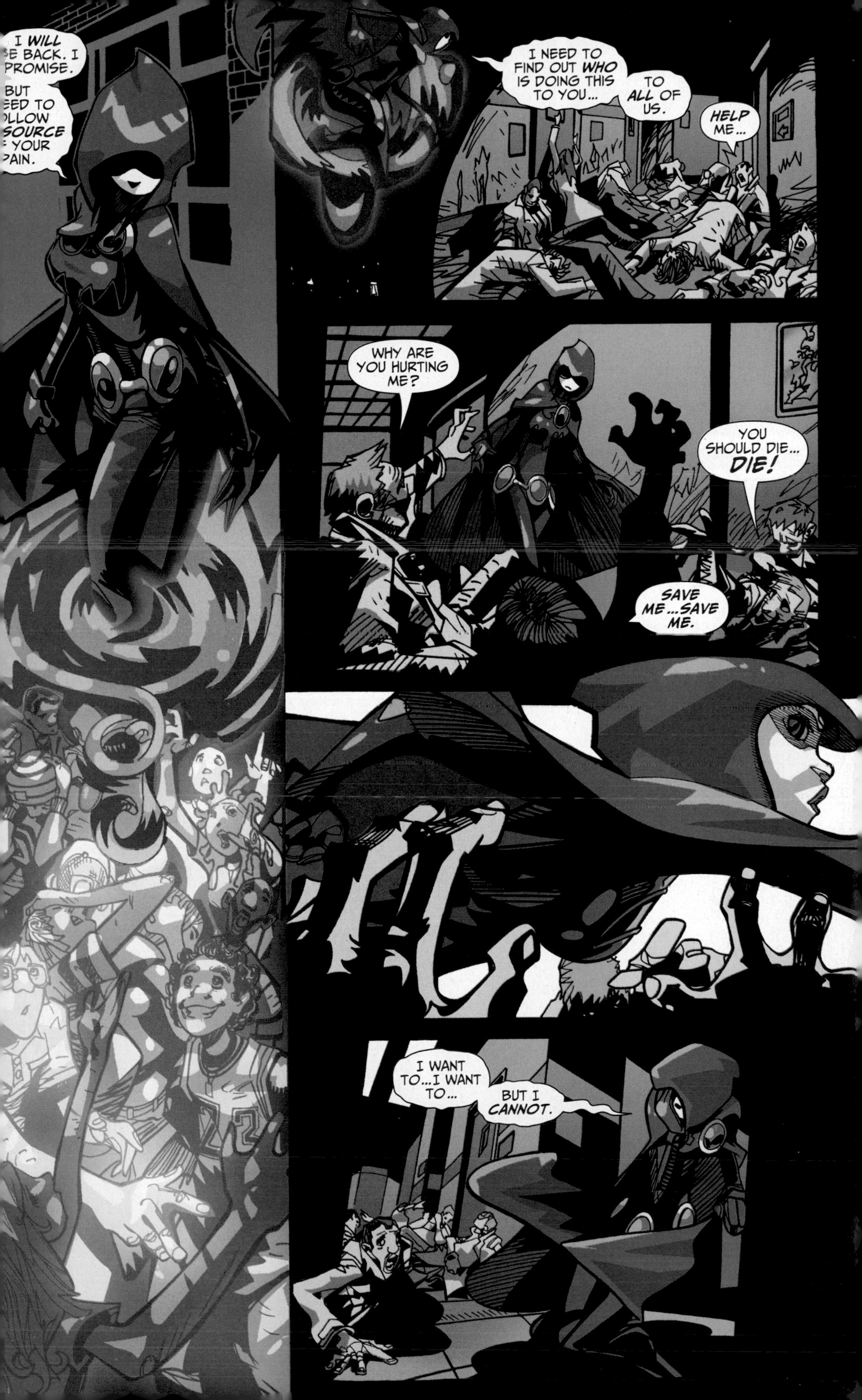

I WILL
BE BACK. I PROMISE.
BUT
EED TO
OLLOW
SOURCE
F YOUR
PAIN.
I NEED TO FIND OUT WHO IS DOING THIS TO YOU...
TO ALL OF US.
HELP ME...
WHY ARE YOU HURTING ME?
YOU SHOULD DIE... DIE!
SAVE ME...SAVE ME.
I WANT TO...I WANT TO...
BUT I CANNOT.

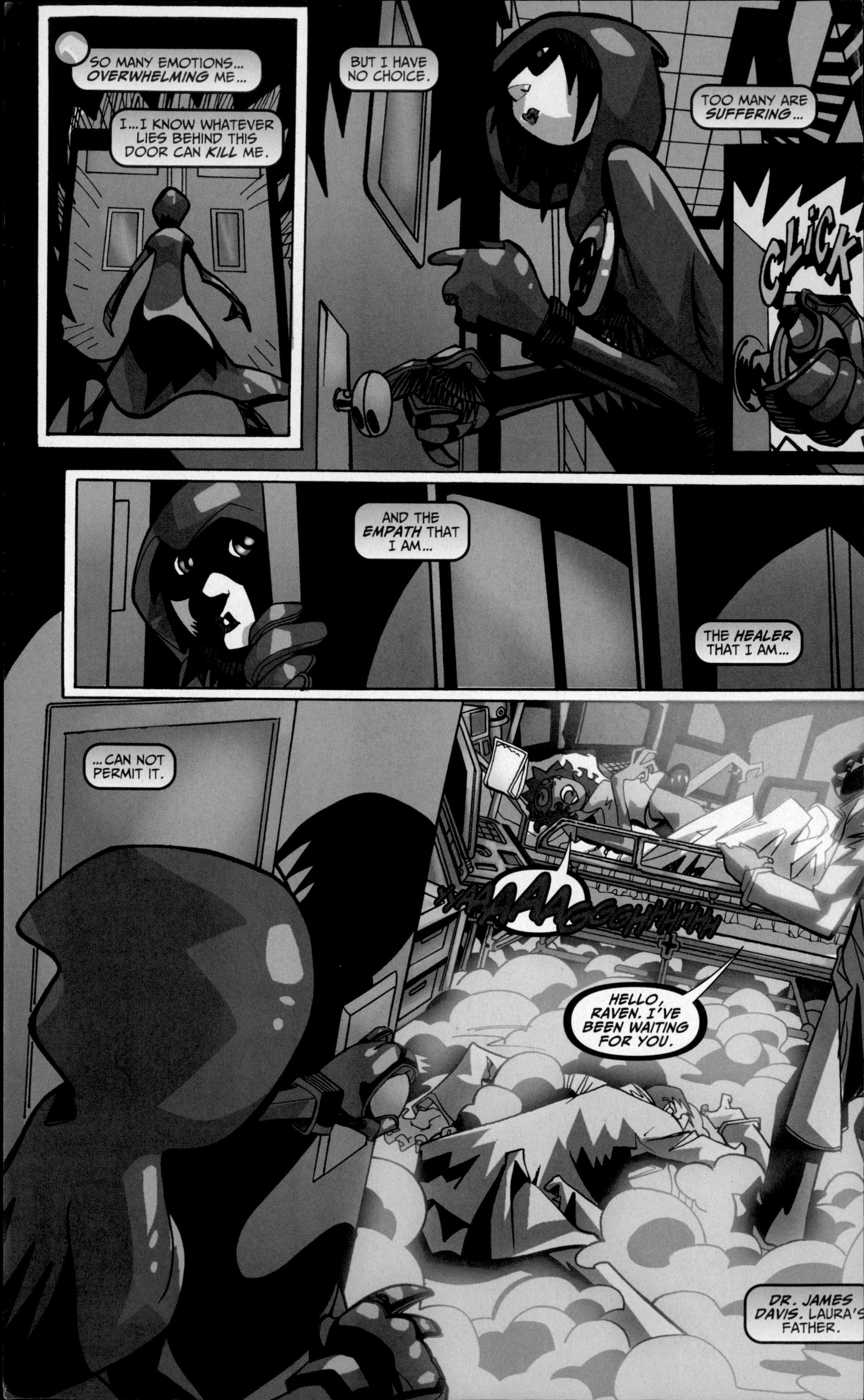
SO MANY EMOTIONS... OVERWHELMING ME...
I...I KNOW WHATEVER LIES BEHIND THIS DOOR CAN KILL ME.
BUT I HAVE NO CHOICE.
TOO MANY ARE SUFFERING...
CLICK
AND THE EMPATH THAT I AM...
THE HEALER THAT I AM...
...CAN NOT PERMIT IT.
YAAAAAAGGGHHHHHH
HELLO, RAVEN. I'VE BEEN WAITING FOR YOU.
DR. JAMES DAVIS. LAURA'S FATHER.

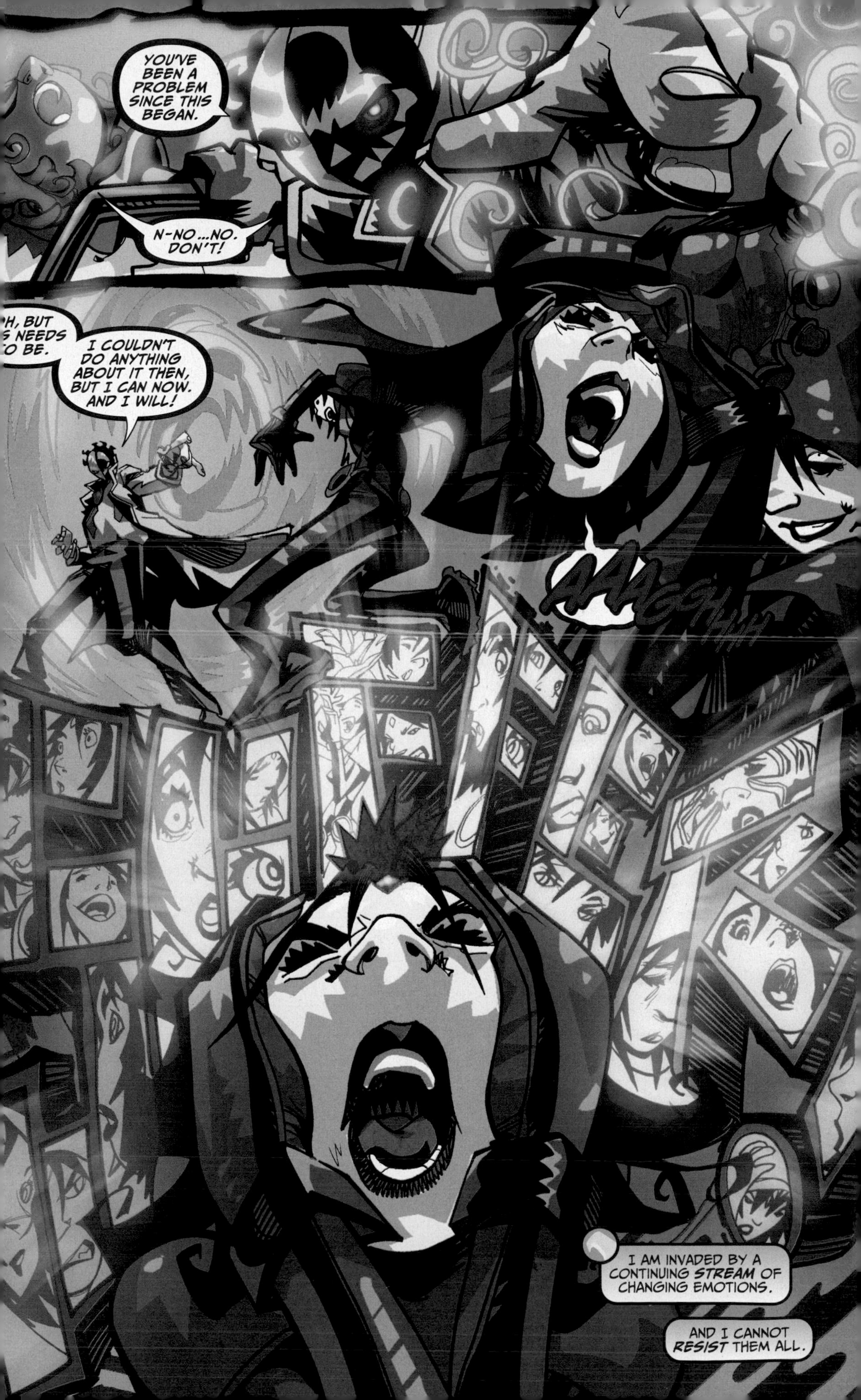
YOU'VE BEEN A PROBLEM SINCE THIS BEGAN.
N-NO ...NO. DON'T!
I COULDN'T DO ANYTHING ABOUT IT THEN, BUT I CAN NOW. AND I WILL!
AAAGGHHHH
I AM INVADED BY A CONTINUING STREAM OF CHANGING EMOTIONS.
AND I CANNOT RESIST THEM ALL.

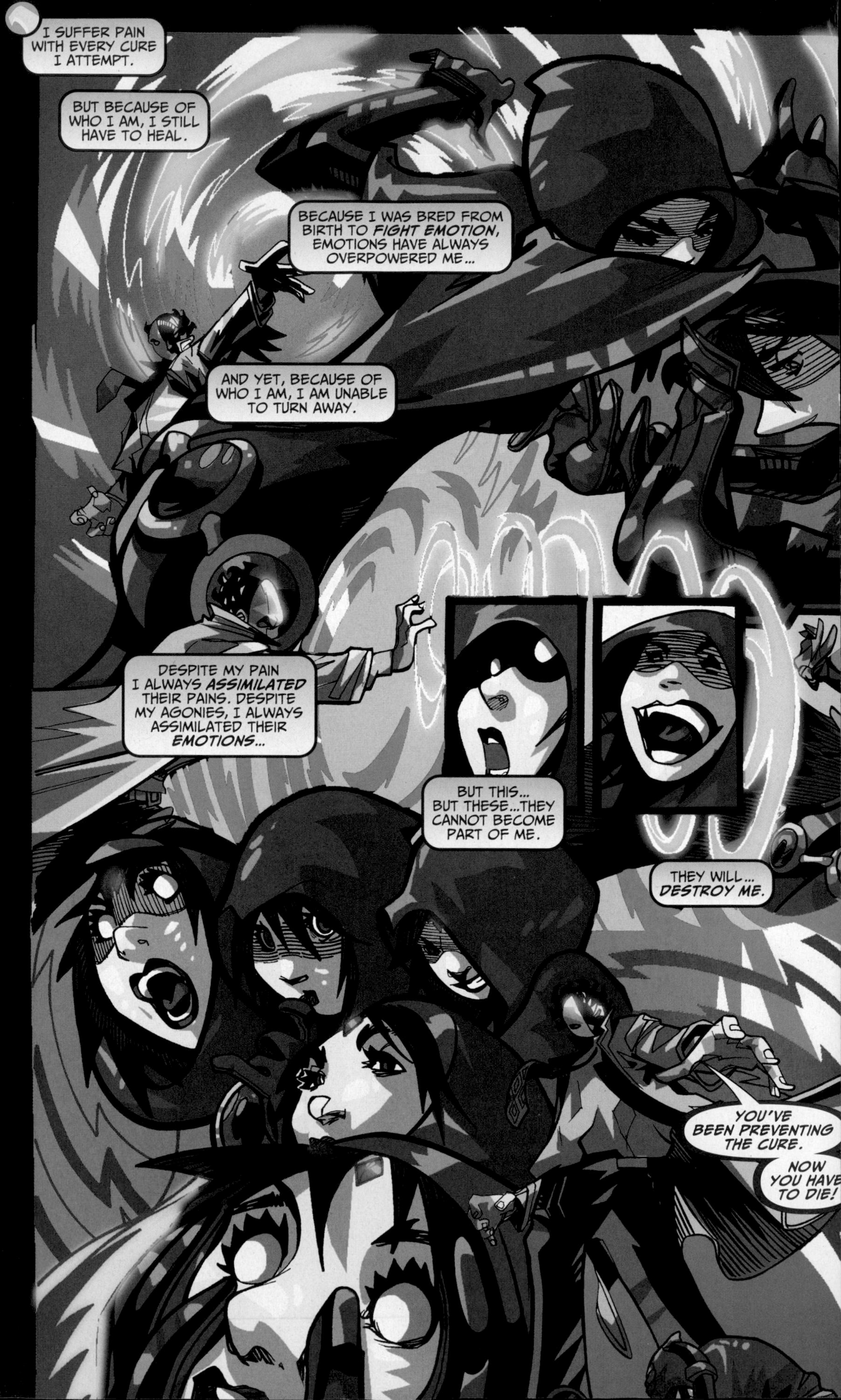
I SUFFER PAIN WITH EVERY CURE I ATTEMPT.
BUT BECAUSE OF WHO I AM, I STILL HAVE TO HEAL.
BECAUSE I WAS BRED FROM BIRTH TO FIGHT EMOTION, EMOTIONS HAVE ALWAYS OVERPOWERED ME...
AND YET, BECAUSE OF WHO I AM, I AM UNABLE TO TURN AWAY.
DESPITE MY PAIN I ALWAYS ASSIMILATED THEIR PAINS. DESPITE MY AGONIES, I ALWAYS ASSIMILATED THEIR EMOTIONS...
BUT THIS... BUT THESE...THEY CANNOT BECOME PART OF ME.
THEY WILL... DESTROY ME.
YOU'VE BEEN PREVENTING THE CURE.
NOW YOU HAVE TO DIE!

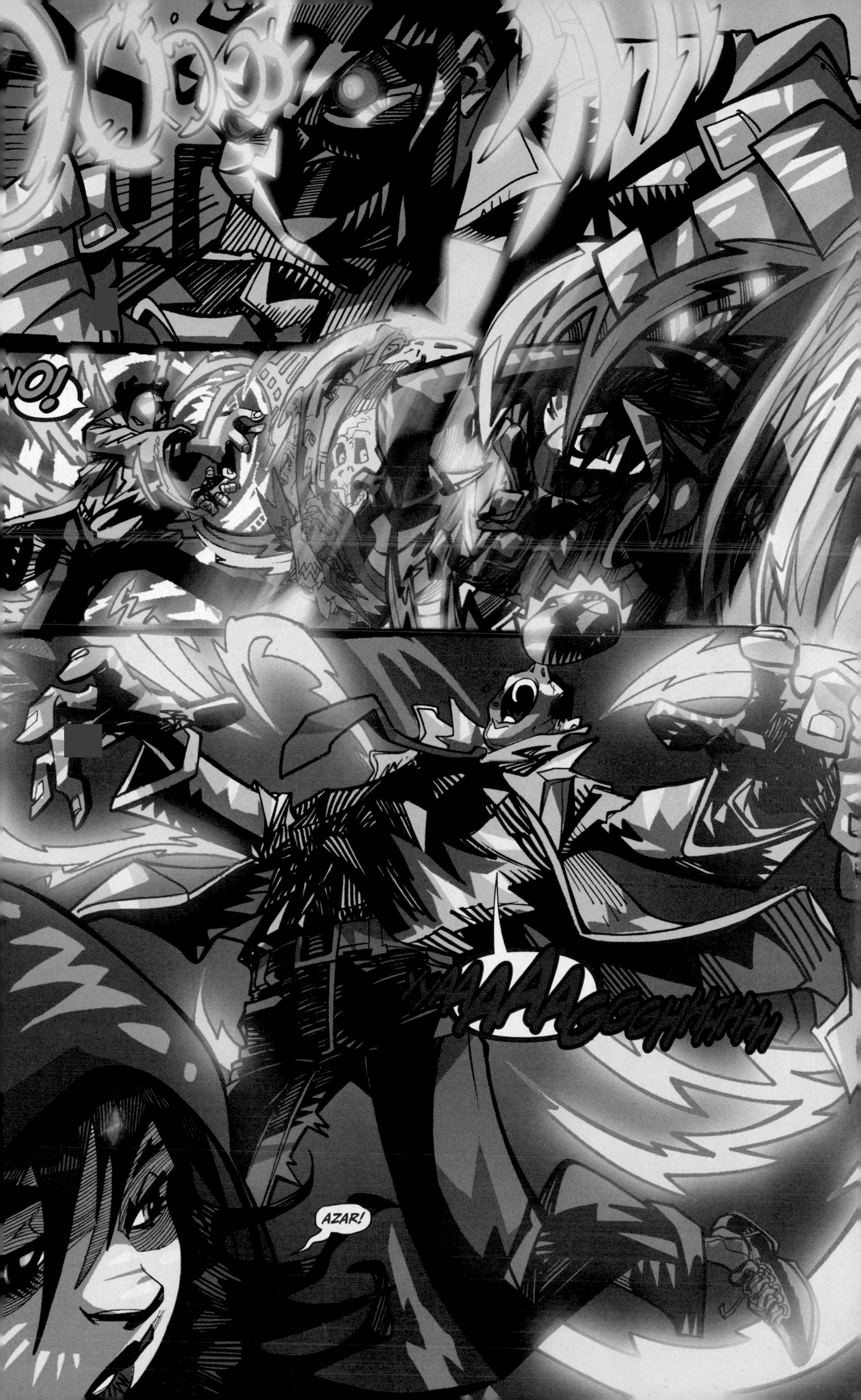
NO!
YAAAAGGGHHHHHH
AZAR!

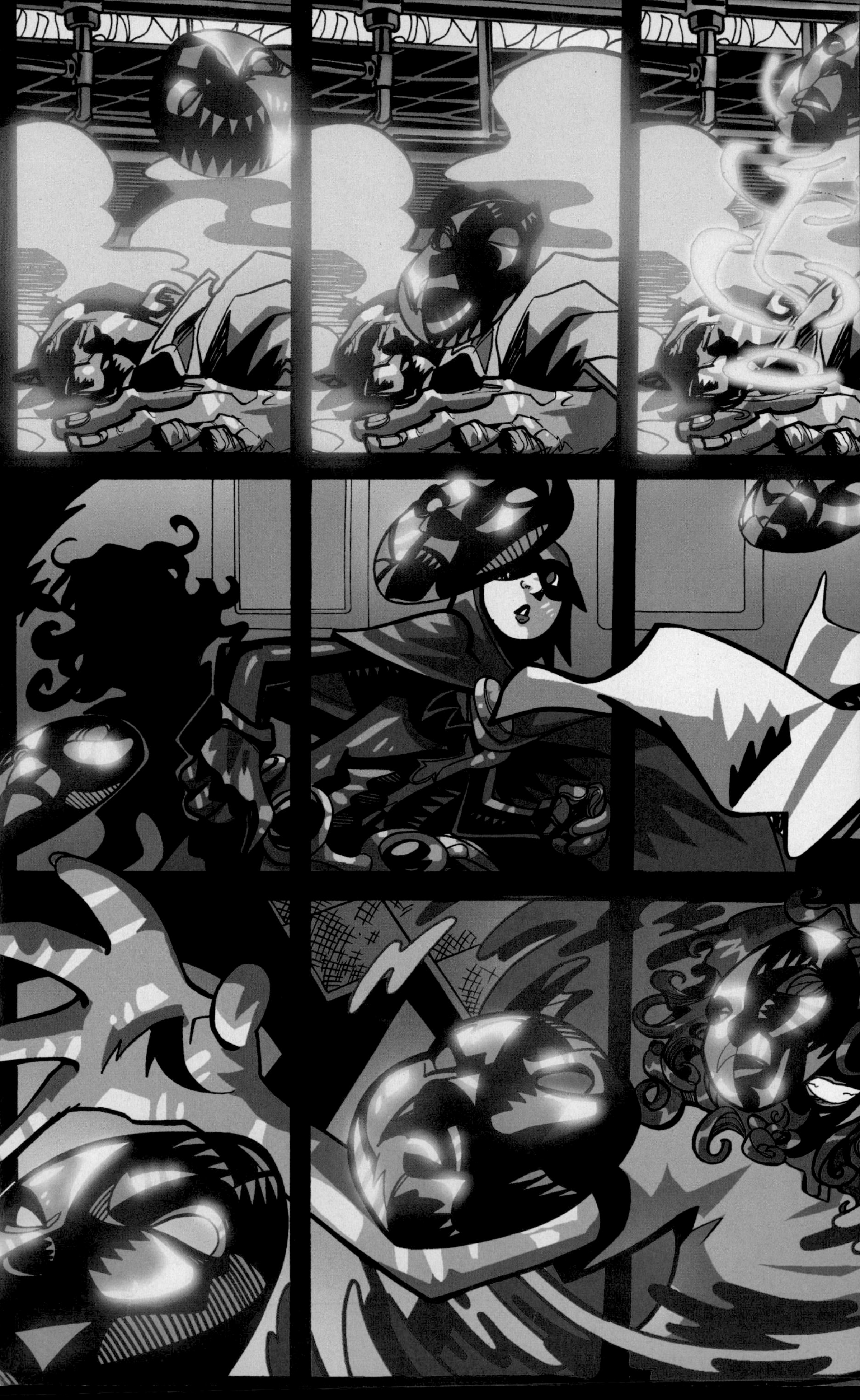

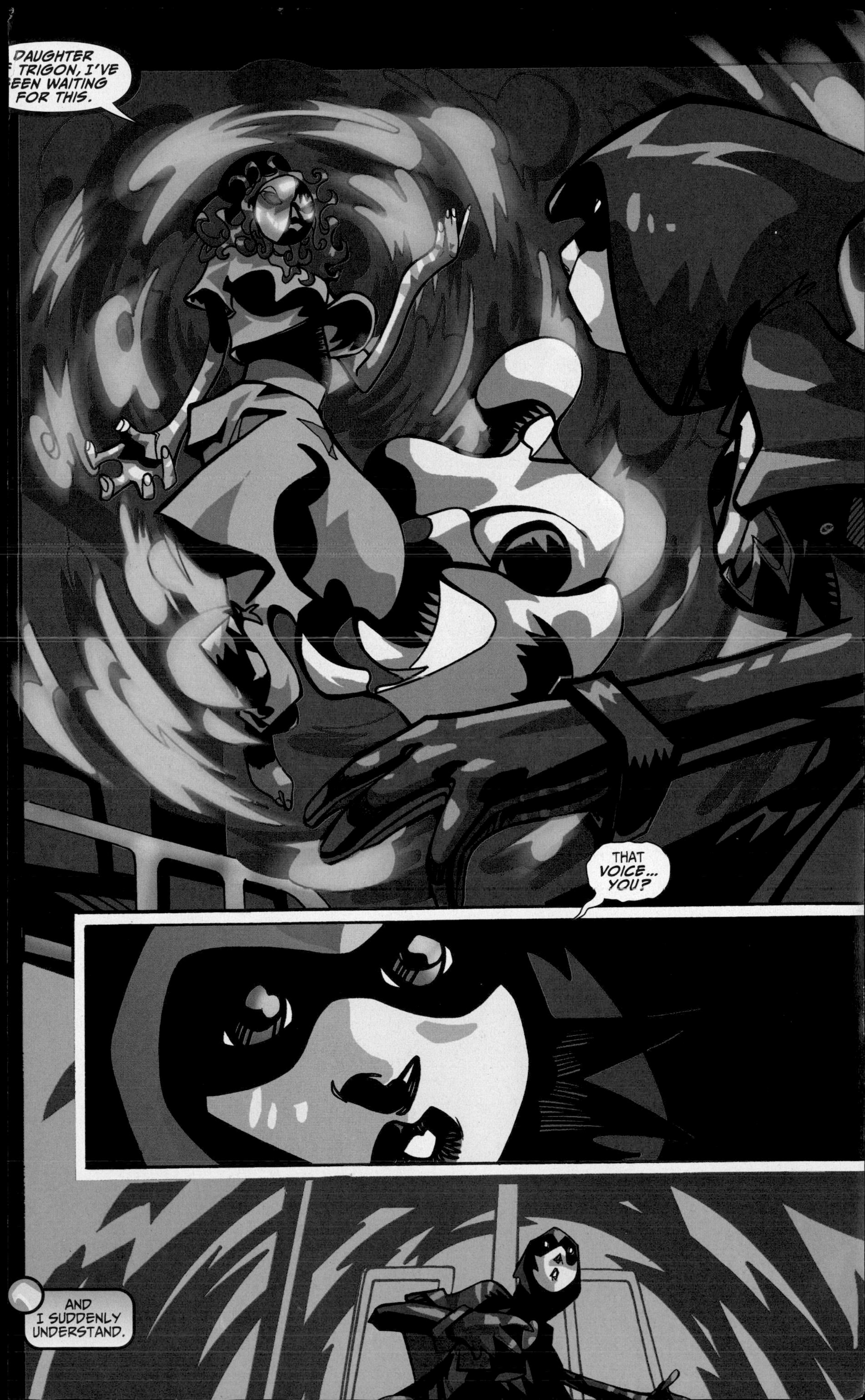
DAUGHTER OF TRIGON, I'VE BEEN WAITING FOR THIS.
THAT VOICE... YOU?
AND I SUDDENLY UNDERSTAND.

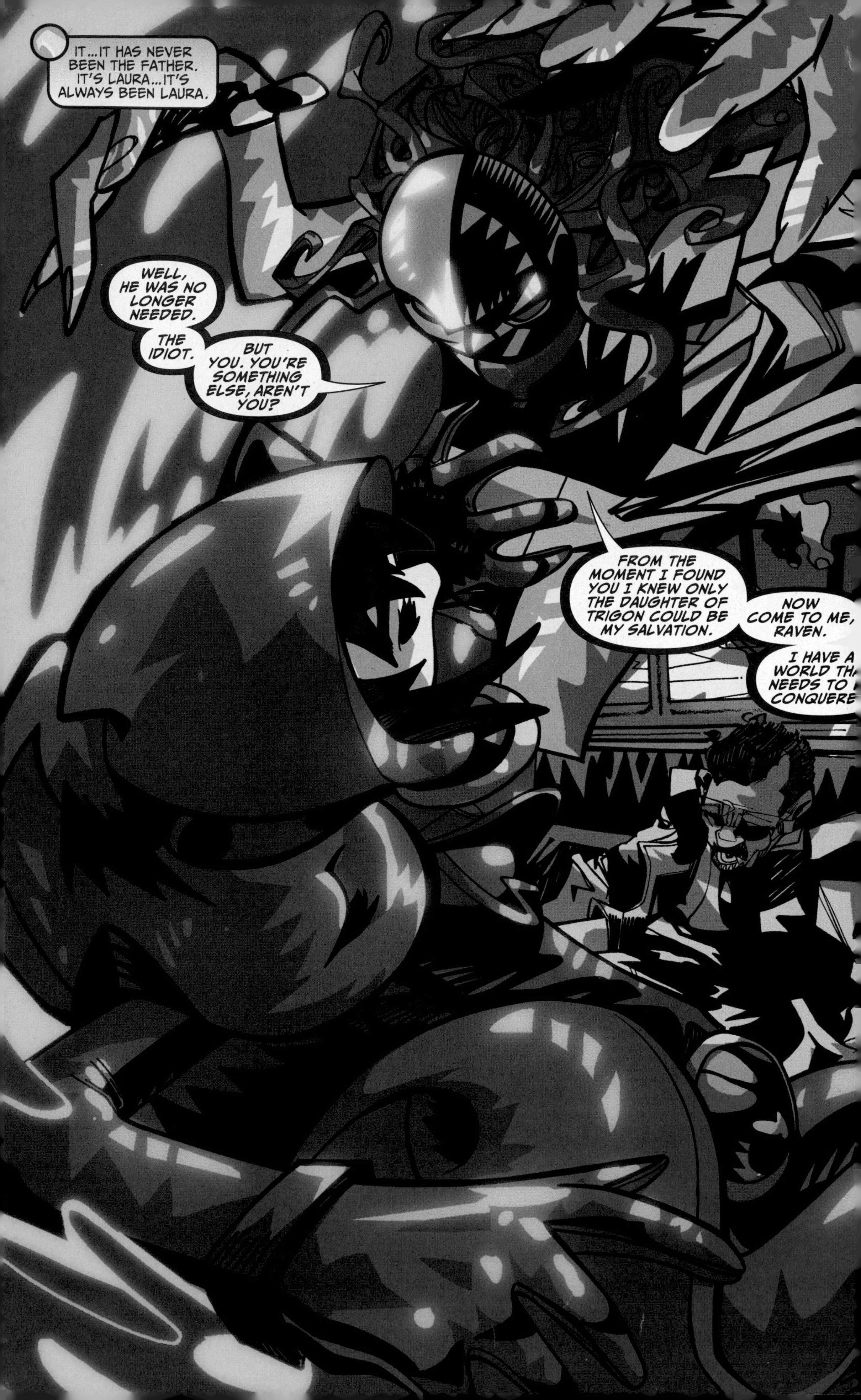
IT...IT HAS NEVER BEEN THE FATHER. IT'S LAURA...IT'S ALWAYS BEEN LAURA.
WELL, HE WAS NO LONGER NEEDED.
THE IDIOT.
BUT YOU. YOU'RE SOMETHING ELSE, AREN'T YOU?
FROM THE MOMENT I FOUND YOU I KNEW ONLY THE DAUGHTER OF TRIGON COULD BE MY SALVATION.
NOW COME TO ME, RAVEN.
I HAVE A WORLD TH NEEDS TO CONQUERE

Part 5: Guilt

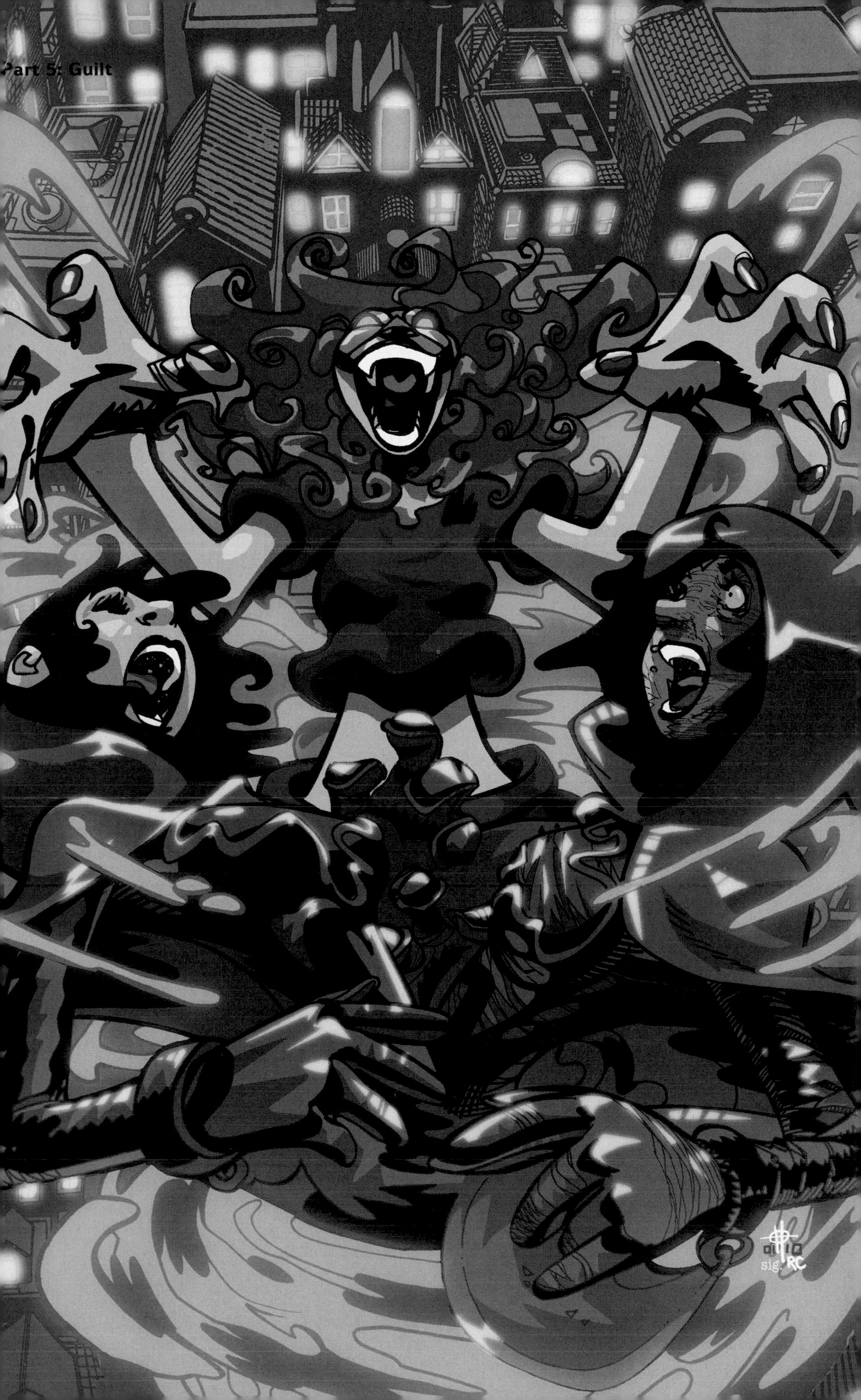

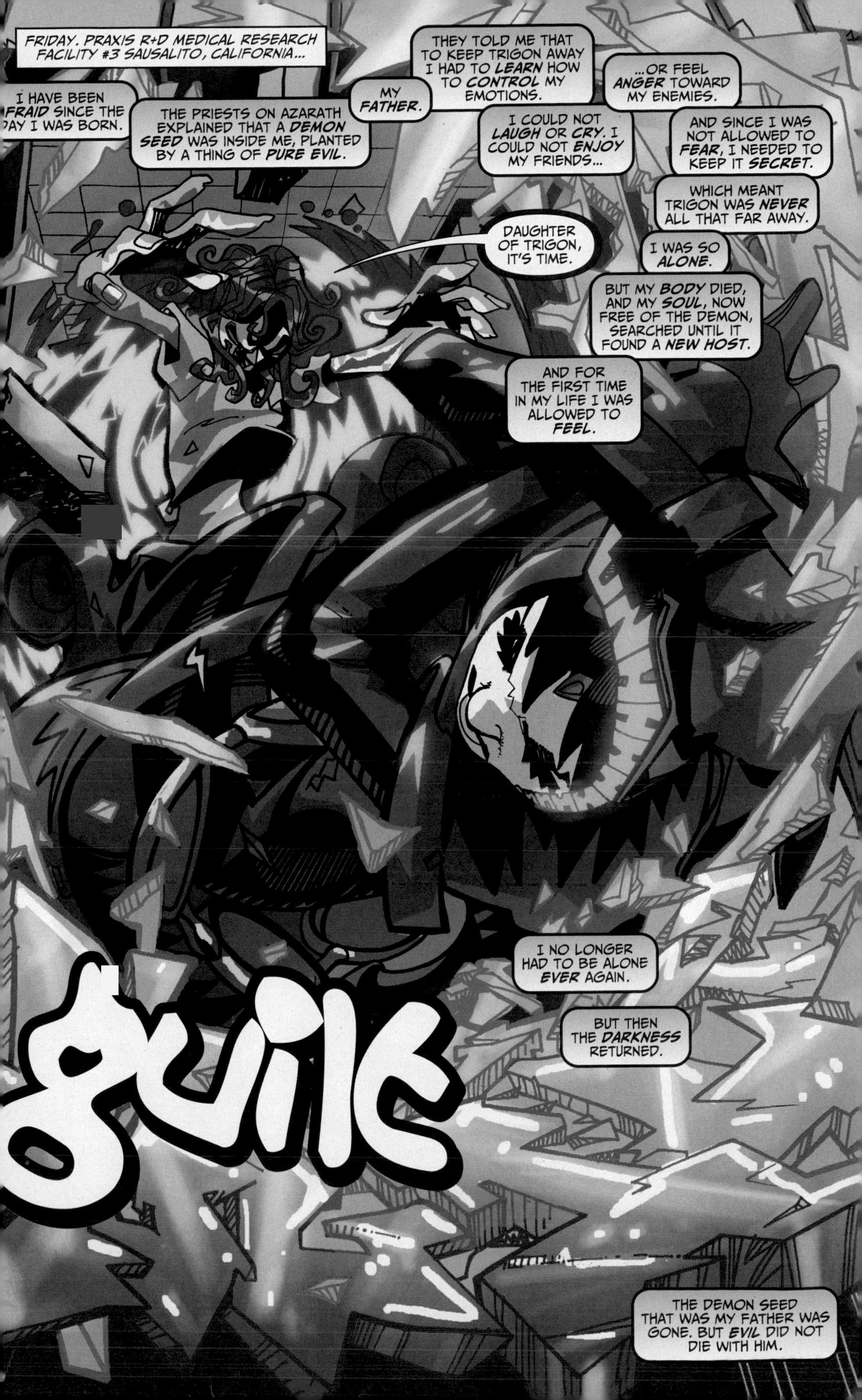
FRIDAY. PRAXIS R+D MEDICAL RESEARCH FACILITY #3 SAUSALITO, CALIFORNIA...
I HAVE BEEN FRAID SINCE THE AY I WAS BORN.
THE PRIESTS ON AZARATH EXPLAINED THAT A DEMON SEED WAS INSIDE ME, PLANTED BY A THING OF PURE EVIL.
MY FATHER.
THEY TOLD ME THAT TO KEEP TRIGON AWAY I HAD TO LEARN HOW TO CONTROL MY EMOTIONS.
I COULD NOT LAUGH OR CRY. I COULD NOT ENJOY MY FRIENDS...
...OR FEEL ANGER TOWARD MY ENEMIES.
AND SINCE I WAS NOT ALLOWED TO FEAR, I NEEDED TO KEEP IT SECRET.
WHICH MEANT TRIGON WAS NEVER ALL THAT FAR AWAY.
DAUGHTER OF TRIGON, IT'S TIME.
I WAS SO ALONE.
BUT MY BODY DIED, AND MY SOUL, NOW FREE OF THE DEMON, SEARCHED UNTIL IT FOUND A NEW HOST.
AND FOR THE FIRST TIME IN MY LIFE I WAS ALLOWED TO FEEL.
guilt
I NO LONGER HAD TO BE ALONE EVER AGAIN.
BUT THEN THE DARKNESS RETURNED.
THE DEMON SEED THAT WAS MY FATHER WAS GONE. BUT EVIL DID NOT DIE WITH HIM.

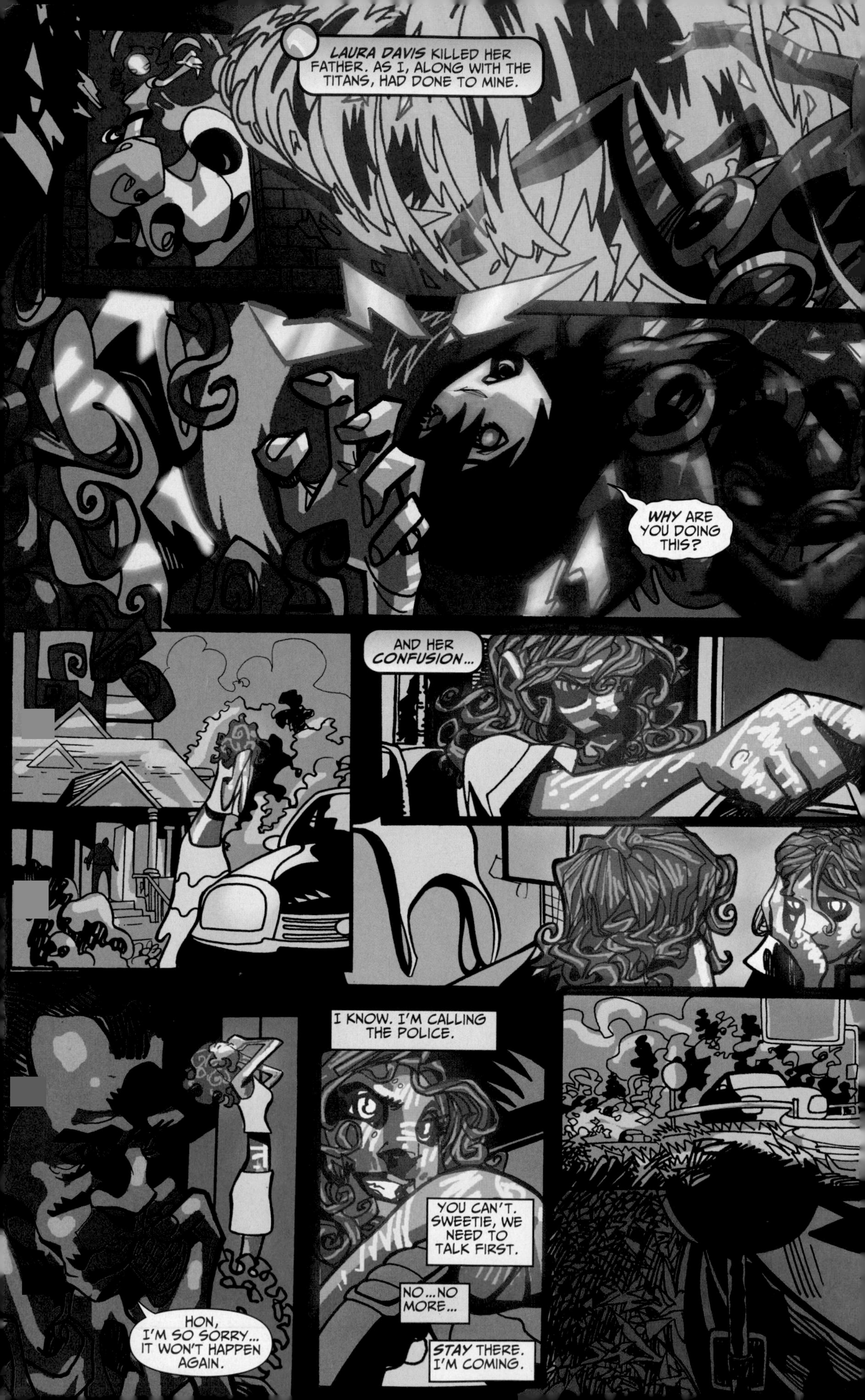
LAURA DAVIS KILLED HER FATHER. AS I, ALONG WITH THE TITANS, HAD DONE TO MINE.
WHY ARE YOU DOING THIS?
AND HER CONFUSION...
HON, I'M SO SORRY... IT WON'T HAPPEN AGAIN.
I KNOW. I'M CALLING THE POLICE.
YOU CAN'T. SWEETIE, WE NEED TO TALK FIRST.
NO...NO MORE...
STAY THERE. I'M COMING.

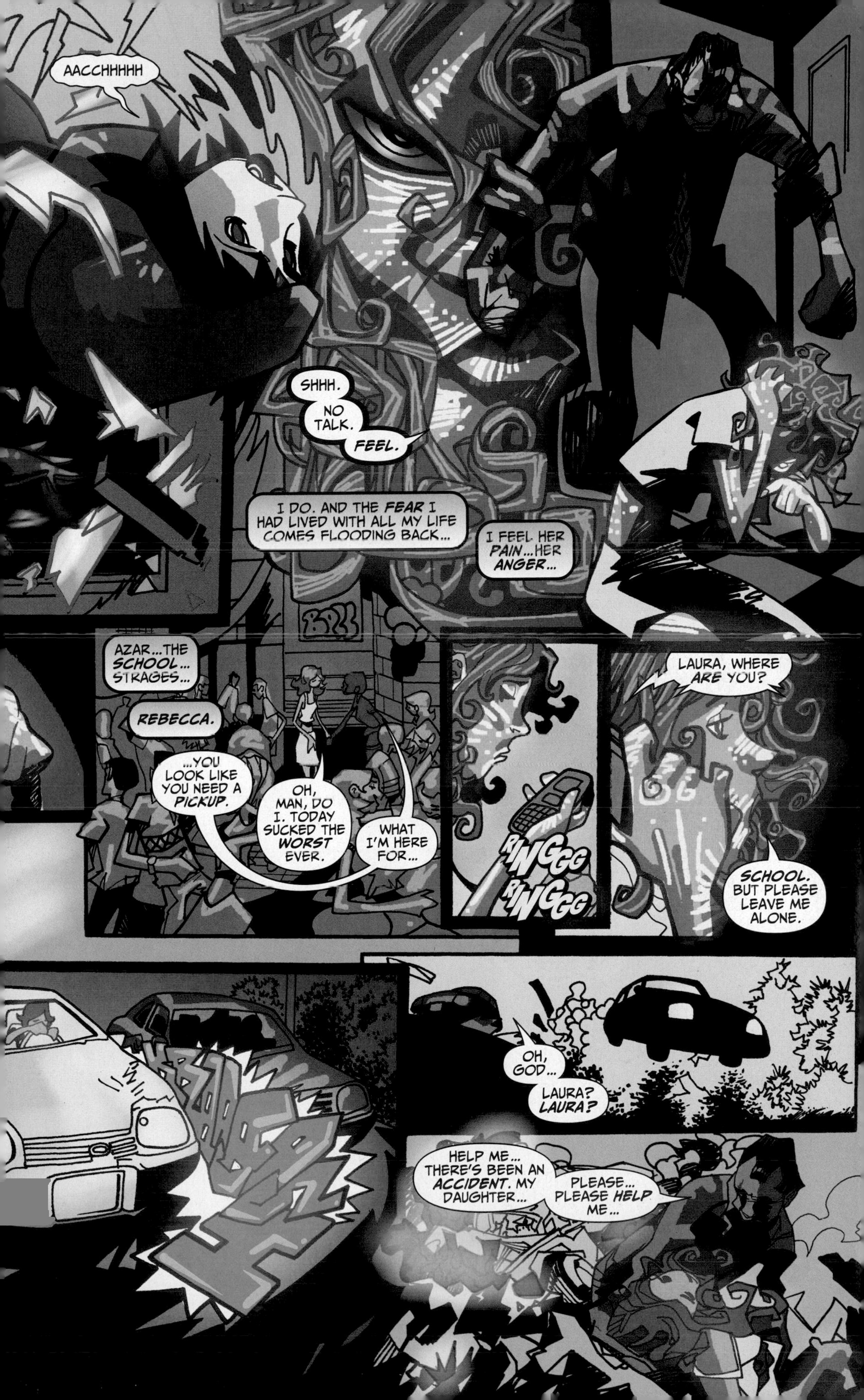
AACCHHHHH
SHHH.
NO TALK.
FEEL.
I DO. AND THE FEAR I HAD LIVED WITH ALL MY LIFE COMES FLOODING BACK...
I FEEL HER PAIN...HER ANGER...
AZAR...THE SCHOOL... STRAGES...
REBECCA.
...YOU LOOK LIKE YOU NEED A PICKUP.
OH, MAN, DO I. TODAY SUCKED THE WORST EVER.
WHAT I'M HERE FOR...
RINGGG
RINGGG
LAURA, WHERE ARE YOU?
SCHOOL. BUT PLEASE LEAVE ME ALONE.
OH, GOD...
LAURA? LAURA?
HELP ME... THERE'S BEEN AN ACCIDENT. MY DAUGHTER...
PLEASE... PLEASE HELP ME...

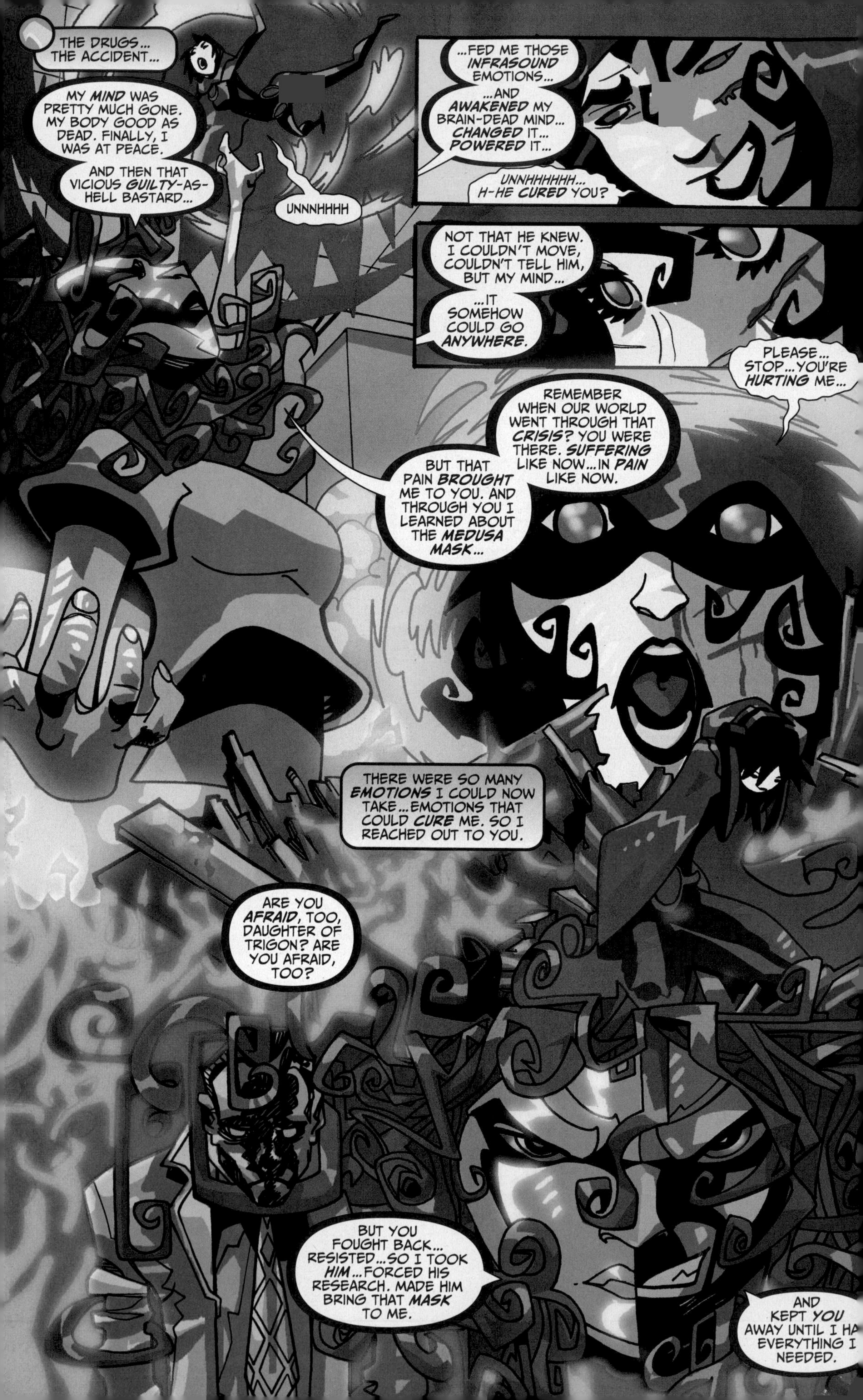
THE DRUGS... THE ACCIDENT...
MY MIND WAS PRETTY MUCH GONE. MY BODY GOOD AS DEAD. FINALLY, I WAS AT PEACE.
AND THEN THAT VICIOUS GUILTY-AS-HELL BASTARD...
UNNNHHHH
...FED ME THOSE INFRASOUND EMOTIONS...
...AND AWAKENED MY BRAIN-DEAD MIND... CHANGED IT... POWERED IT...
UNNHHHHHH... H-HE CURED YOU?
NOT THAT HE KNEW. I COULDN'T MOVE, COULDN'T TELL HIM, BUT MY MIND...
...IT SOMEHOW COULD GO ANYWHERE.
PLEASE... STOP...YOU'RE HURTING ME...
REMEMBER WHEN OUR WORLD WENT THROUGH THAT CRISIS? YOU WERE THERE. SUFFERING LIKE NOW...IN PAIN LIKE NOW.
BUT THAT PAIN BROUGHT ME TO YOU. AND THROUGH YOU I LEARNED ABOUT THE MEDUSA MASK...
THERE WERE SO MANY EMOTIONS I COULD NOW TAKE...EMOTIONS THAT COULD CURE ME. SO I REACHED OUT TO YOU.
ARE YOU AFRAID, TOO, DAUGHTER OF TRIGON? ARE YOU AFRAID, TOO?
BUT YOU FOUGHT BACK... RESISTED...SO I TOOK HIM...FORCED HIS RESEARCH. MADE HIM BRING THAT MASK TO ME.
AND KEPT YOU AWAY UNTIL I HA EVERYTHING I NEEDED.

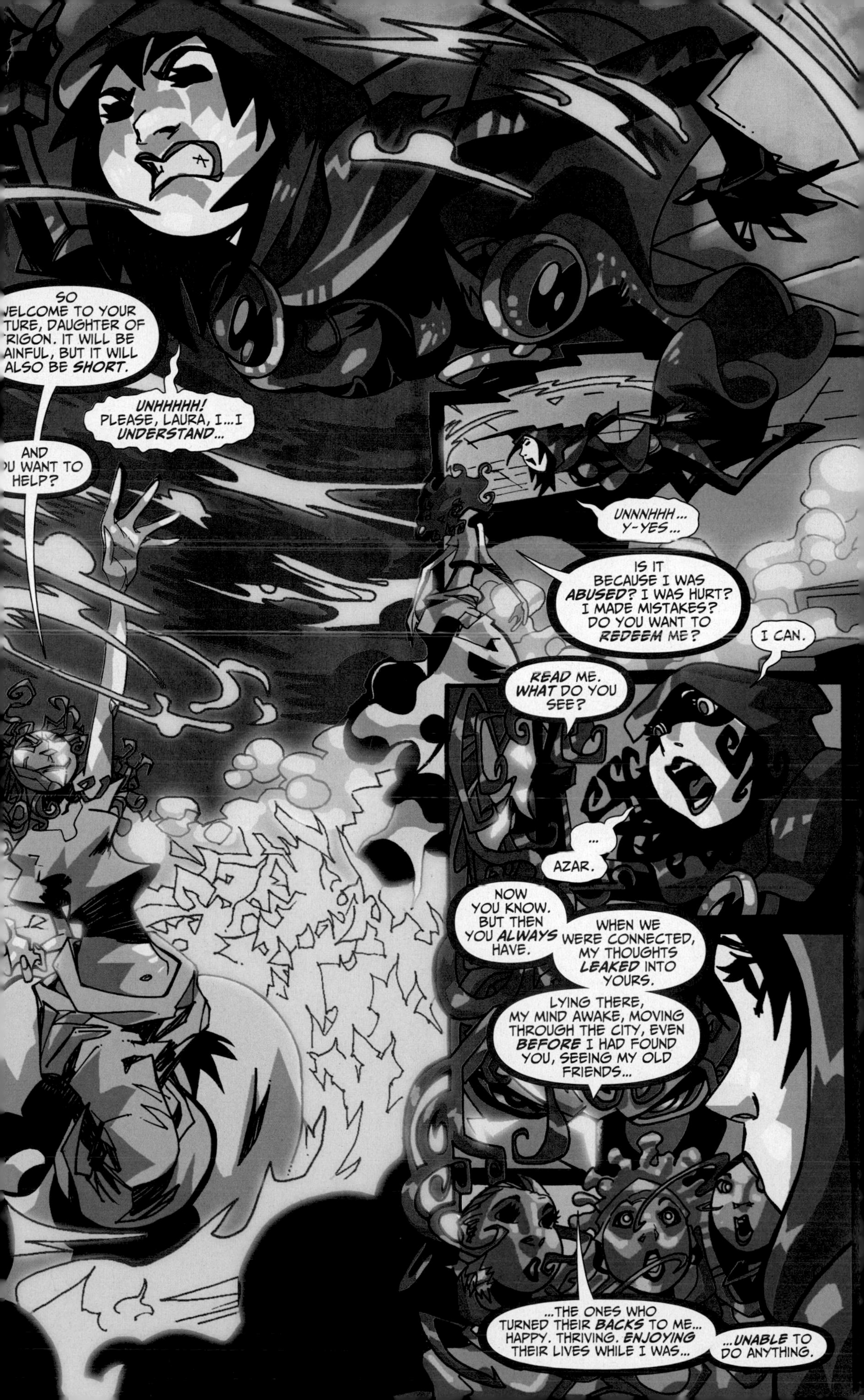

SO
WELCOME TO YOUR
TURE, DAUGHTER OF
RIGON. IT WILL BE
AINFUL, BUT IT WILL
ALSO BE *SHORT*.
UNHHHHH! PLEASE, LAURA, I...I *UNDERSTAND*...
AND
U WANT TO
HELP?
UNNNHHH... Y-YES...
IS IT BECAUSE I WAS *ABUSED*? I WAS HURT? I MADE MISTAKES? DO YOU WANT TO *REDEEM* ME?
I CAN.
READ ME. *WHAT* DO YOU SEE?
...
AZAR.
NOW YOU KNOW. BUT THEN YOU *ALWAYS* HAVE.
WHEN WE WERE CONNECTED, MY THOUGHTS *LEAKED* INTO YOURS.
LYING THERE, MY MIND AWAKE, MOVING THROUGH THE CITY, EVEN *BEFORE* I HAD FOUND YOU, SEEING MY OLD FRIENDS...
...THE ONES WHO TURNED THEIR *BACKS* TO ME... HAPPY. THRIVING. *ENJOYING* THEIR LIVES WHILE I WAS...
...*UNABLE* TO DO ANYTHING.

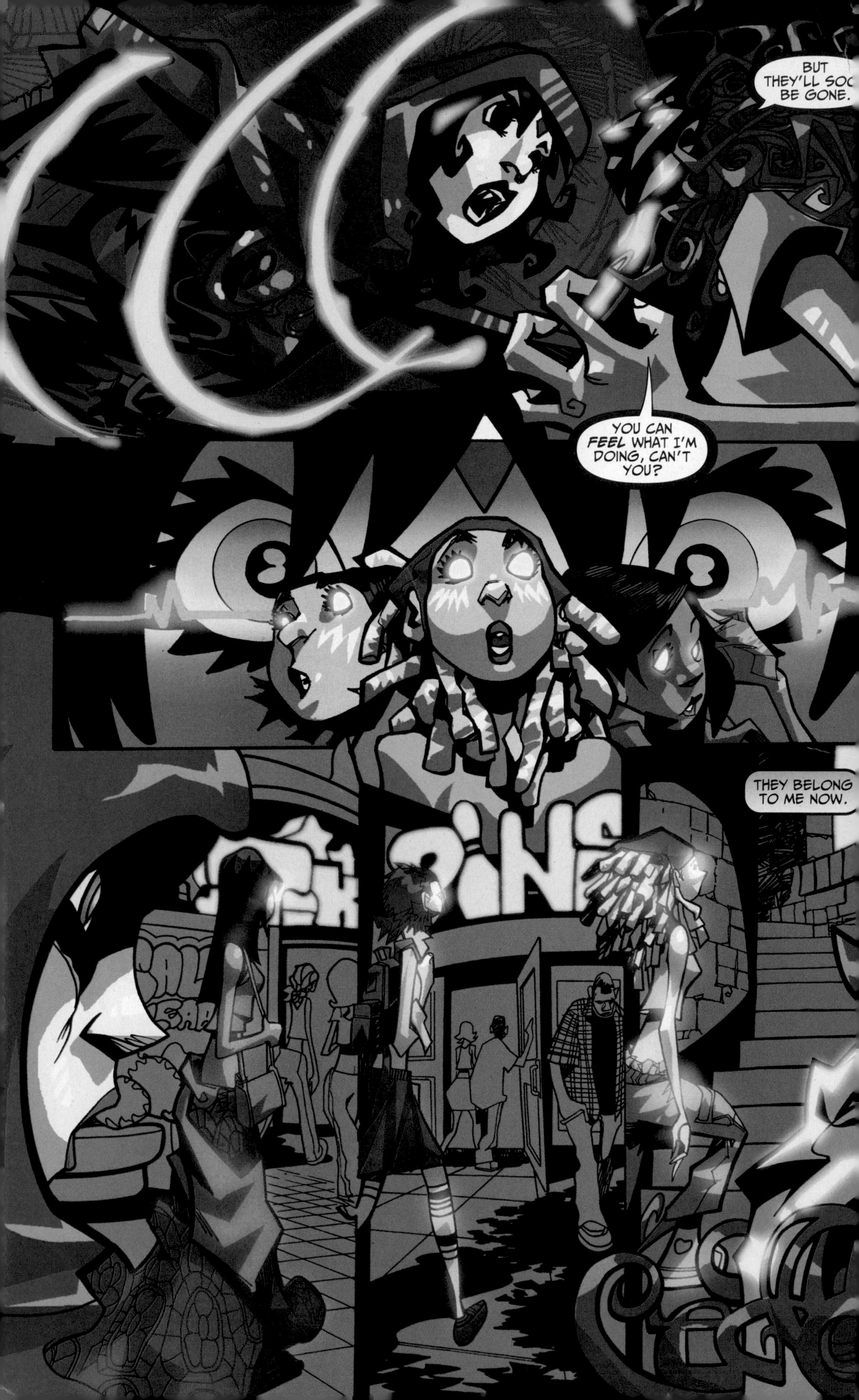
BUT THEY'LL SOO BE GONE.
YOU CAN *FEEL* WHAT I'M DOING, CAN'T YOU?
THEY BELONG TO ME NOW.

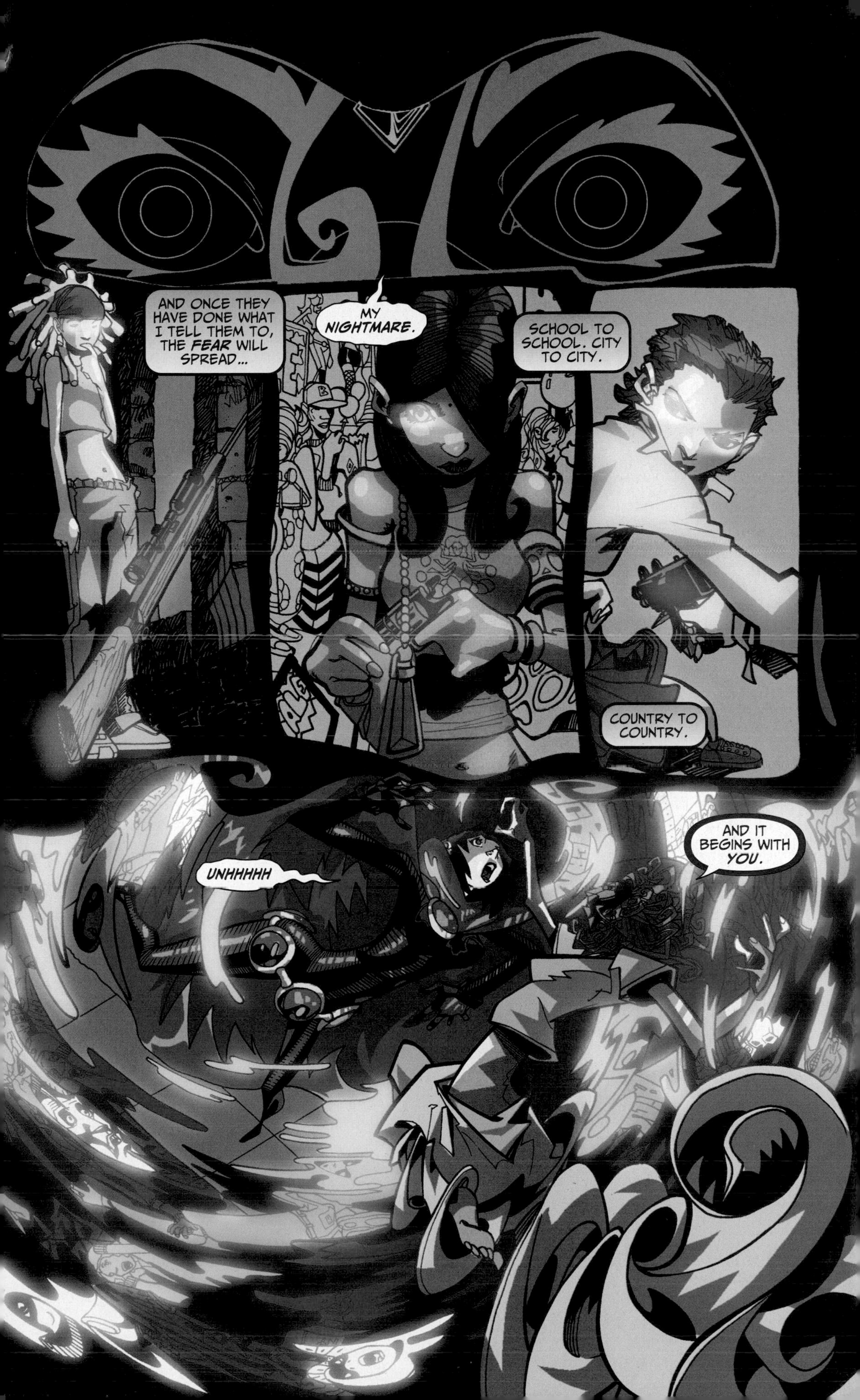
AND ONCE THEY HAVE DONE WHAT I TELL THEM TO, THE *FEAR* WILL SPREAD...
MY *NIGHTMARE*.
SCHOOL TO SCHOOL. CITY TO CITY.
COUNTRY TO COUNTRY.
UNHHHHH
AND IT BEGINS WITH *YOU*.

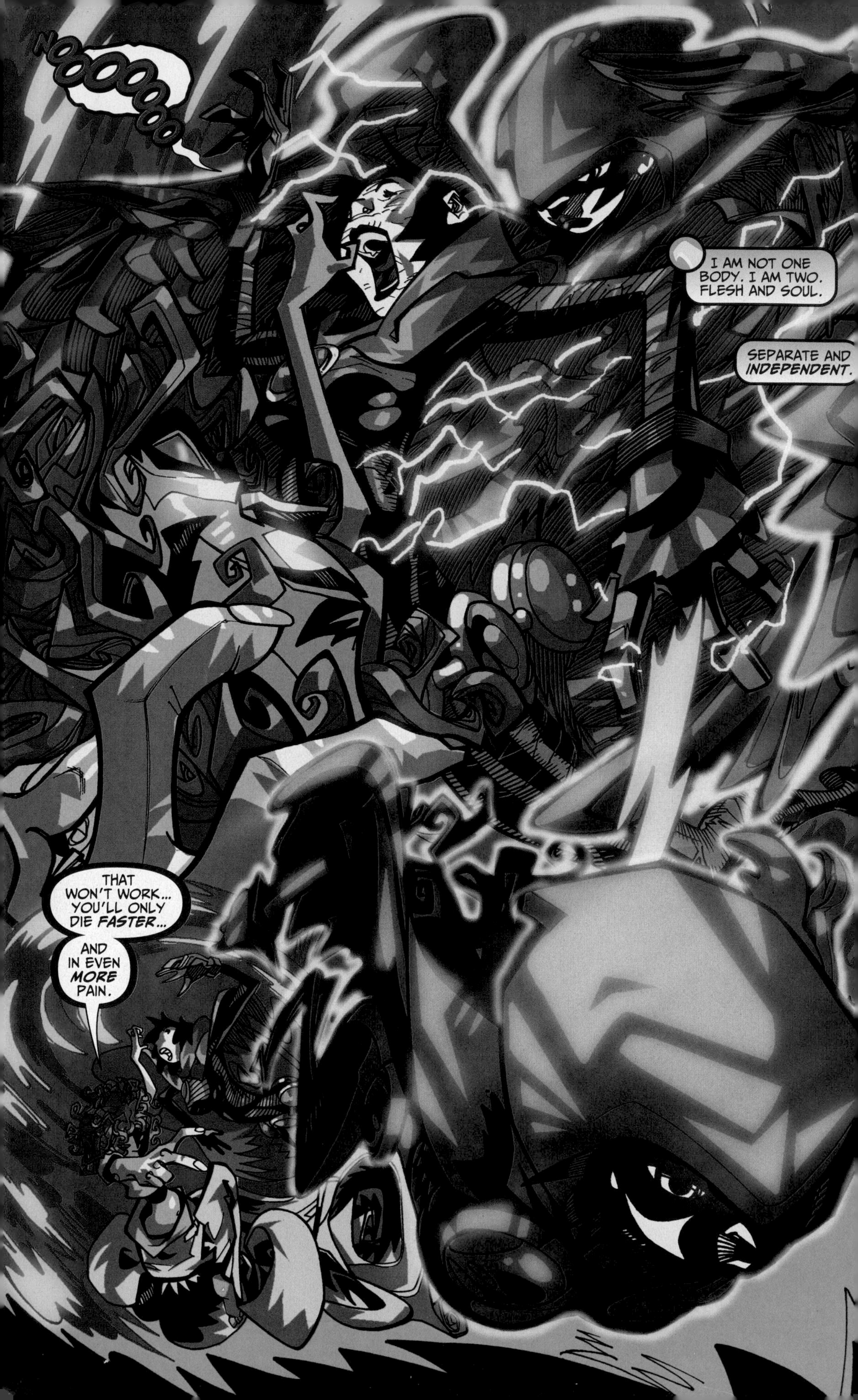
NOOOOOOOO
I AM NOT ONE BODY. I AM TWO. FLESH AND SOUL.
SEPARATE AND INDEPENDENT.
THAT WON'T WORK... YOU'LL ONLY DIE FASTER...
AND IN EVEN MORE PAIN.

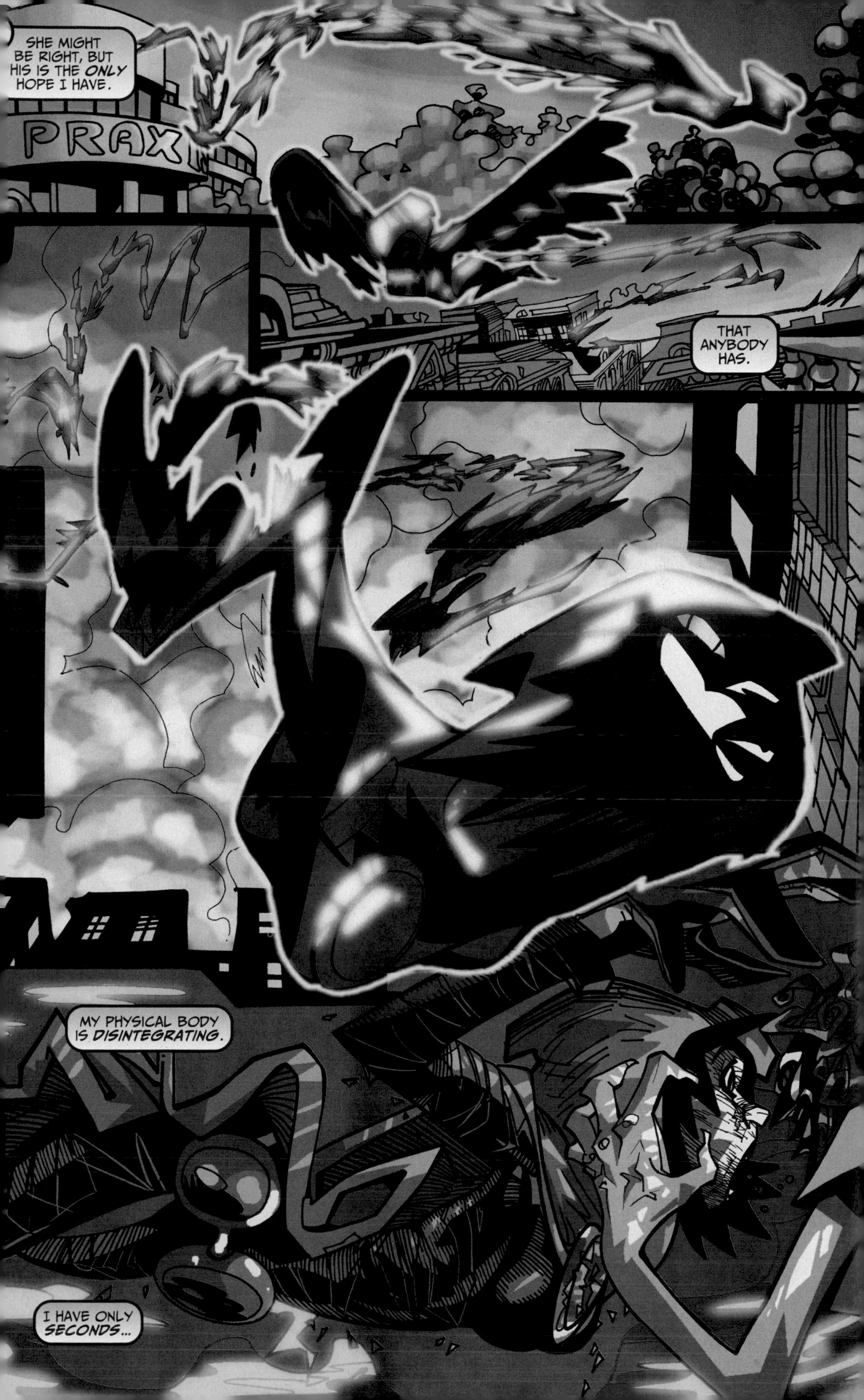
SHE MIGHT BE RIGHT, BUT HIS IS THE *ONLY* HOPE I HAVE.
PRAX
THAT ANYBODY HAS.
MY PHYSICAL BODY IS *DISINTEGRATING*.
I HAVE ONLY *SECONDS*...

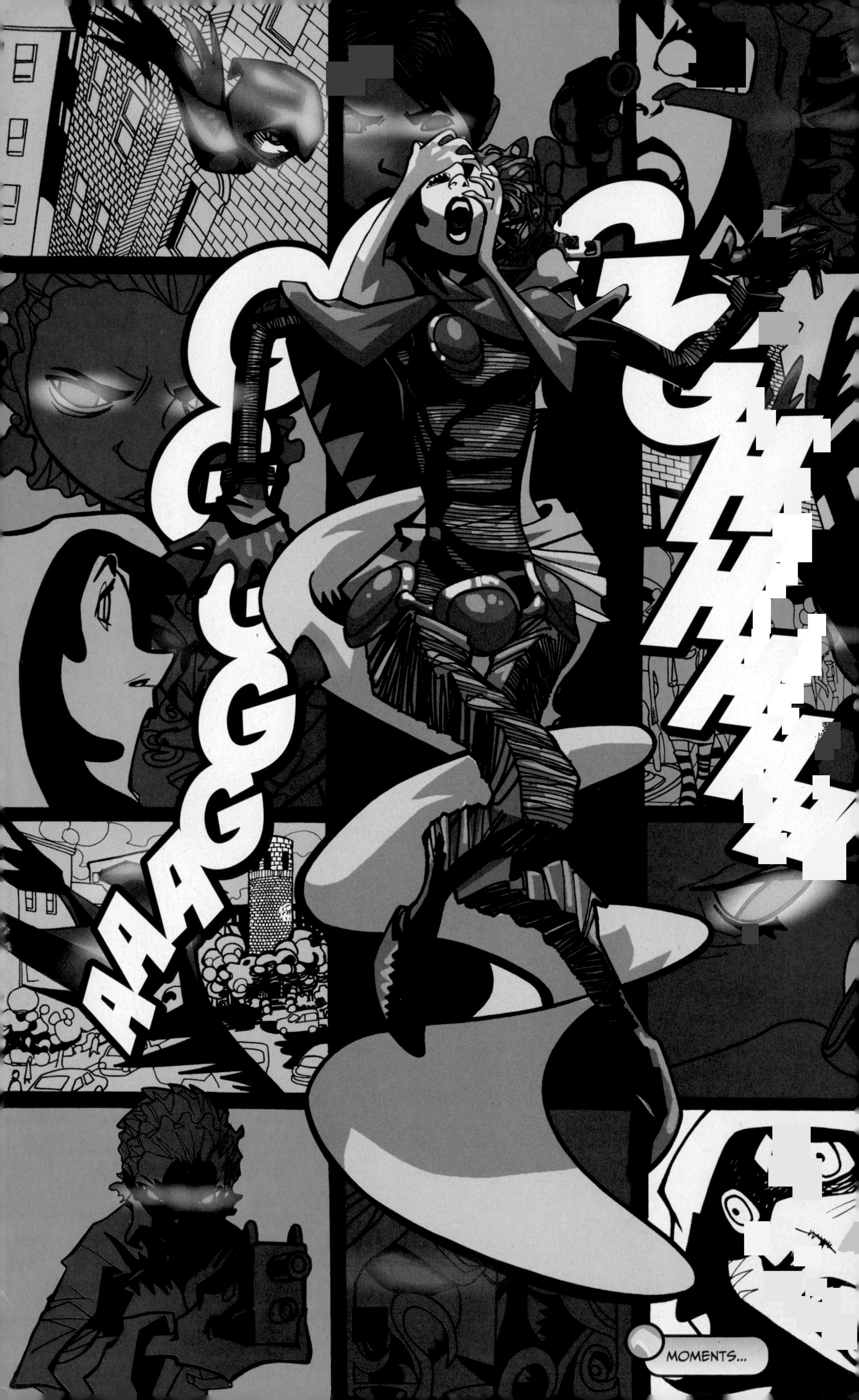
MOMENTS...

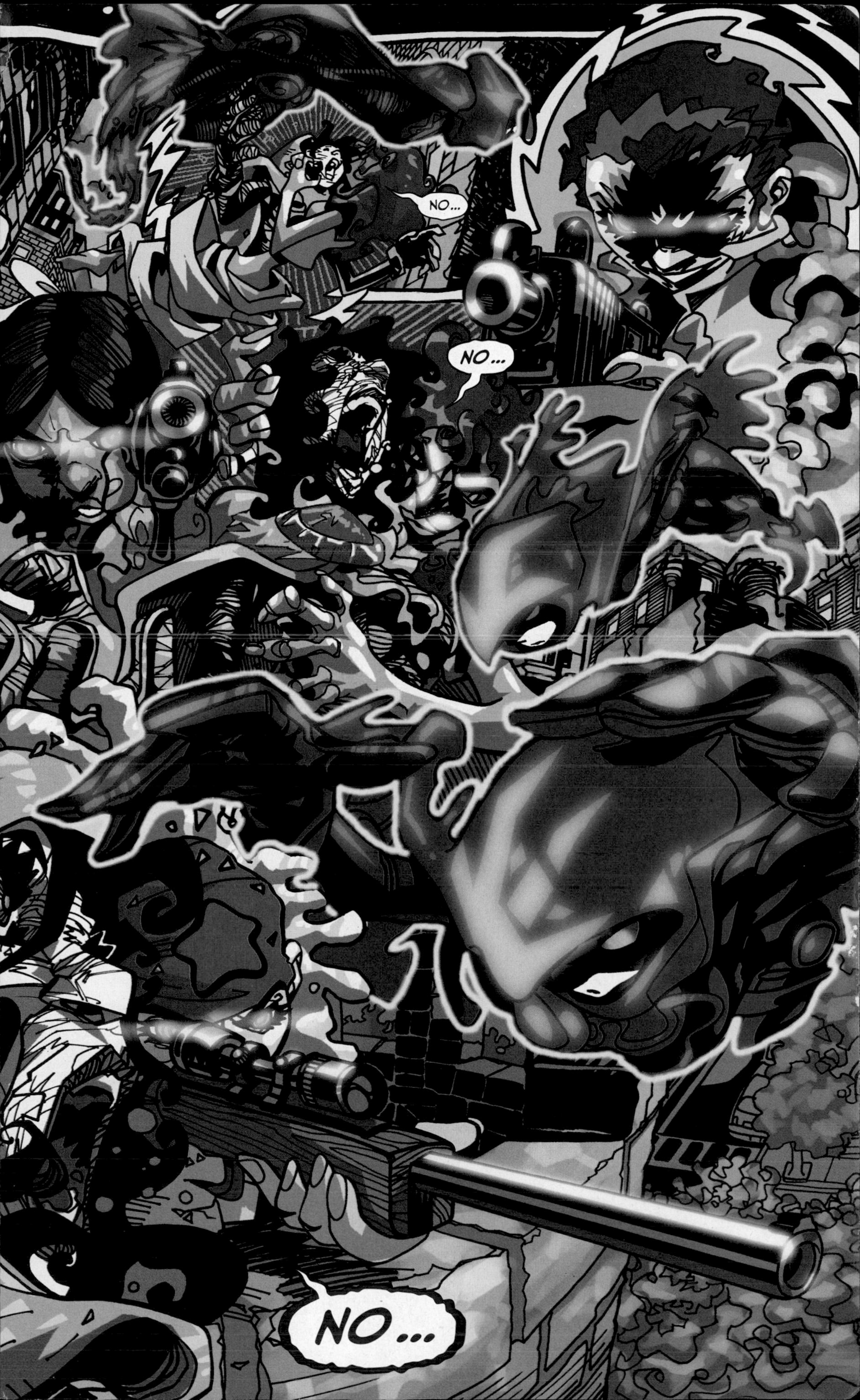
NO...
NO...
NO...

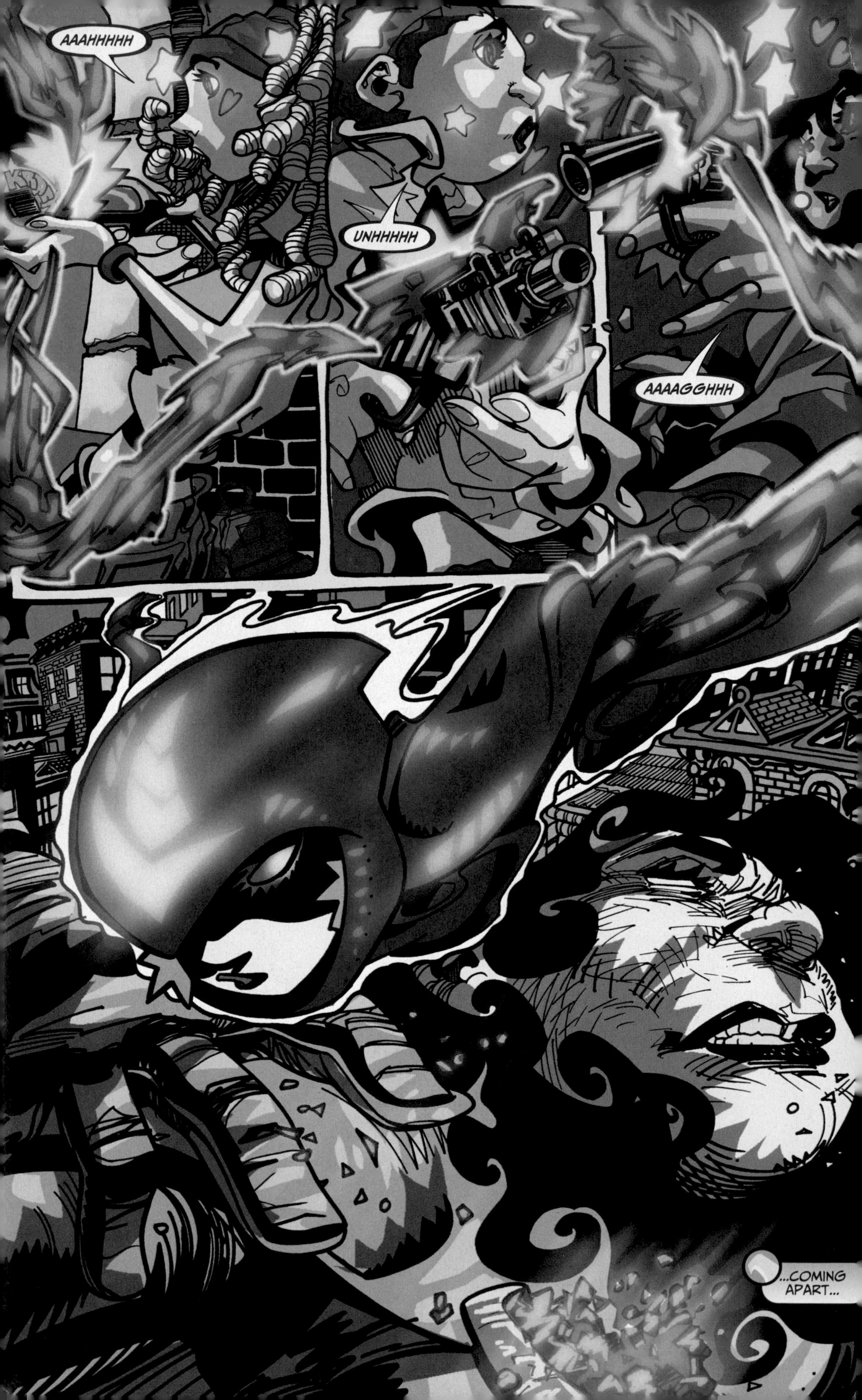
AAAHHHHH
UNHHHHH
AAAAGGHHH
...COMING APART...

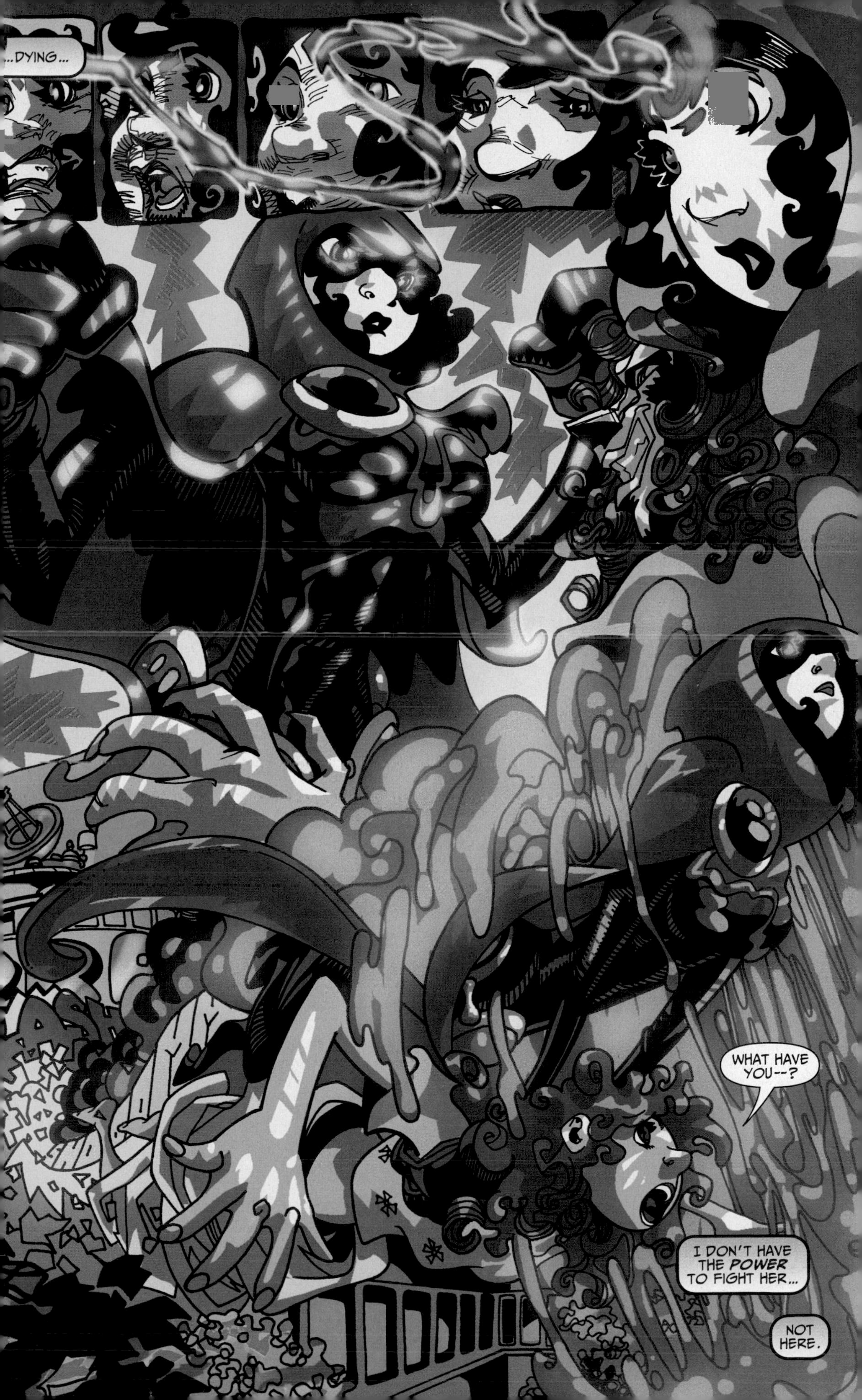
...DYING...
WHAT HAVE YOU--?
I DON'T HAVE THE *POWER* TO FIGHT HER...
NOT HERE.

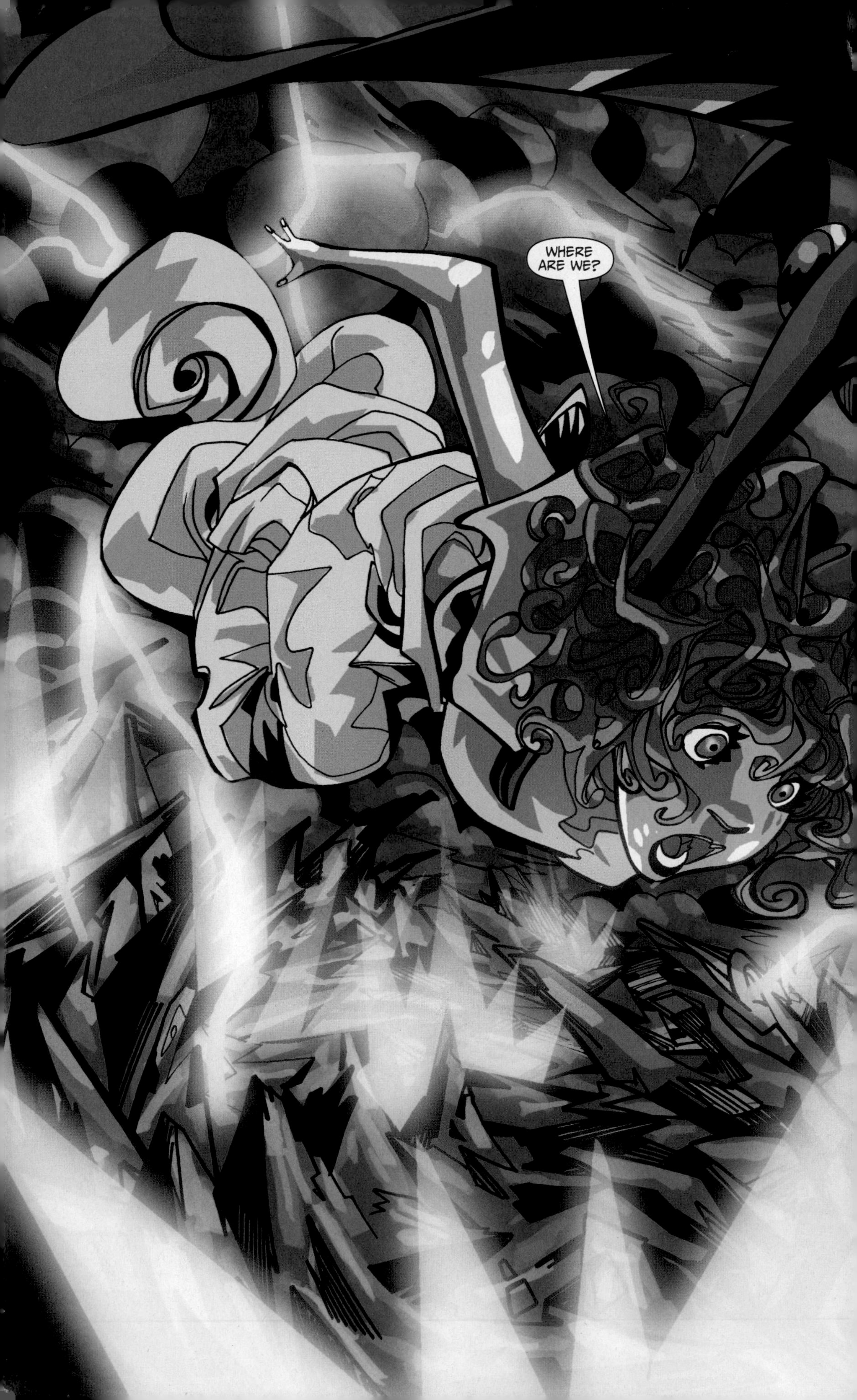
WHERE ARE WE?

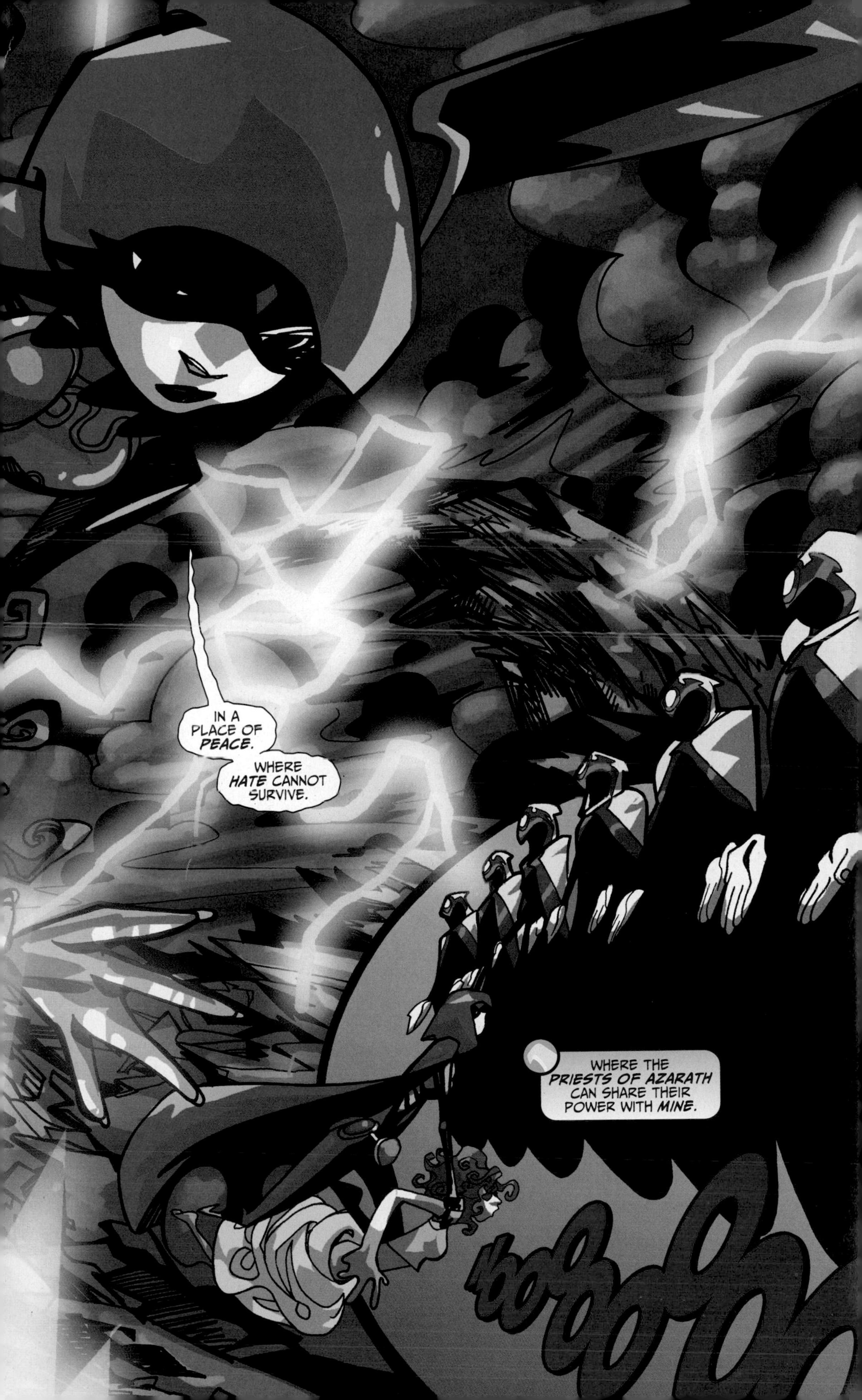
IN A PLACE OF PEACE.
WHERE HATE CANNOT SURVIVE.
WHERE THE PRIESTS OF AZARATH CAN SHARE THEIR POWER WITH MINE.

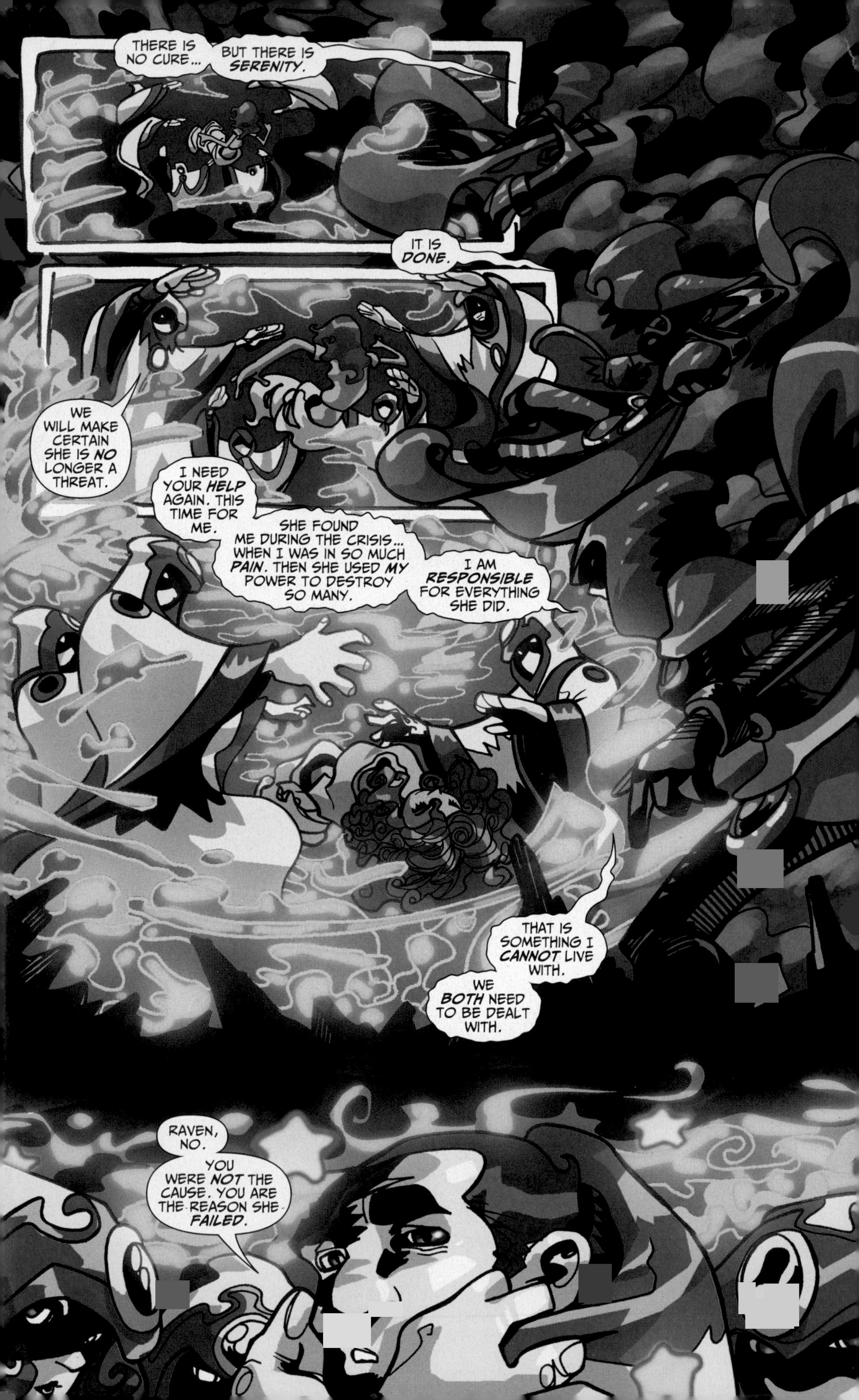
THERE IS NO CURE...
BUT THERE IS SERENITY.
IT IS DONE.
WE WILL MAKE CERTAIN SHE IS NO LONGER A THREAT.
I NEED YOUR HELP AGAIN. THIS TIME FOR ME.
SHE FOUND ME DURING THE CRISIS... WHEN I WAS IN SO MUCH PAIN. THEN SHE USED MY POWER TO DESTROY SO MANY.
I AM RESPONSIBLE FOR EVERYTHING SHE DID.
THAT IS SOMETHING I CANNOT LIVE WITH.
WE BOTH NEED TO BE DEALT WITH.
RAVEN, NO.
YOU WERE NOT THE CAUSE. YOU ARE THE REASON SHE FAILED.

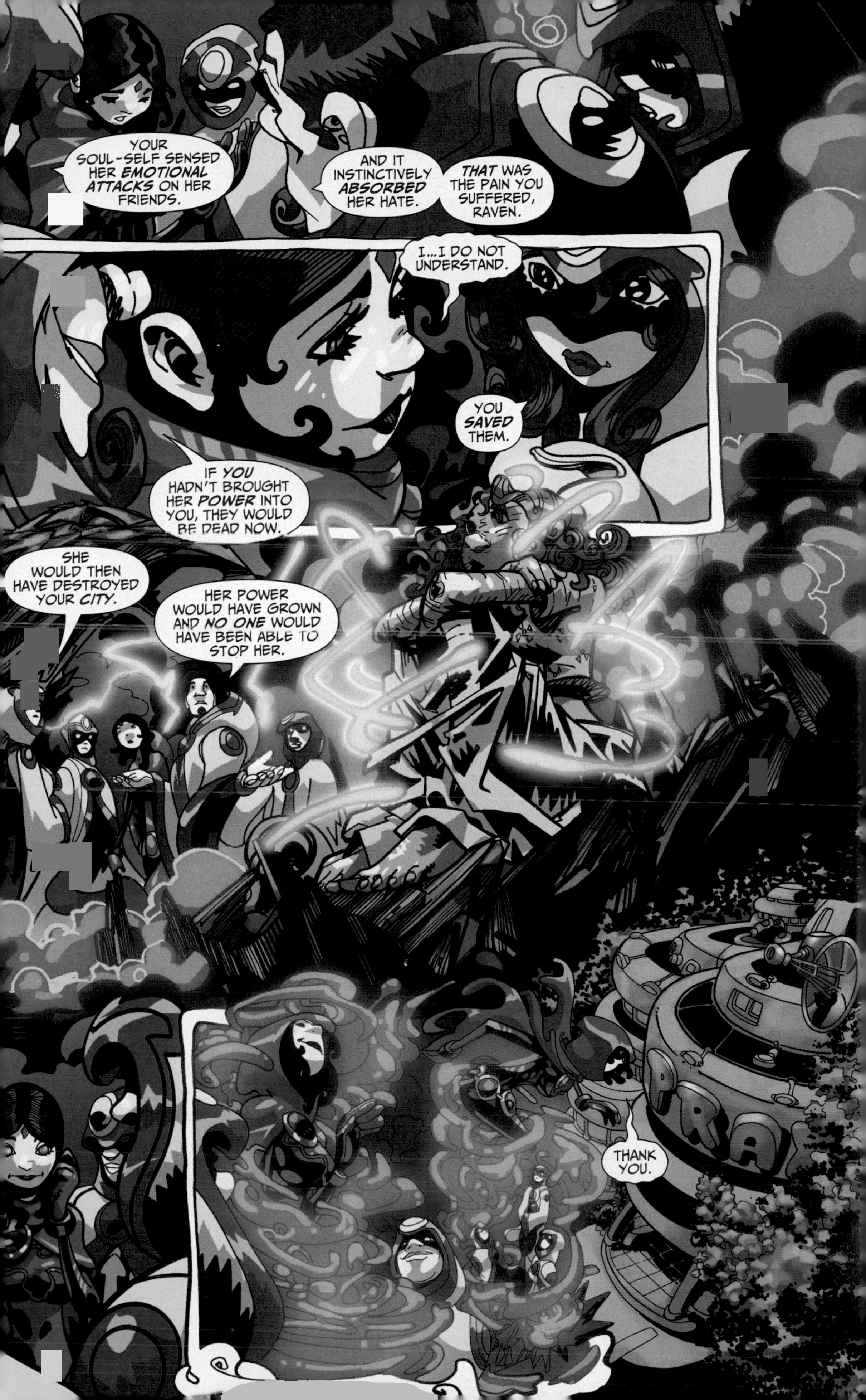
YOUR SOUL-SELF SENSED HER EMOTIONAL ATTACKS ON HER FRIENDS.
AND IT INSTINCTIVELY ABSORBED HER HATE.
THAT WAS THE PAIN YOU SUFFERED, RAVEN.
I...I DO NOT UNDERSTAND.
YOU SAVED THEM.
IF YOU HADN'T BROUGHT HER POWER INTO YOU, THEY WOULD BE DEAD NOW.
SHE WOULD THEN HAVE DESTROYED YOUR CITY.
HER POWER WOULD HAVE GROWN AND NO ONE WOULD HAVE BEEN ABLE TO STOP HER.
THANK YOU.

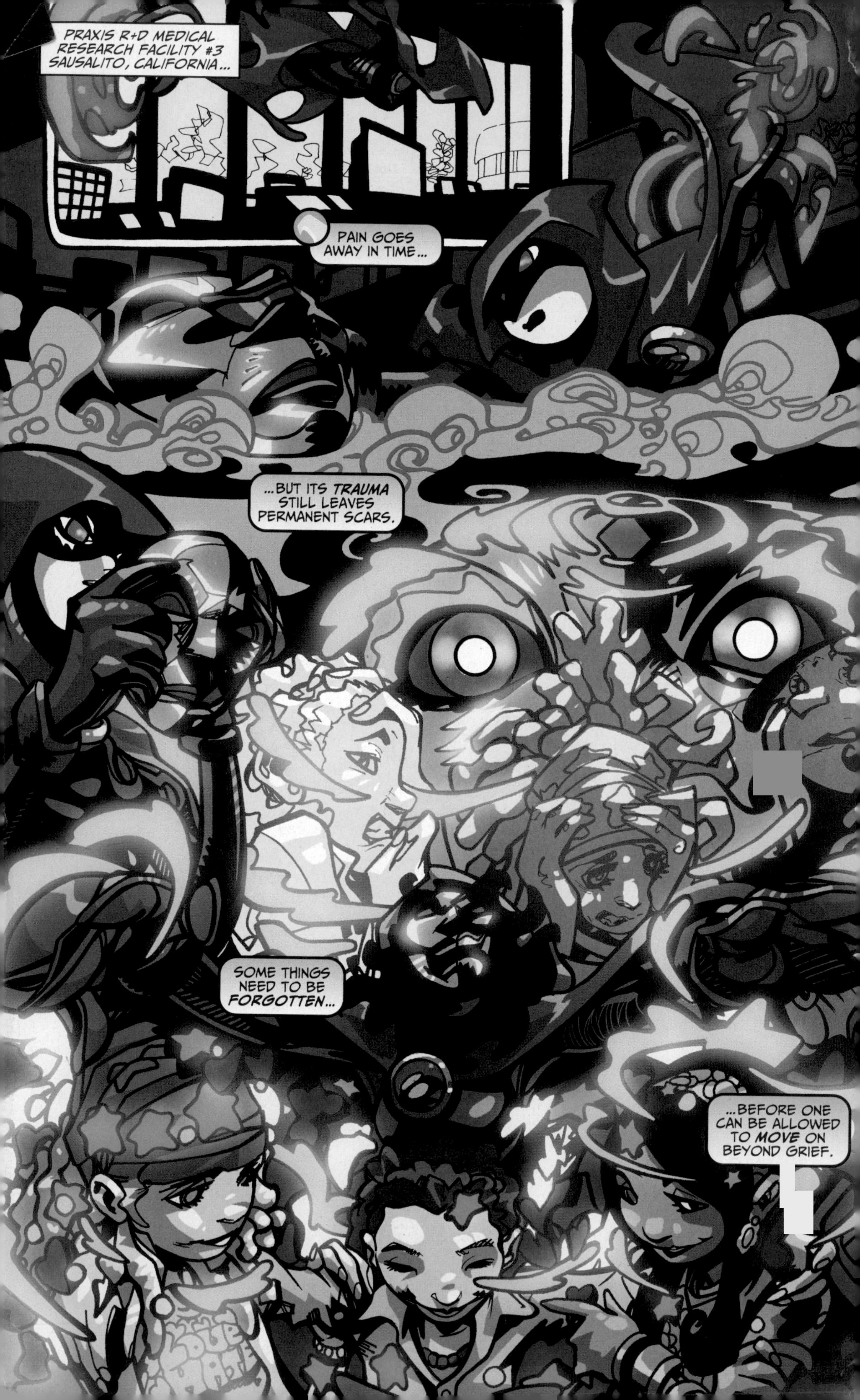
PRAXIS R+D MEDICAL RESEARCH FACILITY #3 SAUSALITO, CALIFORNIA...
PAIN GOES AWAY IN TIME...
...BUT ITS TRAUMA STILL LEAVES PERMANENT SCARS.
SOME THINGS NEED TO BE FORGOTTEN...
...BEFORE ONE CAN BE ALLOWED TO MOVE ON BEYOND GRIEF.

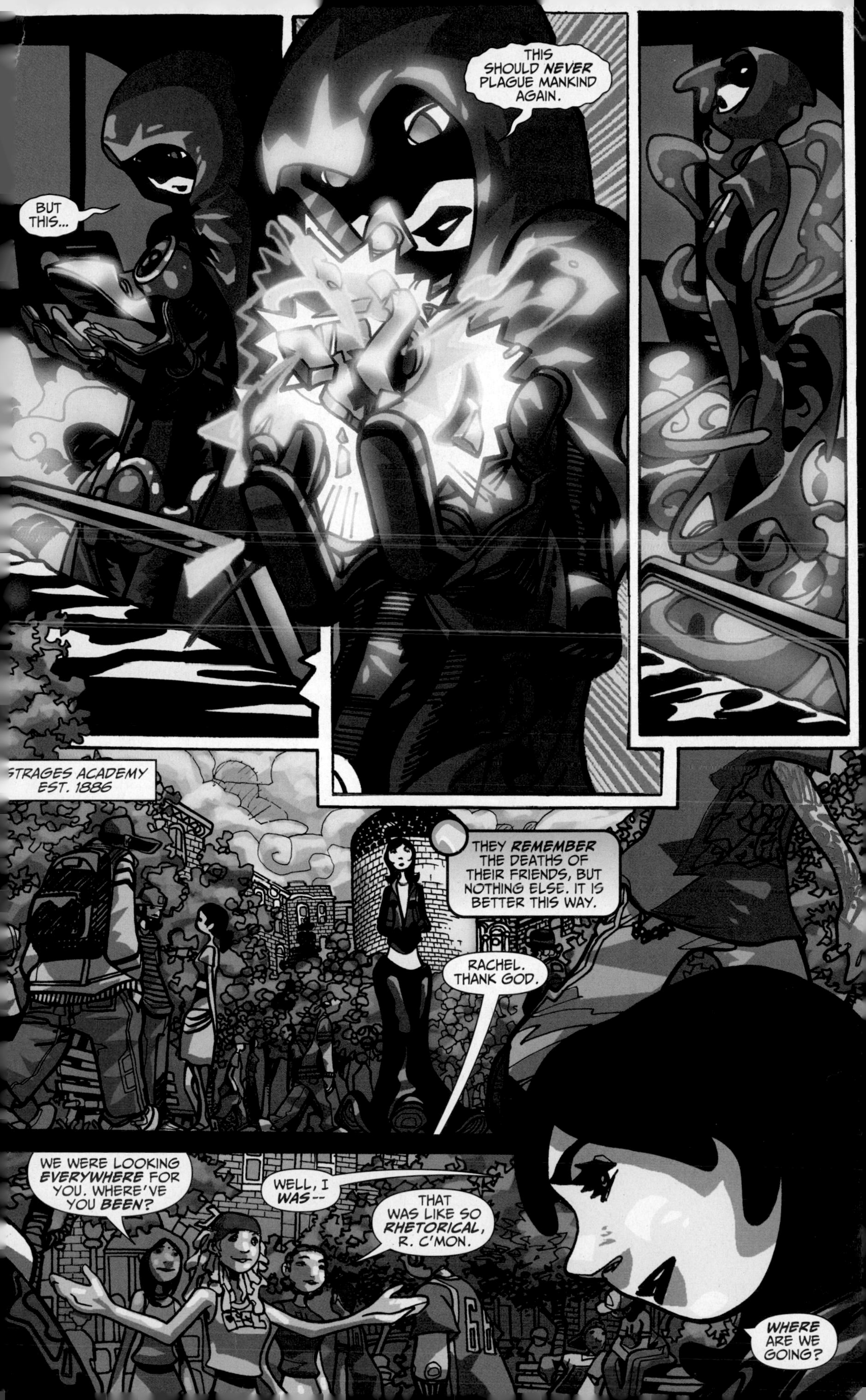
BUT THIS...
THIS SHOULD NEVER PLAGUE MANKIND AGAIN.
STRAGES ACADEMY EST. 1886
THEY REMEMBER THE DEATHS OF THEIR FRIENDS, BUT NOTHING ELSE. IT IS BETTER THIS WAY.
RACHEL. THANK GOD.
WE WERE LOOKING EVERYWHERE FOR YOU. WHERE'VE YOU BEEN?
WELL, I WAS--
THAT WAS LIKE SO RHETORICAL, R. C'MON.
WHERE ARE WE GOING?

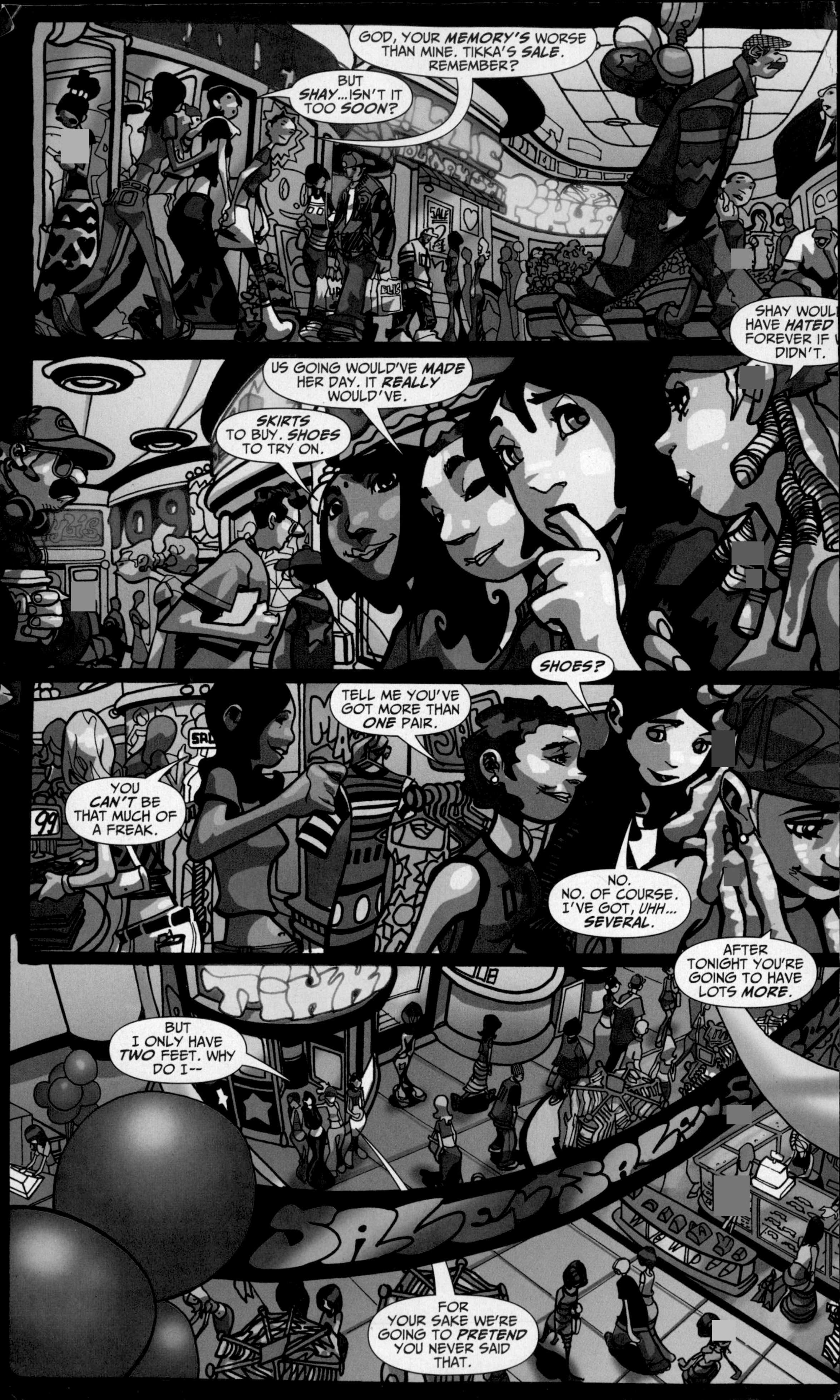
GOD, YOUR MEMORY'S WORSE THAN MINE. TIKKA'S SALE. REMEMBER?
BUT SHAY...ISN'T IT TOO SOON?
SHAY WOUL
HAVE HATED
FOREVER IF
DIDN'T.
US GOING WOULD'VE MADE HER DAY. IT REALLY WOULD'VE.
SKIRTS TO BUY. SHOES TO TRY ON.
SHOES?
TELL ME YOU'VE GOT MORE THAN ONE PAIR.
YOU CAN'T BE THAT MUCH OF A FREAK.
NO. NO. OF COURSE. I'VE GOT, UHH... SEVERAL.
AFTER TONIGHT YOU'RE GOING TO HAVE LOTS MORE.
BUT I ONLY HAVE TWO FEET. WHY DO I--
FOR YOUR SAKE WE'RE GOING TO PRETEND YOU NEVER SAID THAT.

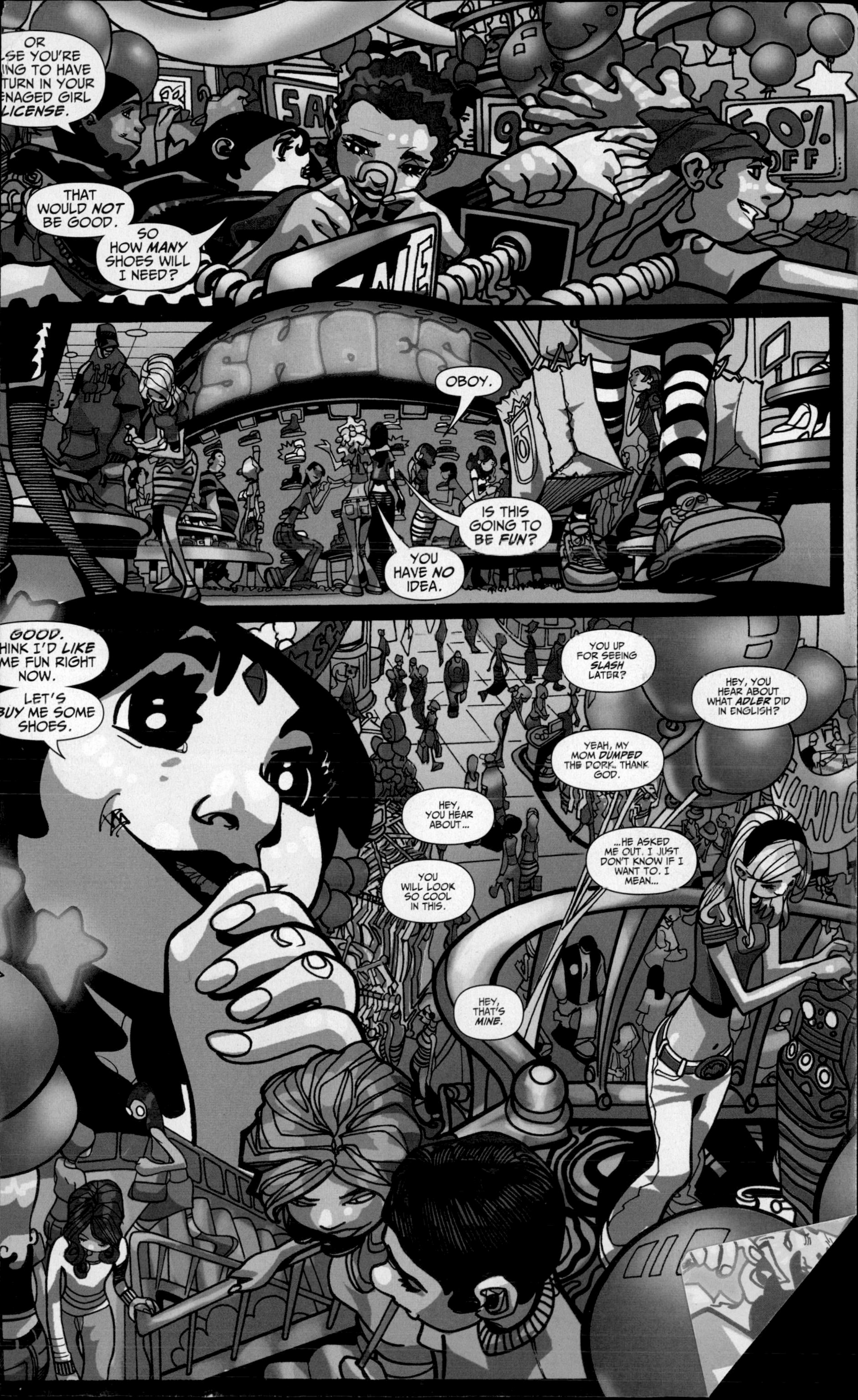
OR
SE YOU'RE
ING TO HAVE
TURN IN YOUR
ENAGED GIRL
LICENSE.
THAT WOULD NOT BE GOOD.
SO HOW MANY SHOES WILL I NEED?
OBOY.
IS THIS GOING TO BE FUN?
YOU HAVE NO IDEA.
GOOD.
HINK I'D LIKE
ME FUN RIGHT
NOW.
LET'S
UY ME SOME
SHOES.
YOU UP FOR SEEING SLASH LATER?
HEY, YOU HEAR ABOUT WHAT ADLER DID IN ENGLISH?
YEAH, MY MOM DUMPED THE DORK. THANK GOD.
HEY, YOU HEAR ABOUT...
...HE ASKED ME OUT. I JUST DON'T KNOW IF I WANT TO. I MEAN...
YOU WILL LOOK SO COOL IN THIS.
HEY, THAT'S MINE.

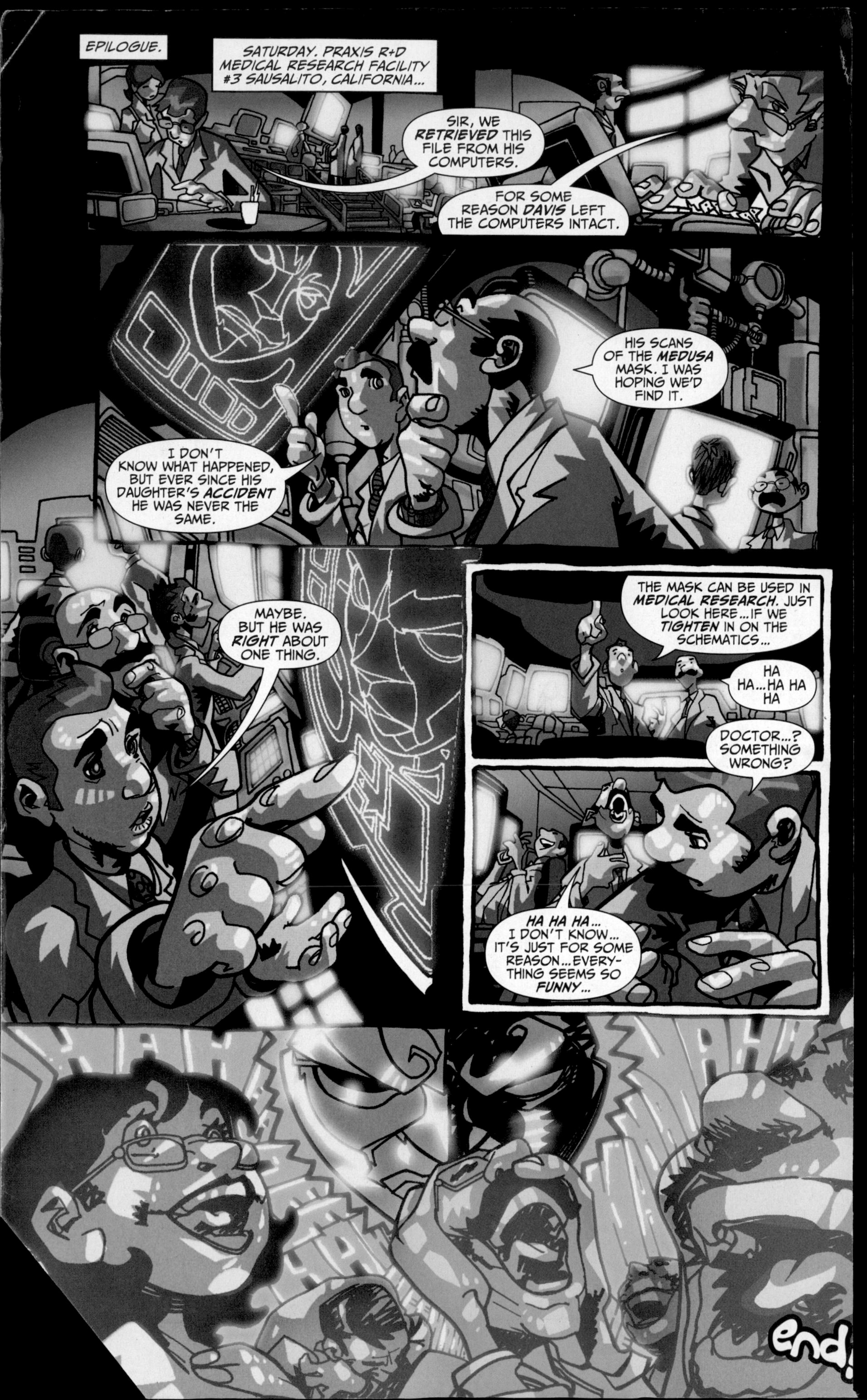
EPILOGUE.
SATURDAY. PRAXIS R+D MEDICAL RESEARCH FACILITY #3 SAUSALITO, CALIFORNIA...
SIR, WE RETRIEVED THIS FILE FROM HIS COMPUTERS.
FOR SOME REASON DAVIS LEFT THE COMPUTERS INTACT.
HIS SCANS OF THE MEDUSA MASK. I WAS HOPING WE'D FIND IT.
I DON'T KNOW WHAT HAPPENED, BUT EVER SINCE HIS DAUGHTER'S ACCIDENT HE WAS NEVER THE SAME.
MAYBE. BUT HE WAS RIGHT ABOUT ONE THING.
THE MASK CAN BE USED IN MEDICAL RESEARCH. JUST LOOK HERE...IF WE TIGHTEN IN ON THE SCHEMATICS...
HA HA...HA HA HA
DOCTOR...? SOMETHING WRONG?
HA HA HA... I DON'T KNOW... IT'S JUST FOR SOME REASON...EVERY-THING SEEMS SO FUNNY...
end!

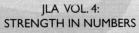

THE WORLD'S GREATEST SUPERHEROES,
THE WORLD'S GREATEST STORIES

JLA: THE GREATEST STORIES EVER TOLD

BATMAN:
THE GREATEST STORIES EVER TOLD
VOLS. 1 & 2

THE FLASH:
THE GREATEST STORIES EVER TOLD

GREEN LANTERN:
THE GREATEST STORIES EVER TOLD

SUPERMAN:
THE GREATEST STORIES EVER TOLD
VOLS. 1 & 2

SUPERMAN / BATMAN:
THE GREATEST STORIES EVER TOLD

WONDER WOMAN:
THE GREATEST STORIES EVER TOLD

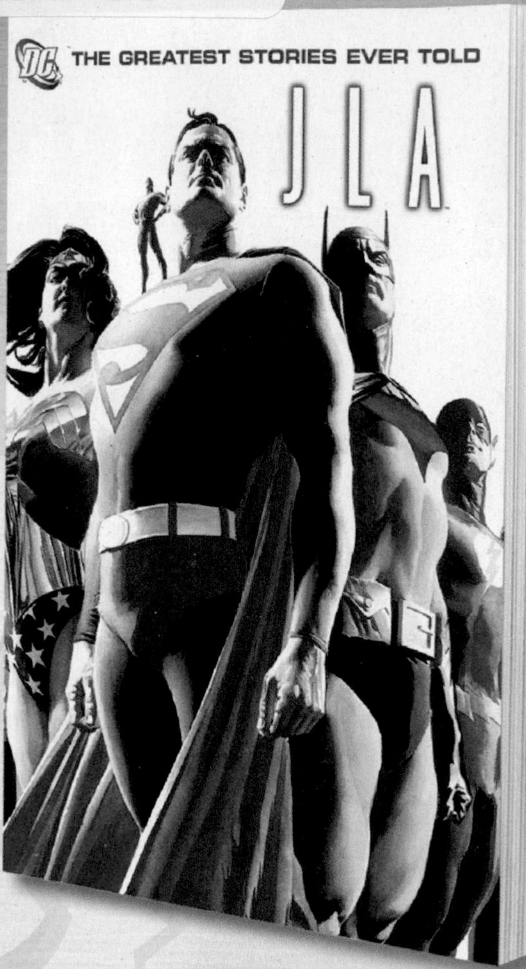
THE GREATEST STORIES EVER TOLD
JLA

SUPERMAN:
THE GREATEST STORIES
EVER TOLD

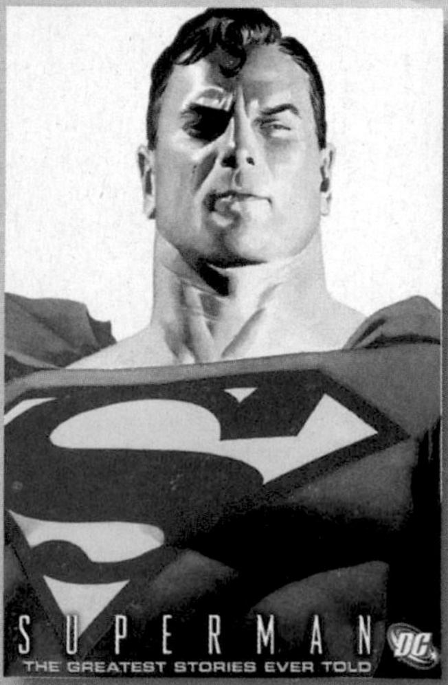
SUPERMAN
THE GREATEST STORIES EVER TOLD

BATMAN:
THE GREATEST STORIES
EVER TOLD

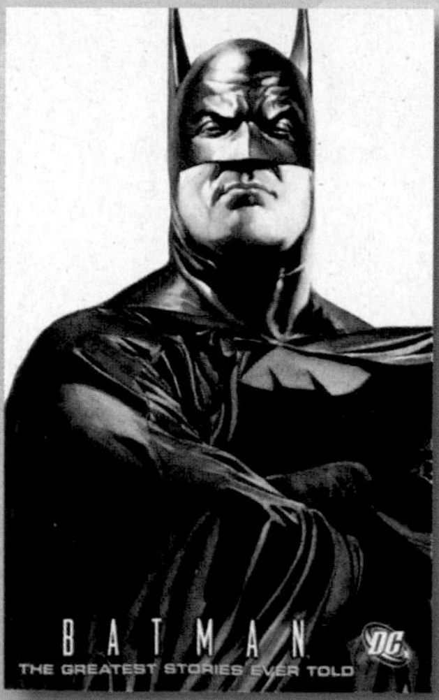
BATMAN
THE GREATEST STORIES EVER TOLD

WONDER WOMAN:
THE GREATEST STORIES
EVER TOLD

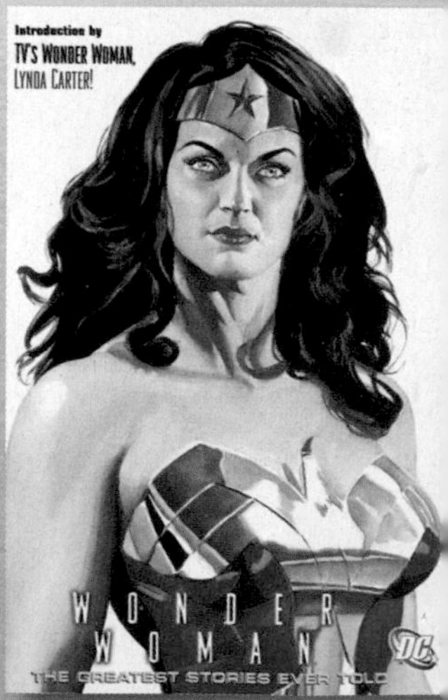
Introduction by
TV's WONDER WOMAN,
LYNDA CARTER!
WONDER WOMAN
THE GREATEST STORIES EVER TOLD

SEARCH THE GRAPHIC NOVELS SECTION OF
DCCOMICS.COM
FOR ART AND INFORMATION ON ALL OF OUR BOOKS!